In the Adirondacks

IN THE ADIRONDACKS

Dispatches from the Largest Park in the Lower 48

Matt Dallos

EMPIRE STATE EDITIONS

AN IMPRINT OF FORDHAM UNIVERSITY PRESS

NEW YORK 2023

Fordham University Press has no responsibility for the persistence or accuracy of URLs for external or third-party Internet websites referred to in this publication and does not guarantee that any content on such websites is, or will remain, accurate or appropriate.

Fordham University Press also publishes its books in a variety of electronic formats. Some content that appears in print may not be available in electronic books.

Visit us online at www.fordhampress.com/empire-state-editions.

Library of Congress Cataloging-in-Publication Data available online at https://catalog.loc.gov.

Printed in the United States of America

25 24 23 5 4 3 2 1

First edition

For my parents

In the Adirondacks

Chapter 1

THE METAL ROOF OF the Red Top Inn had weathered to a dull fuchsia. It looked like a motel I could afford, at least in mid-December, when nightly rates plunged because all the other tourists had fled down to the flatlands. I pulled off State Route 30 and parked in the motel's gravel lot. Across the road, evening fog slithered among tall pines tight against a darkwater lake.

When I opened the office door, the woman behind the desk started. She glared at me for a second too long and then without a greeting asked me what, exactly, I was doing up there at this time of year, summer long gone, not yet any snow to attract snowmobilers, the in-between season when the dull fuchsia roof sat surrounded by six million acres of soggy, leafless forest. All day I had been out walking in that forest. Muddy sand caked my boots and my beard, and I had dropped my worn-out ball cap in a bog. Having grown up in a valley that's all sky, I felt wild-eyed up there hemmed in by so many trees. But she swiped my credit card, verified my signature twice with great care, and across the counter slid me a key to Room #6.

Her husband walked me to it, one room in a long two-story block built sometime after midcentury, a narrow front porch with a vaguely Swiss chalet railing. Evening had dropped to dusk. Raindrops plunked on the metal roof. A row of vacant white rental cabins stood across the parking lot, ghostly. As far as I could tell I was the motel's only guest.

The man demonstrated how to turn up the thermostat. Then he showed me again. He chuckled at his rote repetition and explained that retirees on bus tours had complained the heat didn't work. "But they can turn it up. They can turn it up! The old ladies can turn it up!" Room #6 had one white concrete block wall and three walls of rough-cut boards. The toilet was almond, the shower was almond, the bathroom floor was almond. All I had to do to operate the thermostat was rotate a plastic ring or press an arrow a few times, but he insisted on showing me how to turn up the heat one more time. Looking concerned that I still didn't understand, he wished me a pleasant evening and stepped through the door and onto the porch.

I got back in my car, drove a few miles through the cold dark rain to the nearest village, Tupper Lake, population 3,500. Part of the town stands on a rocky hill and part slumps in a swamp. It feels like a scrap of the Rust Belt hauled to the Great North Woods. Tupper Lake was a settler's clearing until 1890, when a businessman built a railroad and then a giant sawmill. Old-growth spruce all around, there was money to be made. Tupper Lake high school sports teams are still called the Lumberjacks. Fifty years ago, not long after the Red Top Inn was built, logging went bust for what might be the last time. A tall beige brick smokestack still towers over the town, a ruin from a factory that once made millions of disposable wooden spoons. Tupper Lake has been trying to remake itself as a tourist destination ever since. One more attraction, one more real estate venture, one more government grant: Tupper Lake is always just about to be the next hotspot.

That evening Tupper Lake felt dismal, a shade of matte black that consumed any light that had ever struggled to exist in the world. The town sputters through winter on the cash of snowmobilers and a few skiers. That December evening was 50 degrees. An electrical supply shop had used snow-in-a-can to spray-paint PRAY FOR SNOW on its plate glass window.

I hopped over silty, salt-ringed puddles to get to an Italian restaurant. At the bar I ordered a beer, planning to spend the evening talking to locals about what it was like to live here in this town surrounded by so much forest. From where I sat, a thirty-minute drive in one direction would take me to a group of alpine peaks. A thirty-minute drive in the opposite direction would take me to a collection of sandy lakes where I could have paddled for days without seeing a road. I was thrilled to be there, thrilled to have spent the day out in the woods immersing myself in this place.

All around the restaurant, families and couples chatted quietly. The whole room had a pleasant hum to it. One conversation stood out. Against the far wall a table of twentysomethings prattled on about New York City,

Los Angeles, the Bahamas, Austin, Texas—all the places they said they'd rather be.

TO GET THERE FROM any direction, go up. Higher than the valleys all around, the Adirondacks is a place set apart. Where boreal plants venture south to meet temperate. Where the air is chill and the summer short. Where there's a home garden center called Zone 3, and a theme park called the North Pole. Where 1920s silent film directors shot Siberia, Alaska, and Switzerland. Up there, where the frontier held on until the twentieth century. Some people are convinced it still does and always will. Where one county the size of Rhode Island has zero traffic lights. Up there, where you can still see the stars. Where the breeze is balsam and pine. Where the sick went to take the fresh air cure.

Not too far from cities booming with sooty industry and commerce in the nineteenth century, New York and Boston and Montreal, Philadelphia and Rochester and Albany, the Adirondacks was a convenient wilderness where the wealthy could go up to get away. Newport and Saratoga offered society and fashion. The Adirondacks offered an adventurous escape from such things. Even after society and fashion invaded and someone in sweltering New York City could hop onto a train at seven in the evening and disembark before dawn in the chill of the pines, the Adirondacks still felt remote. Despite automobiles and interstate highways and Lear jets, the Adirondacks still feels farther away than it actually is.

I grew up in a gem of a limestone valley a long day's drive south of the Adirondacks. That valley is all sunlight and sweet soil, a valley where you can toss carrot seeds out your sliding glass door and they'll sprout. Every August of my childhood, my parents and I took a vacation. We drove south to Ocean City, Maryland, to spend a week on the beach. Hot sand. Sunburn. Ocean views from the seventh floor of a mid-rise condo. We never considered driving up to the Adirondacks. But I knew the name, one of those iconic places leveraged for lifestyle marketing, places like Yellowstone, Denali, and Montana, parcels of the American landscape elevated to the myth of what we think we want to be. Here's all I knew about the Adirondacks: It was up north. It was cold. It was wild—wild with bears and wolves, wild with gloomy forests and pristine mountain peaks. When I heard a friend or a meteorologist or a passing stranger say the name, it chirped with an enthusiasm not typically granted to place names. It always popped into my head with an exclamation point—the Adirondacks!

A highway rest stop is where I first set foot there. Some college friends and I were on a road trip to a ski resort near Montreal. All day we'd been driving north through ice and rain. I was wedged in the backseat but at least I had a window. We pulled over at the rest stop. I got out of the car, leaned forward to stretch my legs, interlaced my fingers behind me and arched my back. I didn't know where we were at first. Maybe a sign told me. Maybe I saw a rack of brochures for theme parks and motels. Across the four-lane highway, storm clouds crashed into pines and spruce and rocks, and I imagined those pines and spruce and rocks stacked unbroken for a hundred miles. It felt forbidding, gigantic, an enormous bounded object that seemed to have its own gravity, somehow distinct from the rest of the continent, as if the civilized realm had tried to smother the wild but this feral bit had burst through.

We all piled back into the car and sped north. I balled the sleeve of my sweatshirt into my fist and buffed a porthole in the frost on my window. I pressed my forehead against the icy glass to watch the Adirondacks slide by. The land seemed to harbor a secret, something mysterious, even unknowable. I couldn't shake it from my mind. A few years later, I got the chance to go back, finally, and then I went back again, and the more time I spent up there, the more I wanted to see it all. Even after I realized I never could—that no one could see all of the Adirondacks without going mad or broke or both—I still drove up again and again to try.

Now, when I'm not in the Adirondacks, it looms massive up north, spruce-dark and foggy. Up there, I see it choreographed like a stage show: Every neon motel sign hums, flickers, and snaps on, buzzing red in the evening pines. Every real estate agent pounds a sign that says WATER-FRONT into the rocky soil. Every pitcher plant snags a mosquito; every beaver smacks its tail; every porcupine chews on an outhouse door. Every canoeist paddles the perfect J-stroke, and on every pontoon boat, cans of Bud Light pitch in a cooler of melting ice. Wind cuts in from the west: every red spruce leans, every sugar maple creaks, every tamarack sways, and in the last moment before dusk, every lake drops slack, some unknown thousand silver flecks splayed across the Great North Woods going dark.

The Adirondacks!

It's forest, mostly, and lakes and streams and marshes and swamps and bogs and fens and rivers where there's too much water for trees to grow. There are mountains, too, rolling, billowing, peaked. But to call the Adirondacks the Adirondack Mountains is to ignore most of what's there.

Many millions of years ago the metamorphic bedrock of the Adirondacks began to rise. No one seems to know exactly why. Erosion tore into the bedrock dome. Glaciers plucked and grated, gouged and scraped. The bedrock—crumpled and contorted, all zigzags and curlicues—is a billion years old. Fifteen thousand years ago, the most recent glaciers began melting. They took their time. Silt, sand, pebbles, stones, cobbles, and boulders hung suspended in the stagnant ice, dribbled to the ground. I liked to stand on mountains with a good view and imagine boulders hitting bedrock in plinks and bangs. Before trees migrated back north, the Adirondacks was rubble.

All that rock, all that sand, it dammed creeks and rivers, a lake or wetland in every nook. Adirondack bedrock, mostly granite, some schist and gneiss, is impermeable. Every drop of rain and every drip of melting snow either runs off or puddles. If you could pick up the Adirondacks and tilt it, it would slosh. Rivers mingle swampy and then take the long way down, threads of dark water that bow and sweep and curl. Beavers, loggers, and industrialists built a bunch of dams, creating even more lakes that looked a lot like all the others.

"Meet me at the big rock" would be a poor way to make plans in the Adirondacks. The rocks wait where the glaciers let them fall, now capped with ferns and lichen, capped with moss and trees. Others sit balanced on top of mountains. There were more rocks on top of mountains until early hikers reached the summit and wanted to make some noise. Rows of boulder bollards defend the perimeter of hundreds of Adirondack parking lots, as though the glaciers had good aim. In 1932, when Tupper Lake built a golf course, the budget for dynamite was a thousand bucks.

Most of the time, I couldn't see what the glaciers left behind. Too many trees stood in the way. White pine and red pine where there's sand; black spruce and tamarack where the soils slosh; red spruce and beech and maple and yellow birch on mellow slopes with the best soil, which is still quite poor; balsam fir and spruce and paper birch and mountain ash up high where roots crack rock. In that forest that seemed to have no end, there should be more spruce, pine, and hemlock. A hundred years ago, loggers cut so many conifers that they haven't grown back yet. I have a two-year-old child. My great-grandchildren might live to see them.

Even with its two-century-long history of logging—loggers working with axes and then crosscut saws and then chainsaws and then, today, Tigercat 822C feller bunchers that roar and groan and belch diesel exhaust—the Adirondacks might be the largest intact temperate forest left in the world. We've cleared much of the planet's temperate forest to make way for farms, roads, suburbs, cities, and corporate profits. The Adirondacks bucks this trend. It's defined by what we haven't done to it.

When I stood at that rest stop, I assumed the scenery was all the same.

I'd later learn that each region has its own character. More lakes and older trees and millionaires' mansions in the middle. More farms on the fringe. More motels in the southeast. A vast, outwash plain of boreal forest in the northwest, where you're most apt to spot a three-wheeler pulled to parts in someone's front yard and where a flash of luminous blue in the woods is as likely to be a tarp draped over a trailer's leaky roof as it is to be a lake. More hikers in the east, where the High Peaks rise, a cluster of craggy mountains often capped by clouds. Historical, ecological, geological: there are reasons for this variety. The Adirondacks is a cluster of regions glued together with a name.

Owners of souvenir shops revel in the breadth this scenic variety permits their inventories. Forget camping. Forget a weeklong canoe trip. Forget climbing a mountain. The best way I've found to understand the Adirondacks is to wander souvenir shops. Divorced from any limitations of ecology and distance, the whole of the Adirondacks is cataloged there in tight rows, the items on each shelf standing in rank like toy soldiers: balsam-scented knickknacks and maple leaf gewgaws, magnets with sunset lake scenes and mugs painted with loons, faux birch bark picture frames and pinecone drawer pulls, spruce-filled snow globes and napkin holders that read—plagiarizing John Muir but displacing his sentiment—The Adirondack Mountains Are Calling and I Must Go, layer after layer of orange adhesive price labels slapped on the bottom, the price always going down, down until some tourist bites.

With so many ideas and environments crammed into that name, it's hard to tell if someone is referring to one spot or the whole thing. I've never determined whether the name is singular or plural. A fisherman might tell a friend that with every cast in the Adirondacks he pulled out a trout *this* big. A week later, when that friend returns from a trip to a different lake, he might call and disagree. The Adirondacks is a poor place to farm. If you say that to a farmer who husbands one of the two or three cradles of flat, fertile soil, she'll chuck a potato at you. More likely a rock. A photographer in the 1890s captured scenes of the area: lakes and log cabins, streams and bogs. He printed postcards. Hoping to sell them to souvenir shops all across the region and clear a profit, he captioned each of the postcards "In the Adirondacks." A tourist could mail one home and claim she had stood right there.

IN 1892, NEW YORK STATE designated the Adirondack Park. Most people call it the Adirondacks, or the 'Dacks, or the Park. Some call it the A-D-K.

At about six million acres, it's the largest park in the lower forty-eight.

New Jersey, Vermont, and New Hampshire: each state is about the same size as the Adirondacks. Everyone who tries to make sense of its scale notes how multiple national parks could fit inside, arranged like a kindergartener's pasted collage. I'll repeat the calculus because even as a cliché it's astonishing: Glacier, Yellowstone, Grand Canyon, and the Everglades combined. Or Death Valley, Olympic, Yosemite, and the Great Smoky Mountains. You could live in the park for your entire life and still be a tourist on the other side. In the nineteenth century, Adirondack guides would only escort sportsmen through one region. When guides approached the boundaries of their local knowledge, they passed their clients on to someone else. Often I imagined it as much bigger than it really is. It would feel, roughly, the size of Alaska. Alaska is seventy times the size of the Adirondacks. It takes only two and a half hours to drive across the Adirondacks, a fact I try to ignore so I can dwell in my own inflated sense of scale.

It's a park, but not in the way we usually think about parks in the United States. Half is private, half is public.

On private land, there are houses, grocery stores, marinas, nursing homes, car dealerships, industrial zones, garbage dumps (where tourists used to gather on summer evenings to feed marshmallows to black bears, a spectacle I was, sadly, born a few decades too late to witness), strip malls, main streets with rows of local shops, condominiums, camps—thousands and thousands of Adirondack camps: vacation homes available in all sizes, shapes, styles, and price points—playgrounds, theme parks, golf courses, and luxury resorts that boast Big City chefs. For the record, my disappointment in never witnessing black bears eating marshmallows is because I would've enjoyed seeing a bear bounce up and down on the hood of some tourist's cherry 1965 Buick Riviera. Also, I should add, there are a few strip mines, hunting lodges, ice cream stands, neighborhoods, motels, hotels, and hospitals. There's one Walmart.

All of that is the exception. Development clusters in towns and along the few main roads. Trees cover nearly all three million acres of the private land, and most of these acres have been logged at least once and probably will be again, trees ripped into timber, or sliced into veneer, or shredded into woodchips. Fleets of white tractor trailers lug woodchips on the long haul across the Adirondacks, headed to paper mills and biomass power plants. Day and night, white tractor trailers groan through the woods: a downhill, the roar of a Jake Brake, fresh-cut woodchips sprinkled on the road at a sharp turn.

The state of New York owns the other half. It's almost all trees. No one visits most of these three million public acres. Tourists trample the iconic spots bare. By rule, state land is inhabited only by campers and backpackers and hunters, and by white-tailed deer, mink, moose, beavers, foxes, coyotes, pine martens, leeches, ermine, and some birds, like loons and ravens and black-backed woodpeckers and white-throated sparrows and a handful of Bicknell's thrushes: a tiny, pale-brown migratory song-bird that winters in the Caribbean and summers in the zesty chill of the spruce-fir forest that caps the highest peaks—a charmed life if I've ever heard one.

Nearly all state land in the Adirondacks is Forever Wild: no trees may be killed or damaged, a protection embedded within the state's constitu-tion since 1894. Forever Wild trees can't be logged, cut to build a shelter, or hacked down with a battery-powered chainsaw to cook vegetarian bacon on a frosty morning. Forever Wild places this half of the park among the best-protected environments in the nation. Some Forever Wild trees are a few hundred years old, and in a few hundred years many more will be. Forever Wild created a forest that's well on its way to being classified old growth.

That wasn't necessarily the plan. In the 1890s, cut-and-run loggers were shearing the Adirondack forest. Business owners feared this would cause downstate canals to run dry. Proponents of Forever Wild intended the rule to preserve the state-owned forest temporarily, so that in a few years the trees could be managed—that is, logged—according to the nascent prin-ciples of scientific forestry. Fearing corruption, desolation, drought, and inferno, wealthy landowners who loved the wild woods stopped that plan. With the rise of environmentalism in the twentieth century, Forever Wild took on new meaning: an untouched wilderness, an ethos some environ-mentalists like to believe the Adirondacks has always had.

Most Forever Wild trees still stand. But over the years New York has cut quite a few, to build campgrounds and roads and snowmobile trails and ski slopes and fire observation towers and a scenic highway to the rocky, wind-torn top of the fifth-highest peak. Environmentalists often sue. With the exception of rocks, lawsuits might be the most abundant crop in the Adirondacks. Is Forever Wild land a recreational playground or a business opportunity? A remote wilderness or a profitable woodlot? Forever Wild, that Adirondack motto, seen on T-shirts, beer coozies, legal documents, and at least one license plate issued west of the Rocky Mountains: the problem is no one can quite agree on what it should mean.

Between private and public land, no clear line of demarcation ex-ists. The Adirondacks is a fractured mosaic. Timber companies, timber-investment management organizations (TIMOs), private clubs, or wealthy families own many large parcels. New York owns the others. Hodgepodge best describes what remains: chunks and gores and square lots. It's hard to tell what's public and what's private in that forest that goes on and on. It's not like American national parks. They mostly have the tidy boundaries we prefer: private outside, public once you cross a line. This jumble of private and public land makes the Adirondacks the most complicated and contested park in the country. I think it also makes it the most fascinating, a tangle of stories and lives and histories and communities and wild lands.

In the late eighteenth century, the state owned the whole region (after seizing it from the British who had stolen it from Native Americans). That wasteland up north—the state tried to give it all away. No one really wanted it. A few decades later, after realizing its blunder, the state wanted to buy it all back but balked at the now lofty price per acre. (One village is named Speculator.) Over the years, the state has purchased more and more land, parcel by parcel, but long ago gave up on a monopoly. I'm glad they gave up. The Adirondacks would be boring if it were all Forever Wild, if it lacked towns and citizens and motels with metal roofs faded to a dull fuchsia.

At least 130,000 people live in the Adirondacks. Six million acres: that gives each resident roughly forty-six acres of elbow room. That fact didn't strike me as significant until I realized that's half as much as each resident of Montana, a state I think of as being hopelessly expansive and lonely. (Alas, each resident of Alaska has 575 acres.) Most Adirondackers live on the eastern edge and many commute to jobs in small cities outside. Some live in isolated hamlets scattered in the forest like a throw of jacks. In those hamlets, there aren't many year-round jobs, and residents are either retired or work for the local government, work in tourism, or piece together a living somehow. One Adirondacker said he made a living in the 1870s by "guiding, hunting and fishing" and anything he "could turn his hand to in the woods." Which isn't that different from the way many residents in isolated hamlets get by today.

There are even more part-time Adirondackers, around 200,000. They own Adirondack camps as second homes and pay local property taxes but don't get to vote in local elections. At camp, they spend the summer, deer season, snowmobile season, or just a weekend or two. July and August, part-timers outnumber locals in many towns. To locals, how many years you've lived there full-time is a status symbol. It takes at least a decade of winters, mud seasons, and biting black flies before you're no longer a flatlander. Bicknell's thrushes are all flatlanders. I'll always be one, too, and that lady behind the desk at the Red Top Inn knew it.

Here's what really sets the tone of the region: There are eight or ten or twelve million annual tourists. No one's quite sure. Unlike most national parks, there's no entrance gate, no smiling ranger with a badge and a wide-brimmed hat collecting thirty-five bucks and handing you a map. Almost 84 million people live within a day's drive. The Adirondacks is the Northeast's wilderness backyard. Has been for two centuries. Most tourists show up on the Fourth of July. Labor Day is The Exodus. Locals stand on the side of the road to wave goodbye. A tall tale, I thought, until I saw it for myself. Since the 1870s, when the Adirondacks first became a fashionable tourist destination, most people who have seen the Adirondacks have seen it green.

IT PUT ME IN A FUNK, sitting there near the middle of what might be the largest temperate forest left in the world and listening to a boisterous group of young locals making plans to flee. I stood up to go talk to them, to find out what they thought was wrong with this place, to learn more about their complaints, to find out why they wanted to leave an area that for me raised such excitement, that brought to mind images of adventure and relaxation. When I got within a few feet of their table and was about to clear my throat to interject, they all looked up and frowned at me, a flatlander, so I swerved right and pretended I was trying to find the bathroom, stopped to read an advertisement for a yard sale that had happened months earlier, and then made a broad, pointless meander through the entire establishment before I went back to my seat at the bar to brood. Was Forever Wild a worthwhile endeavor if the people who grew up there dreamed about leaving? Could the Adirondacks survive if it was only a getaway for flatlanders? Would this century-and-a-half-long experiment in conservation fail?

Back at the Red Top Inn I watched some television, read for a bit. White tractor trailers hauling woodchips roared by on the road every thirty minutes or so. I could hear them from a long way off, and I imagined those white tractor trailers barreling through a sodden, dark forest the size of New Jersey: headlights and taillights, splash and clang and a Doppler-effect rumble. This was a land of leisure and wilderness, I had thought, a place to be enjoyed, a place to escape the modern world. There I was sulking about brain drain and poverty and jobs and woodchips in white trucks while I stared at the glint of silver insulation in the uneven gaps between the rustic boards on three walls of Room #6. What was I doing up there? Why did I care about this region and its past and future? What was I looking for? These weren't just questions about me. They were about wilderness and culture and America, about the way we look at the land and how we're drawn to what's wild and what we think is unknown, and about what that means for how we value the world around us and what we choose to protect.

Trying to fall asleep on a flimsy mattress under a roof once red, I thought back to my history in this place. After college, my girlfriend, now wife, and I had spent a weekend up there each summer, camping, hiking, wandering souvenir shops. Two weekends if we were lucky. After the long drive up, Erin and I would park next to a lake and get out to gaze at pines and rocks in the fading light. We felt as though we had entered another realm. A loon would wail or a coyote would yap, as if the moment had been queued up for our arrival. We'd inhale the tangy balsam air and make big eyes at each other, awestruck by the scenery, the silence, the heft of so many trees. I remember feeling a giddy sense of wonder that this place existed, that it was open for the public to explore. I didn't yet know the history of the area. I didn't even consider that it had a history. It seemed it had always been and would always be a wilderness open to tourists. Open for tourists. I remember seeing a real estate ad that boasted about a camp that sat within six million acres of wilderness. A lark, clearly. Even back then Erin and I laughed it off. But it seemed to speak some truth about the way many flatlanders felt about the area.

A few years later, we moved to Ithaca, New York, a few hours south of the Adirondacks. Erin landed a job. I lingered a bit too comfortably in grad school. When Erin couldn't sneak away for a long weekend, I started driving up by myself. A perpetual Adirondack tourist, that's what I wanted to be. I wanted to be surprised by what I found. I wanted to be open to the possibility that around the next corner there waited a geyser or a waterfall with a perpetual double rainbow or a range of alpine peaks. About this time, standing in line at a Big Box home improvement store in Ithaca with Erin, she smirked at me and glanced at another shopper's cart. Tucked on the bottom rack was a ceiling fan in a box. The model was named Adirondack: rustic wooden blades and antler pulls, a scene of silhouetted moose and bear and spruce wrapped around the faux animal hide light shade. On the way into the store we had seen a stack of those outdoor chairs, usually molded plastic now, that weren't first built in the Adirondacks but still got the name so the chairs made people think of fresh air. I began to wonder why this geography had weaseled its way into American culture.

Go back further.

My history in this place precedes my time there.

At the age of thirteen, standing in the limestone valley, the exclamation point I saw was because of the myth Americans have made of the Adirondacks: that it's a pure wilderness of balsam breezes, a playground of adventure, an empty land of leisure and health, free of all concerns and cares. Glance at any of the dozens of landscape photography books or scenic calendars of the region—all cascading streams and precipitous peaks and remote forests. They illustrate the myth. I fell hard for that myth before I knew anything about the Adirondacks. I was still seeking the myth when I walked into Room #6 and endured repeated thermostat lessons. I had a fairly average White, American, suburban, middle-class childhood in the 1980s and 1990s. I was more interested in Paperboy and the $999,999 SimCity cheat code than campfires and trails to alpine peaks. I went to Boy Scout camp one summer, where I could have learned to spark a fire with sticks or navigate by map and compass. At lunch one day two boys made fun of me because my mom had packed me a box of animal crackers. I didn't go back.

Why did a kid whose backyard was a cornfield attach an exclamation point to the name of a forest he'd never seen? This strikes something vital about the place of the Adirondacks in American culture. The Adirondacks rose to popularity in the late nineteenth century just as some people said the frontier in the West was closing and more Americans were beginning to appreciate the experience of wilderness rather than trying to subdue it. In the Adirondacks—the Adirondacks!—they had a chance to do that whole frontier rigamarole all over again, this time without having to traverse a continent. With less risk of getting a slug to the gut. With a lower chance of starving alone in some parched wasteland and having coyotes and vultures pick your ribs clean. With enough potential danger to brag about going there but not enough to be, well, dangerous. That idea has persisted, shifting into a love of the scenery and wilderness, and then was handed down to me in the excitement the name brought to my mind. The Adirondacks is a geography that has skewed American thought. It wasn't the first large, wild park in America, but it was the first that could be easily reached from East Coast and Midwest cities.

Out of all the rural areas of the United States, including those in the West, which are bigger and propped up by more pervasive myths about adventure and nation and wilderness and freedom, why has the Adirondacks accumulated such a well-known identity beyond its boundaries? There's no chair named after the Sandhills of Nebraska. No rustic ceiling fan sitting on Big Box shelves named after the Colorado Plateau. In the nineteenth century, there were other popular highland destinations near the East Coast. The Poconos. The Allegheny Mountains. The White Mountains. Why is the Adirondacks still so widely known? How had it escaped obscurity? Why do so many flatlanders still go there?

One way to think of the Adirondacks is as a resort region many decades past its last prime, now a tired, gimmicky area of only regional interest. Just another state park. Another way is to think of the Adirondacks as an idea diffused throughout the nation, permeating the meaning of forests and outdoor recreation and parks and preservation and wilderness. That's the more accurate tale. Every park and protected environment in America contains a faint echo of the Adirondacks. How else to explain that the myth of the Adirondacks reached me, a failed Boy Scout, in that limestone valley?

Listening to white tractor trailers and fretting over seasonal employment and the profit margin of a roadside motel and the public relations problems of thermostat control, and wondering what that guy across the restaurant would think when he first encountered fire ants in Texas, I had to admit that what I had found up there didn't match the myth. That was disappointing but not too surprising. The myths of places always prove specious if we look too closely. That's why we work so hard to prop them up. That's why we don't often bother to look too closely.

I'd later realize what I had found up there was more complicated than the myth, more dynamic and undergoing change, grittier, like glacial sand in your right shoe, and full of people and their stories and competing histories, packed with conflicting visions of what the region had been and might yet become. Except—sometimes it did match the myth. Sometimes it matched the myth exactly, or at least for a fleeting moment it did, as if the myth weren't even a myth. Long after I thought I had learned too much and seen too much to fall for the myth, long after I thought I was too informed and too level-headed to sucker for such hackneyed nonsense, I did just that: fell for that myth like a fool of a tourist feeding a marshmallow to a black bear at the town dump. Car window rolled down. Arm outstretched. Eyes closed. Sweaty palm open and facing up. Hoping for drool but not fangs.

That melancholy night in Tupper Lake forced me to find another way to think about the Adirondacks and its history. Which meant thinking about why I was drawn to this place. Which meant figuring out that exclamation point. Which meant rethinking how I thought Americans had enjoyed the wild outdoors. Which meant that everything I thought I knew about the Adirondacks had to go. I'd have to start again.

I LEFT ROOM #6 BEFORE dawn the next morning, drove through Tupper Lake, and parked at an empty trailhead. That's why I had driven up—to hike a mountain that a friend told me had the best view around.

By the light of my headlamp I walked a trail through a towering forest of Forever Wild hemlock, birch, and maple. If they somehow escaped climate cataclysm, these trees would be here in three hundred years, rotting on the ground, harboring the next generation. The forest smelled good. Wet trees. Wet leaves. Cold, wet rock. The trail kicked up a gully; the foot-worn path kinked and dodged. I hauled myself from rock to rock, happy to forget my concerns of the night before.

In a plush, mossy nook the trail leveled off. I snuck through a notch in a cliff and scampered up a slope of greasy mud, birch roots for handles, to the summit. Southeast I looked up to the sharp ridges of the Adirondacks' highest mountains wrapped in agitated clouds. I turned around. The horizon jumped thirty miles away. Up on that bare dome of gray rock I stood perched high above distant knobby hills that kneeled in a murky forest pocked with dozens of lakes, each lake a glint of pastel light amid wisps of fog. In that eerily temperate December dawn, there was an uncanny peace.

Chapter 2

OVER THE PAST TEN THOUSAND years or so, this is what's happened in the Adirondacks:

Native Americans lived there. They still do and have since not long after the glaciers melted. The Haudenosaunee and Algonquian peoples and their predecessors traded, hunted deer and moose and maybe caribou, fished by wooden torch, sang, danced, died, gave birth, told stories, hunkered down out of the winter wind, slapped mosquitos and blackflies, chipped stones into points, grew corn and then ground it with stone pestles. I often wondered about their names for lakes and mountains. Rocks, too. If the next nineteen pages of this book were filled with the unrecoverable traces of that time, it would more accurately display the scale of Indigenous Adirondack occupancy.

Europeans arrived on the fringes about four hundred years ago. To more accurately display the scale of European occupancy, that sentence would dangle, alone, at the end of those nineteen pages.

The Europeans purchased every beaver pelt they could. Various would-be colonizers dreamed it a virgin land of jewels and precious metals. The Dutch feared it might harbor unicorns. The first European to cross the Adirondacks, long before it was called that, was either an ambitious trapper or an abducted French missionary. Official maps depicted the region as a few rivers scattered on a blank spot. Native and European trappers scratched more accurate maps on birch bark.

Of the recorded voices from that time, not one really knew what was there. Some said it didn't exist, that it was all a ploy. In 1755, a map of the region noted: "This Country by reason of Mountains, Swamps & drowned Lands is impassable & uninhabited." Either a lie or an oversight or a way to stake claim by falsely calling the land empty. But the sentiment stuck and still resonates with many flatlanders. If that were now an Adirondack marketing slogan, I believe it would boost tourism 20 percent.

After the Revolution, wealthy men from coastal cities speculated in their convictions about what the region should become. They purchased expansive tracts and then sold them without ever setting foot there. One bought four million acres or so for eight cents per acre. Another group went into the interior to survey one million acres. After they drank the last of their rum, they climbed a low mountain with a good view, decided to eyeball the rest, and went home.

The region was a harsh but appealing refuge for Native Americans whom colonists had violently evicted from New England. The same goes for European outcasts and hermits. To disappear, there was plenty of space.

Settlers wriggled up river valleys, hearing panthers shrieking in the night, and lived alongside Indigenous families who were already there. Swinging an ax, gardening, hunting, scraping deer hides, raising livestock, trapping, boiling maple syrup, baking potash, and sewing with sinews— all were necessary for a family to survive. A farmer could clear three or four acres of forest per year. Loggers cut the tallest, straightest white pines—pines three to five feet in diameter and a hundred feet high—and on spring freshets floated them to flatland cities. Farming, logging: after a few decades, the result was only a few clearings around the fringe and a few incursions up river valleys, like a chipped rim and a crack or two on a dinner plate.

From the interior, forest of mystery, arrived reports of volcanoes, a red, turbulent glow on the horizon. False, those reports, but it took a long time for flatlanders to find out for sure. The Erie Canal whisked most restless New England farmers to flat, fertile, rock-free Ohio. The Adirondacks became an eddy in America's rush west.

Scientists, artists, and writers discovered the region. They wanted it to be a wilderness. So that's what they called it, and that's what most flatlanders have called it ever since. Scientists measured elevations and wanted to open it to progress, profit. Artists painted scenes: big rocks, shadowy pines, penumbral dusk light, and the luminous crescent of a sandy shore.

One geologist, Ebenezer Emmons, named the Adirondacks the Adirondacks in 1838. Emmons considered naming the Adirondacks Aganuschioni because he thought Aganuschioni had a better sound.

"Adirondacks" might have been a corruption of the name of a tribe that never lived or hunted anywhere in the Adirondacks. It might also have been an Anglicization of a derisive title the Haudenosaunee called some Algonquin tribes, meaning, possibly, bark eaters, because that's how those tribes survived famine, or because they dwelled in the forest, or because they cut fallen trees to clear a route down narrow rivers. It might have been a generic term for foreigners. Translation between languages might have confused the root for "tree" with the root for "rock," and the phrase might originally have been about a people who lived in the land of rock. That's the story I like best. Emmons intended for the name to apply to a single range of mountains. Later writers stretched it out.

In 1840, a surveyor wrote that the region was "as little known and as inadequately appreciated as the secluded valleys of the Rocky Mountains or the burning plains of Central Africa." Shocked that such a wilderness remained in the East, wealthy sportsmen had to see it for themselves. *Ho! For the woods!* (In this era, exclamation points first appear in Adirondack writings.) Wearing coarse woolen shirts and cowhide boots, the sports, as they were called, ventured along rough paths into the wilds, often sleeping in settlers' log cabins. In the interior, if the sap was flowing and the bark would peel, a guide, usually a farmer, a trapper, or a Native American—sometimes all three—built a spruce bark shanty. Over an open fire the guide cooked trout stuffed with salt pork.

A few sports wrote poetically about what they saw and felt: "It was wonderful how those solemn mountains, swelling and rolling, with the forests draping them to the summits, and heaving, rising and sinking into ridges and gorges . . . seemed animated by a presence which we all felt but none could define—a something that awed us though we could not say why." The sports fished and shot deer (relying on the expertise of their guides), looked at the stars, listened to guides tell stories, and expected to bump into warriors and trappers around the next gooseneck bend in the river.

Loggers cut all of the region's biggest white pines along rivers and streams, so they started cutting spruce until they had cut most of those, too. *Cut out and get out.* More sports showed up after reading published tales of Adirondack adventure. Sports slept on loose boards across the rafters of a boardinghouse. If too many sports showed up, the porch became prized real estate, buggy but typically dry.

Some said the Adirondacks was now ruined, trampled, overbooked, civilized. Arcadian days gone for good. Every summer, newcomers showed up giddy at the gates of a wilderness untouched.

After the Civil War, the nation antsy and eager to get away, more and more people ventured north. Some went west, too—to the Rockies, to the Sierras—but the Adirondacks was easier to get to and still felt wild, a chunk of the unexplored West displaced to the domesticated East. That story still has traction. I took my first trips to the Adirondacks when I wanted adventure but couldn't afford airfare to Colorado.

Some tourists longed to gaze at scenery and breathe pristine air, not shoot deer or hook trout. This must have struck locals as odd, since they cut a living from land that was ice for six months and mud for another three, but they were happy to take flatlanders' money.

Tally-ho stagecoaches, like in a John Ford western, replaced wagons, and steamboats paced lakes and rivers. The Adirondacks was a wilderness with steamboat tickets. Some steamboats were not much bigger than a rowboat. Worried that steamboats would ruin their business, guides sank a few in protest. Tracing the most tortuous, shallow streams, sometimes a steamboat got stuck. Passengers shifted to the high side to get it out of the mud and moving again.

On a date that's still disputed, someone shot the last Adirondack moose.

The state of New York stopped selling land at bargain prices and called the region a park and imposed regulations and game laws. Flatlanders applauded the state's prescience. Locals protested. With good reason. No one had asked them what they thought, and no longer could they walk out back and cut trees or kill deer or catch trout where and when they pleased. Some still did. Most got away with it. One resident got caught cutting Forever Wild trees, was fined, and then cut more Forever Wild trees to pay the fine. Hotels still served poached venison. On menus it was Mountain Mutton.

Before the twentieth century, railroads skirted the region, and then one sliced right through. The Adirondacks was a wilderness with a timetable.

Developers sold lakefront lots, and loggers chopped down more trees, shipped them out. More and more flatlanders built camps. Something about the Adirondacks made people want to own a piece of it. That something, it might have been—and might still be—the Adirondack mystique: unicorns, volcanoes, Indians, trappers, and hermits. It might also have been increasing disposable income, faster modes of travel, a growing national appreciation of the outdoors, anxiety about industrial society, and the lingering influence of Romanticism.

Luxurious hotels popped up in scenic spots near railroads. Guests spent three weeks or a month or the whole summer. Wooden, most hotels burned. Some were rebuilt. Some burned again. At one hotel, dinner on July 24, 1909, was boiled red snapper with lobster sauce, iced cucumbers, and Hollandaise potatoes. For dessert, bread pudding with brandy sauce. Many hotels mounted a moose head above the fireplace or the front desk. Importing mounted moose heads from wilder places where moose still roamed, Maine or Canada, a local likely turned a profit.

Some said the Adirondacks was now ruined, trampled, overbooked, civilized. Arcadian days gone for good. Every summer, newcomers showed up giddy at the gates of a wilderness untouched.

When automobiles became affordable in the 1920s, the middle class drove up. CABINS—BEER—POP—FOOD—GAS: signs on the roadside. The wilderness could be seen in a day or two, cruising right on through. Locals built rows of one-room white cabins along tourist routes. Even more flatlanders built camps, and real estate developers caught on.

After World War II, neon motel signs hummed, flickered, and snapped on along the busiest roads, now smooth and fast. The Adirondacks was a wilderness with tourist traps and bumper stickers: FRONTIERTOWN— ENCHANTED FOREST—THE NORTH POLE—ANIMAL LAND. And yet parcels of forest felt untracked, wild, strange creatures howling. Adventurous families spent their vacations paddling aluminum canoes, sleeping under the stars, eating oatmeal and Spam, and expecting to bump into warriors and trappers around the next gooseneck bend in the river.

A four-lane interstate highway—still the only one—cut through the eastern edge in 1967. The Adirondacks was a wilderness with exit ramps and rest stops.

Today, some say the Adirondacks is ruined, trampled, overbooked, civilized. Arcadian days gone for good. Every summer, newcomers show up giddy at the gates of a wilderness untouched.

1

On almost every drive up, the first Adirondack lake I saw was plastered on a billboard. Six real estate agents dressed in business casual stood thigh-deep in the water, everyone smiling, waving to the camera. They'd been standing there for quite some time, so it seemed. Water had wicked a good distance up each agent's pants. Stuck into the sand in front of them, a sign said SOLD.

2

Against a good gale, I paddled across Fish Pond, oblong, trees tight to shore, a few miles from the nearest road. A teenager in a much larger canoe waved, changed course. He paddled over to chat. Shouting, we talked about the wind.

"I've heard it's always like this, up here," he said.

I tried to tell him that wasn't true, that last fall I was up here when the water was glass. He wouldn't hear it. His myth of the Adirondacks demanded a remote lake where the brisk west wind never flagged.

3

Sucker Lake: Locals had named it after gullible flatlanders, like myself, I was sure. It's actually named after the lake's abundant leeches.

4–16

One day I drove past thirteen lakes not visible from the road. Each lake was hidden in the forest, somewhere. All I saw of each lake was a roadside real estate sign that said WATERFRONT. One said PRIVATE WATER-FRONT—the ultimate feature in Adirondack real estate.

Chapter 3

A LATE-AUGUST DRIVE to the gates of a wilderness untouched:

Strap canoe to top of car. Tighten and twist the two blue straps so they don't whine. Head north, merge onto the interstate. Get cut off by a black pickup truck with an ADK sticker.

Raining, concrete wet and glossy. Windshield wipers scattering wild reflections, headlights and brake lights, traffic cones and giant arrows blinking orange.

Vehicles and signs along the way north:

Whitehawk tow-behind camper just as I find the Beastie Boys' "Intergalactic" on the radio. I turn it up.

SUMMER MEANS CAMP

An older couple in a bus-like camper with a flat, someone already stopped to assist.

YOUR GUIDE TO THE ADIRONDACKS

Pickup truck pulling a camper called Wildwood, two jet skis shoehorned into the truck's bed.

ADIRONDACKS' BEST PIZZA

A Prius capped with a canoe, the canoe a good bit longer than the car.

KEITH'S TAXIDERMY

Just before entering the park, I pass The Wigwam, a restaurant. The tail of a plane sticks through the roof, as if the plane crashed propeller first. Flash of a silver lake through a wet forest of pine and spruce. A herd of wooden moose in front of a rustic furniture store. Cross bridge over Moose River.

Flip through the radio stations. Can only find NPR. Up here it's like pirate radio, broadcast from every rock, every tree. Traffic jam: an RV is slowing down a line of fifteen vehicles, including a dump truck and an appliance delivery van. Something bulky in the back of the van makes a hollow thunk at each bump.

FOR SALE 92 ACRES

Stop at a grocery store to buy food for the next few days. The store is packed with tourists who don't know where anything they want is shelved. Lady in front of me in the checkout line says to cashier, "Hang in there." Cashier rolls her tired eyes, gives a smile that seems to wink. The busy season is a sprint. Next weekend it ends. The green will go away. Swiping my credit card, I complain about the tourists. The cashier frowns, ferrets me out as a flatlander.

SOUVENIR VILLAGE

Rain again.

WELCOME TO

LEISURE SHORES

Hazy pines strung along a ridge.

PROSPECT POINT COTTAGES

NO VACANCY

—on a canoe-shaped sign. In the winter, it's on a snowshoe.

WATERFRONT

Sun sneaks out. Black glossy shadows in the wet woods.

SECLUDED RUSTIC HOMESITES

—which means they're dry.

Onto a back road I turn left: asphalt then gravel then sand but it's wide and smooth, flowing through unbroken woods. Windy, trees slashing back and forth: creaks, sharp cracks, branches crashing to the ground. I'm concerned the lake where I'm headed with my boat and gear and food for a camping trip will be all chop. Around a turn, a white tractor trailer barrels toward me on my side of the road. The blurry bulk doesn't budge or even bother to honk. Dust swirling. Stones flying. I swerve into a ditch. I get out to check on my boat and find the two blue straps still snug. A whiff of freshly chipped trees.

I park in a gravel lot with fourteen other cars and walk down a short trail to check out the lake. It's broad, ringed by tall pines. It's the myth spread out before me. In the limestone valley at the age of thirteen, this is what

I thought the Adirondacks would look like. Nothing but water and rocks and trees and sky.

Two middle-aged guys stand nearby on the beach, along with a canoe and bags of food and coolers and clothes and tents and two titanium camp-stools, the price tags still attached. They're headed out for a few nights of wilderness camping. We've all crossed into a designated Wilderness Area along our walk from parking lot to lake. Decision time for them: Should they cram all the hamburger patties and bacon into one cooler and stack the beer in the other cooler? Or use lake water to later chill the beer?

I jog back to the parking lot, unstrap my boat, lift it off my car. Sleeping bag, tent, and food, I pack them all in those waterproof bags that you fold three times and then click the black plastic buckle. I can't find my stove. I unpack everything, toss it on the ground, find stove on the bottom of the last bag. Fold, fold, fold. Click. Carrying my bags, my boat, and my paddle, I walk back down the trail to the lake. Those two guys, they're still standing there trying to figure out what to do. I set my boat in the water, load the bags. I wade shin-deep, launch, glide, hop in: slick, like I know what I'm doing.

The lake is glass. Where's the wind? A nearby island is all slabs of gray rock, and plush, pale moss and trees somehow holding on. I round it. A gust lashes me. Dip one end of the paddle and pull. Dip the other end of the paddle and pull, trying to keep the boat head-on to the waves. White-caps, spray stinging my face, a roller coaster of a ride. A far shoreline of pines leans away from the wind, and I don't know if they've grown like that or if the wind has them pinned down.

On an island near the middle of the lake I find a vacant campsite. The island is long and skinny, tapers at both ends, a spine of bedrock that peers above waterline. There's a stone fire ring, a flat spot beneath pines to pitch a tent, a rocky point facing west, and a small sand beach with a far view to a forested shore, rolling blue ridges in the distance. It's the only site on the island. For free for the night: my own Adirondack island.

Set up camp. Listen to the waves, to the wind. Roam the island. Nap on waterfront rocks. Wake up just in time to see those two guys paddle by, a case of beer wedged between one guy's knees.

All afternoon, sunlight strikes the far shore of pines and then slips away, and then strikes the far shore of pines and then slips away.

TWO BALD EAGLES LAND in a lightning-struck pine and fluff their feathers above the rocky point where I sit to watch sunset. The wind has died. Bald eagle feathers grating lightning-scorched pine bark, that's all I can hear.

It's wilderness reverie, an escape, a moment to reflect on the quiet places where we are fortunate enough to still find a scrap of calm that grants us peace. I recline on the still sun-warm shield of gray rock and tuck my hands behind my head, take in the view. Sunset blushes a neon pink beyond gray ridges, and when I trace the shapes of the ridges, which roll and dip and rise all across the panorama I can see, I think about the underside of the glacier that sculpted them, think about this landscape as the inverted form of the Ice Age, think about how all that ice pressed down and melted to leave this puddle hemmed in by rock and sand.

Then on the far shore I see it and it snaps me out of the myth. In some book I had read about it but had forgotten it would be there. Across the lake, in a break in the forest, there's a weedy clearing that was once a close-cropped lawn. The lawn once held a mansion, the wilderness retreat of a man who had married a Vanderbilt and then managed the construction of the only railroad to cross the Adirondacks, which opened the whole region up to tourists. In the living room there had stood a chimney of massive, rough-cut rocks, more crag than chimney. I've seen a photograph. A stuffed panther crouching on one ledge. Two stuffed bear cubs hiding in the nooks. Three bear rugs on the floor, and in the corner, on top of a cabinet, a stuffed fox standing alert. The panther might have been the last killed in the Adirondacks. It stood stuffed in a hotel, and then in someone's attic, and then William Seward Webb, the railroad man who owned the mansion, bought it.

How was I supposed to feel about this presence of the human past here in the wilderness? I tried to ignore it. By the time the pink had drained out of the sky and the eagles had moved on I had changed my mind, and I wished the state had let the chimney stand, those craggy blocks of stone where the stuffed carcass of what might have been the last Adirondack panther crouched, as a reminder of what this lake once was. I didn't have any particular affection for Webb's story, although I do appreciate that before he died he arranged to have a boulder from this property hauled to Woodlawn Cemetery in the Bronx as a footstone for his grave. There's a township named after him, and his story—rich man opening up the woods for more people to get there—is the type that Adirondack history tends to valorize. But I didn't want the land wiped clean. I wanted the chimney to be a ruin, a reminder of what it once was—a rich family's PRIVATE WATERFRONT, and before that the realm of a hunter and trapper who occasionally wore a cloak of furs, mangy and rank, and roamed down to the settlements to flaunt his collection of bird and animal skins, and before that a homeland of Native American tribes. I wanted to have land that could feel wild and still have a past we acknowledged. The state torched the mansion when it bought the land in 1979 and made it Forever Wild.

Forever Wild, that radical act of not cutting trees, is often viewed as a landmark victory in natural preservation, a turning point in the way we treat the land. If the Adirondacks appears in history textbooks, it's for that triumph. Forever Wild is framed as part of the inevitable progress we've made as a nation to take better care of the environment. But it also tends to cloak histories that don't match the escape from the world most of us think we want this place to be.

At dark the wind dies. I launch my canoe and float in a stillness that's a lapse in the progression of time.

LET'S TALK ABOUT BOATS:

Two months earlier, I had parked my car at an outfitter next to a different large lake. Late June. A day of blue sky and puffy clouds, forest clicking and buzzing with bugs and birds. For thirty dollars I rented a kayak for a few hours. The man working the counter walked me over to a storage room to find a musty lifejacket and a paddle. He told me my boat was stashed near the dock.

Walking toward the water, he started coughing—hacking, really, phlegmy and gruff. I joked that there must be too much fresh air up here. He caught his breath and then kindly told me he had been a first responder on 9/11. He had moved up here to heal his lungs. I felt like walking into the lake and wedging myself beneath a big round rock.

A clunker, that's what the boat was, a plastic kayak so heavy and boxy I was paddling a forty-gallon insulated cooler with a two-by-four. I was smitten, threading my blocky craft along the shadow line of the shore. Rocks and trees and camps lined most of the lake, ridges and a peaked mountain beyond, and the mirror of a lake reflected the punchy green and blue of the forest and the sky.

Until that afternoon I had seen the Adirondacks mostly from my car or on foot. That afternoon wised me up, made me realize that in a land with so many lakes and rivers I needed to spend more time in a boat.

A guideboat, I desperately wanted to buy one. Guideboats were the Adirondack boat of choice in the late nineteenth century. Sleek, sturdy, relatively light, an oar to each side, a guideboat rowed by a guide could make good time up long lakes when loaded with a sport and a week's worth of gear; could cut through the chop when the afternoon wind kicked up; and when the lake ended, the guide could pick up the boat, set the yoke across his shoulders, and haul the boat to the next lake. A wooden shell walking. There are no portages in the Adirondacks. Up there, a path that connects two lakes is called a carry.

Guideboats were endemic to the Adirondacks. Before roads, the region was too swampy and too thick with trees for wagons to roll. Lakes and rivers: water was the quickest, smoothest route. But the lakes are staccato, streams and marshes strung between, and the rivers drain in a radial pattern rather than slicing through. No unbroken water route exists. Every route involved a series of carries. Native Americans had once used rocks to sink dugout canoes at each end of every carry. Some White trappers adopted bark canoes from Native Americans, but birch trees of the necessary size were rare. Other trappers, taking inspiration from boats they had seen elsewhere, cobbled together boats from pine and spruce and cedar, proto-guideboats. When sports from the cities showed up in the 1830s and 1840s looking for adventure, looking to shoot moose and deer and bear, looking to hook trout, Indigenous and European trappers became guides. They brought their boats along.

In its mature iteration, which first appeared in the 1860s and was perfected by the 1890s, a guideboat is a series of wooden ribs with perpendicular planks pieced together to shape the hull. The middle of the boat yawns, broad and low. Both ends are slender, sharp, with an upward kick like a canoe. A guideboat looks mellow in the middle, frisky and excitable at each end, as if it might get spooked and try to run both ways. Looking down into an empty guideboat is like looking at the rib cage of some lithe beast after scavengers have picked the carcass clean. Twelve to fifteen feet long, typically, guideboats weighed between sixty and seventy-five pounds.

Much to my disappointment, I've never sat in a guideboat. The closest I've been to a guideboat was standing behind velvet ropes in a museum. In my head, if I twice rapped on the planks with the knuckles of my right hand there would be a raspy, tense resonance that would echo pleasantly against a shore of pines.

The ribs of guideboats were cut from spruce crooks. A crook is the flare of a spruce trunk where the wood grain curves to transition from trunk to roots. Bracing the tree against wind, crooks grow strong. Builders scoured the woods for the perfect spruce. A crook is shaped like half of a smile. Two cuts from a crook made two ribs; placed end to end across the boat, they shaped the hull, rib after rib down the spine, each curve bent by the wind and refined to a pattern by a metal blade. Builders honed a boat's hull planking to minute tolerances. The best builders cut planks only a quarter of an inch thick, each plank curving to match the shape of the spruce crook. Where plank met plank, builders planed a fastidious lap. A few thousand tacks and screws held the boat together tight. Some boats were varnished. Some were painted. Most villages had at least one guide-boat builder. Which village built the best guideboat was a never-ending Adirondack argument.

Guideboats were the pickup trucks of the nineteenth century Adiron-dacks. They fit the category of the everyday. The writer of the definitive historical account of guideboats grew up around them. He once said that as a boy he didn't pay much attention to guideboats until they leaked. Gradu-ally guideboats became pleasure craft. Instead of hauling supplies, guides rowed sports out into the wilderness to kill deer or rowed tourists from hotel docks to pick water lilies, maybe out to a rocky point for a picnic. In the early decades of the twentieth century, guides replaced guideboats with outboard motors.

It's a good story, an endemic boat built to facilitate travel in a soggy land. I mention all this for another reason: I ached to row a guideboat. I'd see one strapped in the bed of a pickup truck driving to a lake, or I'd see one on a rack in a boathouse, or I'd see an 1890s photograph of one loaded with two guides, two sports, four dogs, and a dead deer, and I'd go weak in my knees. I searched everywhere for a camp rental that in the list of features included: guideboat. Contemporary guideboat builders craft them with Kevlar shells. One company sells a Kevlar guideboat for about $6,000. I drive a 2008 Subaru Outback, gray, black cloth interior. It has plenty of rattles and clunks and the rear windshield wiper only works when the car is in reverse, but it still passes state inspection. It's worth less than half of a Kevlar guideboat. A company sells a cedar guideboat, ribs and planks varnished—the look that really caught my eye—for about $15,000. Historic guideboats in good condition built by well-known builders in the nineteenth century can sell for thousands more.

I've never cared much for boats. It took me a while to figure out why I longed for a guideboat, why a historical craft seemed to influence the way I experienced this place. In the late nineteenth century, sandy shores near hotels on the fringes of the Adirondacks filled with sports and guides and guideboats, all ready to set off on an adventure up in the wilderness. That excitement! That anticipation! That sense of teetering on the edge of the unknown beyond! I thought a guideboat would let me experience that. Guideboats felt like a vehicle of the frontier, which made them part of that American tale of exploration and adventure and conquest. They might as well have been Conestogas.

Today there are many more gasoline-powered pontoon boats and clunker kayaks, but the guideboat remains the region's emblem for many people. The logo of the preeminent Adirondack museum was a guide carrying a guideboat above his head, a wooden shell walking, until the misguided intervention of a marketing firm. There's a Guide Boat Realty. Driving around the Adirondacks, you might see a sketch of a guideboat on one of their For Sale signs. Browsing real estate listings, I saw a few six-figure camps that included a dusty guideboat suspended between salvaged barn beams above the living room. When someone rows a guideboat onto a public beach near a road, she draws a curious crowd; traffic backs up, like a bison jam in Yellowstone. Nostalgia for the Adirondacks in the time before cars and roads and cell phone towers, that's why guideboats haven't yet been relegated to the pages of hobby boat building magazines. Those boats of the wind in the spruce, they bring that time before back.

Which never struck me as odd until I realized something: Most people, including myself, who today desire guideboats wouldn't have been able to afford to vacation in the Adirondacks when guideboats were the primary mode of travel. We would've roasted all summer in flatland cities.

The canoe I bought a few weeks after I paddled that clunker of a kayak, the canoe I anchored to my car's roof rack with two blue straps before I drove north to the gates of a wilderness untouched, four scraps of foam pipe insulation to cushion the gunwales, that boat has a different lineage.

Guideboats were expensive, even in their time, and they demanded strength and skill to pilot. In 1908, the *New York Times* ran an article titled "Adirondack Boats Cranky: Easiest Thing in the World to Get a Ducking, If You Are Not Careful." Not many people had the skills to show up and set off alone into the wilds in a guideboat without a guide, and only the well-off could afford to hire one.

In the 1880s, George Washington Sears, widely known by his penname, Nessmuk, who had written extensively about outdoor adventure and woodcraft, ordered a series of light solo canoes from boat builder J. H. Rushton. Rushton had built wooden canoes before. Nessmuk pushed him to build them lighter, smaller. Rushton joked to Nessmuk, "If you get sick of this as a *canoe*, use it for a soap dish." Rushton's canoes cost less than a guideboat. A novice could paddle one of the canoes with a double-bladed paddle, much like a kayak. Between nine and ten feet long, the canoes ranged in weight from sixteen to twenty-two pounds, light enough for even the frail and aging Nessmuk to haul from lake to lake on his sojourns. This was Nessmuk's point: his boats were easy to carry from one lake to the next, encouraging solo adventures in the Adirondacks. He hoped to make wilderness voyages affordable for more people, like shop clerks and craftsmen. For their health, for their vigor, Nessmuk wanted to get this class out of the sooty, sickly cities and into the fresh balsam air. The wilderness was then a rich man's playground. Nessmuk wanted to change that. His boats were as much vehicles of social change as they were vehicles of exploration.

Twelve feet long, my boat weighs about eighteen pounds. The designer, the late Peter Hornbeck, partially modeled it after one of Nessmuk's boats. Layers of Kevlar and carbon fiber bonded by epoxy form the hull, yellow on the inside, an inky gray-green exterior. It's no boat of the wind in the spruce, but it didn't cost more than my car. For the first year I owned it, I stored my boat in my garage, balanced on a blue wheelbarrow and a cedar chest Erin bought on Craigslist but hadn't yet refinished. Anytime I wanted to haul mulch or dirt, I had to pick up the canoe and place it in the grass. When I picked it up, Adirondack sand drifted out: glacial dust on the garage floor. My neighbor Alphonse, out for an afternoon stroll with his dog Zeus, would ask how I could so easily hold that boat above my head.

Paddling, I sit on the bottom of the hull on a foam pad, my legs extended in front of me, my knees comfortably bent, my feet resting on foot pegs. One of my favorite Adirondack sounds is the gentle grating of the last few grains of sand on the hull when I paddle away from shore. About one of his boats, Nessmuk said it was "a one-fool power in the middle, gets over the water like a scared loon." Ditto. And I've not yet taken a ducking.

THE LAKE ALL AROUND my private island roared in the middle of the night. Thunder. Lightning. Cloudburst. I scrambled out into the wet black roar to drape a tarp over my tent. At dawn, the storm clouds frayed. The sun reflected off the mirror lake to glimmer on the underside of the pines, the day a brisk fresh green.

To the far shore I paddled, looking for any sign of the chimney and then into the lake's narrow outlet. Pines reflected glossy on the water at each twist, each twist a scrolling reveal: crooked pines, dark spruce shadows and two blue skies, sandy shallows and pools of deep murk. Which tall pines still standing had witnessed the progression from dugout to Kevlar?

According to my map, the river left the lake and flowed sluggish for about a mile to another lake. It then left that lake to flow a bit faster and straighter until it reached Stillwater Reservoir, a shallow, long body of water, shoreline mostly uninhabited. I wanted to paddle through, look around. There's private land between. Nessmuk could've paddled through, but current interpretation of property law argues the route isn't public. If

I had gone that way I might've seen a wire strung across the river, a big orange sign; a remote camera might've snapped my picture, and I might've been sued for trespass just to make a point.

A WEEK EARLIER, I HAD driven up the long gravel road to Stillwater, a lodge, a gas station, a store, and a gravel parking lot clustered at the far end of the reservoir. I was there because I wanted to visit the hamlet of Beaver River. Looking at a map one day, I noticed no road connected to Beaver River's small black dot. A cartographic error, I thought, a missing line, a mapmaker's Monday morning mistake. I decided I'd better go check it out.

It's not a mistake. There's no road. To visit Beaver River, you have a few options. Walk seven miles along a trail through a Wilderness Area. Boat six miles up the reservoir from Stillwater. Charter a floatplane. Drive along the railroad tracks, which by law you're not allowed to do anymore. Or, in the winter, snowmobile across the ice or along the snow-covered tracks. You could ride a train until the 1960s, since Beaver River was a stop along the main line to Montreal. Once there was a road. New York raised the dam and the reservoir swamped it. If you call ahead, you can drive your car onto a barge at Stillwater, float over the flooded portion, and then drive the remaining six miles to Beaver River. This abundance of options makes it sound like there's an overwhelming demand to get there.

At Stillwater I parked my car and boarded the Norridgewock Riverboat. A shuttle to haul guests to a lodge in Beaver River, the oversized pontoon boat also offers narrated, scenic cruises. A round-trip ticket cost me eighteen dollars. Set in rows, the seats are wooden, with slats like park benches. The captain sits up front in a padded white chair, flanked by two screen doors of the type typically found in stock at Home Depot. Walls of wood paneling that's been wet a few times, orange life jackets stashed on the ceiling, a decorative pilot's house welded to the roof, the boat felt like a landlocked clam shack that aspired to be nautical. Generous windows offer passengers panoramic views of the scenery. A few more passengers boarded. One, having just rattled up the long, dusty road to Stillwater, complained that each eighteen-dollar tour should include a free car wash. Scott Thompson, the captain, frowned. He squirmed in his white padded chair, expecting a mutiny, a demand for car wash coupons at the nearest car wash. The nearest car wash is a fifty-minute drive down a different but equally long and dusty road.

A logging town, Beaver River boomed and went bust, and then boomed again and went bust again. All along, sports visited Beaver River to shoot deer and bear, and to listen to guides tell stories about panthers and wolves.

As in most of the Adirondacks, tourism was the economy that endured. After the last logging boom, Beaver River became a real estate scheme. In the 1940s, a prospectus claimed Beaver River was *In the Heart of the Frontier*. As far as I know, there's no Sucker Lake nearby.

Today, Beaver River is less than a square mile of private land packed with a community of one hundred private camps. Thompson's lodge and the Thompson family are the community's focal point. The year-round population of Beaver River is four. Beaver River is an island, surrounded by water and Forever Wild forest. That's why a new road can't be built, and while Forever Wild has never applied to the subaqueous realm— given the amount of fish culling and restocking that's been done over the past century and a half—I bet building a floating bridge would trigger a lawsuit.

For a few decades, locals have been sparring with the state over construction of a new road. Many locals and part-timers either want a new road or want the railroad tracks torn out so the right of way becomes a road. When Thompson saw me scratching notes in my yellow notebook, he asked, bluntly, which side I was on. He contorted his face into a sharp look of scorn, as if he knew for certain I was an anti-road flatlander, that I didn't know the mental and physical demands of living up here. Maybe I projected that insight because I thought it was true: that I couldn't comment critically about the situation of locals because I lived in a neighborhood where I could take a stroll to buy milk and bread and organic goat cheese. I didn't have to board a boat and then drive twenty miles to get to a grocery store. About the new road, I dithered. Thompson dropped it. An apologetic smile snuck back onto his face, probably because I wasn't among the passengers demanding car wash coupons.

My dithering wasn't intended to be diplomatic. I didn't yet know how I felt about the issue. After my visit I hoped a road would never be built. Before roads crossed the Adirondacks, visitors boarded a guideboat at the end of the road to reach the interior. Here was a place where that was still somewhat true, even if it was artificial, Forever Wild trees the only obstacle. I never got over my regret that I felt this way. Even if the lack of a road added to the atmosphere of the area, was that worth the inconvenience and potential danger it created for locals? Was I being too sentimental about this town that had no road? What was I even being sentimental about? You can reach Beaver River via motorboat or snowmobile. This wasn't the frontier. Would Beaver River somehow feel less like the Adirondacks if I could drive there?

Thompson told stories while he piloted the boat. For many years, residents and camp owners in Beaver River modified old trucks with small metal wheels so they could drive on the railroad tracks. Tighter regulation ended that practice, officially, but he made it sound like some people still do it when no one's looking. Most of the time no one is looking. A construction company drained the reservoir in 2001 to repair the dam. In the exposed sandy bed of what used to be the Beaver River, Thompson found discarded modern camping gear. He also found logging tools and horseshoes, as if artifacts from the past century and a half had dropped from the sky. I enjoyed that image: each Adirondack lake not only an accumulation of rock and sand and silt, not only layer after layer of pollen pressed into rank, benthic muck since the glaciers had melted 15,000 years earlier, but also a stratigraphic record of the objects locals and flatlanders had used on or near the water: carbon fiber tent poles, bamboo fishing lures, hand-carved canoe paddles, maybe a bottle of whiskey or a logger's leather boot, maybe a dugout canoe sunk with rocks, some arrowheads a few hundred years old, some arrowheads a few thousand years old. All of human history along this lake was pressed down there in laminations I wanted to mine. I looked down into the water and thought about mammoth tusks, even though I didn't know whether mammoths had lived there or even, if they had, whether their tusks would still be intact.

Cruising up the middle of the lake, Thompson said a moose had been spotted nearby recently, and that the reservoir had the highest population of loons in the Adirondacks, and that every boat tour so far this year had seen a bald eagle. Everyone on the boat perked up. Thompson spoke quickly, and he mumbled sometimes, which is a trait I notice about people because I'm an inveterate mumbler, and he didn't like it when a passenger interrupted his narration by asking an unexpected question—such as, Where do you go when you want to go out to eat? (admittedly, an inane question to ask a person who has to board a boat to reach a road)—but his words held some unexpected authority of not only the boat but of this reservoir. Each time he mentioned an animal, everyone on the boat glanced out the boat's big windows, as if Thompson's words could cue that creature to show itself.

Thompson said a fleet of limousines was waiting to take us the remaining half mile into Beaver River. One woman looked at her husband in a way that suggested they had just won a free Caribbean cruise. We docked, disembarked. Everyone formed a line and climbed aboard a short white bus. The bus rattled and clanked and eventually got going, rolling dusty down the gravel road along the railroad tracks. I walked.

Camp after camp along the road, Beaver River felt like a suburban neighborhood that might be called Forest Grove, built when asbestos still seemed like a good idea. The day was hot. Shade felt good. Beaver River's lawn ornaments were propane tanks, generators, solar panels, and outhouses: off-grid idols.

(It's been nineteen pages.)

Most other passengers went to Thompson's lodge for lunch. If I went inside, I thought I'd be expected to buy something, a hamburger or a postcard, a time share. Along the roads I walked, through a cluster of camps, down to the dock where most Beaver River camp owners arrive by boat. That sandy road was where toads went to die. Every toad that had ever been flattened on the road remained, desiccated, like old scraps of leather in the dry, soft sand.

A clutter of stashed cars and trucks marked the end of the road. A 1980s GMC Eagle station wagon spray-painted orange, "09" in white paint on the side. A green 1950s Dodge truck with Wyoming plates. A golf cart wrapped in a beige vinyl cover, the left front wheel chocked with a coordinating beige cobble. Rocks and logs, divots and mounds, the lumpy surface of the woodland clearing heaved the vehicles askew. A front end pushed up, a wheel dropped down, a tire pinched to the rim, a bumper bent: the vehicles looked more expressive than a typical collection of worn-out cars. They seemed to be singing some strange song of the north woods. In this parking lot at the end of a road beyond the end of any road, most vehicles lacked registration or an inspection sticker. Most looked like they could putter about fifty feet. Almost far enough. Camp owners only drive them to haul supplies from dock to camp a few times each summer.

In the week ahead, after I drove around the Adirondacks for a few more days and then drove back home, planted some spinach seeds in my garden and mowed the grass, and then drove back up to camp at the lake where I would see those two guys trying to decide about where to chill their beer, I spent an unreasonable amount of time thinking about those cars. A few years earlier, I would have called them an eyesore, petitioned the state to clean them up, plant some trees and native grasses, post No Parking signs. The cars didn't match the aesthetic associated with environmental protection or wilderness. That's why they stuck with me. They were something almost forbidden, something I had been told not to praise, especially not here in one of the cradles of the American environmental movement, one of the places that had shaped the way so many Americans thought about wild land and what it should look like.

The more I thought about the cars, the more I realized they spoke to the Adirondacks and its history and how people interact with the land in a way that we too often overlook. They were about the necessity of moving supplies around in a remote area that felt wild and was hard to get to. Guides had always helped flatlanders overcome distance, by rowing them or hauling their gear, and now that guides are rare and there are motors and cheap gasoline, the worn-out cars help with that hauling. They'll never be romanticized like guides and their boats. No museum will ever ring them in velvet rope. The junk cars conflicted with the myth and yet presented a way of being in the woods that deserved more consideration. They made me wonder if Forever Wild and the myth had restricted the recent and future Adirondack story to the narrative of wilderness versus development, good versus bad, pristine versus developed—an increasingly trite narrative as the planet warms and the oceans rise. Here was a place between. It felt wild but wasn't pristine. Why couldn't it fit into the American story of what the outdoors should be? I guess it did, since the families here already enjoyed it. But the American story of the outdoors is so often one of an empty, timeless wilderness. The Adirondacks and its history—if you really paid attention to the details rather than just to the myth—pushed back, offered appealing alternatives. Was what America had so far extracted from the Adirondacks only the myth? Rather than really looking at the Adirondacks and the various ways that people have interacted with this wild land, had we called it a wilderness so it matched our expectations? Had we written the eccentricities and possibilities out of this place?

As I stood there looking at those cars, a family arrived on a pontoon boat. A guy hopped off and trotted uphill toward the vehicles. He opened the door of an unlocked SUV. Before climbing in, he briefly bowed his head to pray, maybe curse. After some coaxing and a few squeaky stomps on the gas, it started. Quivering, brakes shrieking, slabs of rust rattling, the SUV rolled downhill to the dock.

Swatting all the time at gnats, the family loaded heavy crates into the back of the SUV. Enough food for a week at camp. Some bedsheets. Plastic jugs of booze. Firewood. An entire crate of store-bought cookies. Because of the bugs, the family moved fast. Loaded, warmed up, and running quite a bit smoother, the SUV heaved and creaked uphill, belching and growling, trailing a pale blue haze of burnt oil. It looked like a good time, and it made me wish that I had a Beaver River camp, that I had been coming here since I was a kid. I liked that Beaver River didn't pretend to be the frontier or the wilderness and yet embraced that it was a significant departure from the everyday. A week later, watching sunset from my private island just a few miles up the river that might have a camera to catch trespassers, it must've been my time at Beaver River that made me want to see that chimney. What I most appreciated was that Beaver River and that island could be just a few miles apart and yet tell such different stories of the outdoors. I liked that the geography of the Adirondacks could put those two places into conversation, could show us that it didn't have to be one or the other.

Two women hopped off the boat and started walking toward their family's camp. They dragged wheeled suitcases behind them, two sets of parallel lines in the soft sand, the lines swerving frequently to avoid flattened toads.

17

Owners of waterfront camps on Star Lake build floating decks that motor. Wooden floor, wooden railings—about twelve feet by sixteen—chairs and a beach umbrella, coolers, and sometimes a propane grill, the floating decks all look nearly the same, an outboard motor bolted on the back. They go slow, chug along creaking. The first one on Star Lake floated on empty maple syrup barrels in the 1960s. An 1894 guidebook says, "Star Lake, *star*-like in form, purity and brightness is one of the fairest of all the galaxy of gems adorning the Adirondack wilderness." There's a sandbar, one arm of the star, and on perfect summer days, that's where floating decks gather. Maybe two, maybe eighteen. One with a waterslide. One with a second story, stairs to the top. One with a radio playing Florida Georgia Line at a perfectly reasonable volume. Three or four decks lashed together form a barge. Out there on the sand on an arm of the star, it's a party. A plastic table and some plastic chairs dropped in the water, waist deep: people sit there all afternoon drinking beer, filling empties with that gem of a lake so the cans don't blow away.

18–24

Nick Stoner discovered a chain of three small lakes in the early nineteenth century. A flood had washed hundreds of fish over a beaver dam. Dry, the fish had died. Stoner found the fish in putrid heaps. He named the three lakes Stink. Stoner was probably a hardscrabble farmer who turned to trapping because the stony soil wouldn't yield. Adirondack literature later mythologized Nick Stoner as a type of Adirondack Daniel Boone. Stink Lakes, again smelling like spruce, became Stoner Lakes. In the 1920s, a real estate developer (ignoring at least ten thousand years of Native American residency completely) hoped to augment the area's natural scenery with some human history. He latched onto Stoner's life story. The developer donated land for a golf course, named after Stoner, and dedicated a bronze statue of Stoner at the top of a low rise on the course.

South of Stoner Lakes: Broomstick Lake, Goose Egg Lake, Nine Corners Lake, and Pine Lake. On a sandy shore of Pine Lake, there's a cluster of mobile homes made into camps. There's also a pizza shop, a mini-golf course, and a dance hall. Pinesap and sun-hot sand, the whole place smelled like that when I drove to Pine Lake one afternoon to look around. Off-season, the place was empty. I parked next to the dance hall. On one side of the brown building, large brown letters read: ADIRONDACK PARADISE.

25–83

Forty-three Mud Ponds, and sixteen Clear.

84

Jonathan Wright, known as Jock, walked out of the woods lugging a basket of trout he had caught in a lake no one else had ever seen. (Typing those words, I think: the Adirondacks!) Veteran of the Revolutionary War, marksman and hunter, scout and trapper, Jock roamed the wilds. In town, Jock drank rum. As he drank more and more, the water of his lake became more crystalline, the beaches more golden, the trees taller, the deer faster and fatter, the fish larger and in such shocking abundance that on buggy evenings in June the lake appeared to boil. ADIRONDACK PARADISE. Sloshed or sober, Jock refused to reveal the location of his lake. I would've done the same. Sometime later, someone found Jock's lake. Likely that ruined Jock's day.

About sixty years later, a man named Dut built a hotel on Jocks Lake. When guests arrived at the end of the road, they summoned a boat ride to the hotel by blowing into a horn. Bright and pleasant, a large porch fronting the water, Dut's hotel sat on a spit of rock sheltered by a grove of hemlocks. For the first season, the cost to stay at this scenic, remote getaway on Jocks Lake up in the Adirondack wilderness, all meals, all activities, all adventure, and all advice included, was zero dollars per night, and the cost of whiskey, by the glass, was zero dollars. Always there was a crowd, a party in the wilderness. Most nights a group chaired by Dut stayed up all night playing poker and, probably, shot their guns into the forest, water, and air.

In 1890, a group of wealthy men formed the private Adirondack League Club and purchased a 90,000-acre retreat that included Jocks Lake. The club built pricey rustic camps on the shore. Delmonico's in New York City hosted the club's Winter Camp Fire Dinner. Adirondack red spruce tips formed each table's centerpiece—the club a bit of the city in the woods, the spruce tips a bit of the woods in the city. I'm assuming the spruce tips were Adirondack. I don't have evidence to prove the spruce tips weren't cut in Central Park. Shipping red spruce branches from the wilderness to the city seems like the type of outlandish gesture a group of rich nineteenth-century men with a taste for the Adirondacks might make.

The club changed the lake's name to Honnedaga Lake, thought to be a local Native American word for "clear waters."

I TRIED ONE DAY to drive to Honnedaga Lake, down the long, rough gravel road. The lake was still privately owned, I knew. I hoped the club was magnanimous, that they allowed the public to pull into a parking lot to gaze up the long wild view where people going to Dut's once blew the horn for a ride.

Nowhere near the lake, the road dead-ended dry at a gate:

NOTICE!

This is a

PRIVATE PARK

These posted private lands and the private waters therein contained are
and will be used as a Private Park for the propagation and protection of
fish, birds and quadrupeds, and
All persons are hereby warned
against hunting, fishing or trapping
thereon, or trespassing thereon for
any such purpose or for any other
purpose whatsoever.

85–98

Lost Pond: there are fourteen.

99 & 100

Driving a slow loop around two small lakes, I caught a glimpse of a waterfront camp through sun-dappled maple leaves. The roofline resembled a pagoda. That's odd, I thought, in this region famous for its rustic architecture of birch bark and logs and twigs.

Later I'd learn that the roofline's story began with a name change. In 1924, a real estate developer, Lyon de Camp, successfully petitioned New York to change the name of Hellgate Ponds to Okara Lakes. "Okara" might be a Haudenosaunee word for "The Eyes." I've never found any record of what the Haudenosaunee called the lakes. De Camp probably hoped "Okara" sounded more romantic and mystic, traits that would allow him to sell more lots to suckers. De Camp owned 17,000 acres. He planned to develop the tract into Ga-Wan-Ka, a wilderness playground of estates and camps. Okara was phase one. De Camp dedicated Ga-Wan-Ka as a memorial to the League of the Iroquois. At the dedication ceremony, the crowd feasted and watched smoke signals rise from a nearby peak. The cover of the Okara sales brochure depicted a Native American. He wore a long feather headdress, the type worn by Native Americans a thousand or so miles west on the northern Great Plains.

De Camp hired architect Harold Van Buren Magonigle to design camps to build there. Magonigle thought the region looked a bit like Japan, so he mimicked elements from traditional Japanese architecture. Magonigle could make that stylistic leap because flatlanders have always seen the Adirondacks as a big green blank where any style might stick. All along, the Adirondacks has required invention and humbug. In that theatrical type of truth-seeking that infects many architects, Magonigle spent months exploring "to find the true Adirondack color." He found it: a pale blue-gray, the color of a misty ridge. In my view, Magonigle made the right call. He had the exterior walls of his camps painted that color, and the trim painted red and orange and gold, the colors of sugar maples after the first hard frost. All those bright camps were built around the shoreline of two lakes once thought dark enough to be the gates to hell.

101

Frederick M. Heath inherited most of a lake from his uncle in 1892. It had been called Big Pond, Brown Pond, and then Trout Lake. Heath built a fourteen-room hotel, Fernwood Hall, with an observation tower and a long porch looking to the lake that Heath called Lake Ozonia, a name that still rings with the zest of the woods. Rates at Fernwood Hall were modest. Heath wanted guests to rest and recuperate, even if they weren't rich. I have to admit: that's probably not what I would do if I inherited an Adirondack lake. I'd tack up signs. NOTICE! THIS IS A PRIVATE PARK. Heath once wrote, "Every leaf of this vast forest gives forth Ozone, that intense form of oxygen that is the sworn foe of disease and the very elixir of life."

Heath wanted to impose his vision of what the lake should be. When he built Fernwood Hall, he displaced locals, made them move their ramshackle hunting and fishing camps to another shore so they didn't spoil the view. Heath preferred silence. Locals sometimes rowed onto the lake at dawn—a mirror surface, a thick fog, a hush of a breeze in the pines: a peace that matched the myth—and started hollering, just to make Heath mad.

102

Rich Lake: when sunlight strikes the sandy shore, flakes of mica glint like gold.

103

Eskers are ridges of sand. When the glaciers melted, water rushed away, hauling sand and gravel that the glaciers had plucked up in their advance. Some got left behind. Eskers are the shape of glacial meltwater cast in sand. They weave and squiggle, porpoise and dive, only to pop back up farther along. Eskers lace the Adirondacks.

Long and thin, topped with pines, an esker arcs through Rainbow Lake. Paddling along the esker, I didn't know whether to credit the lake's name to the shape of the esker or to an afternoon thunderstorm sometime in the late nineteenth century.

104

A hunter shot a moose and hung its antlers in a tree near a lake. Sometime later, no doubt, another hunter said, We're going to that lake where that other guy shot that big moose: Big Moose Lake.

105

Black Bear Lake exists, but not by that name. Dr. Anne LaBastille, writer, adventurer, wildlife ecologist, and a licensed Adirondack guide, invented the lake's name to protect her privacy. In 1976, LaBastille published a book titled *Woodswoman: Living Alone in the Adirondack Wilderness*. The story goes: she grew up in a New York City suburb, took a summer job at a resort in the Adirondacks, fell in love with the land, fell in love with her boss, married her boss, got divorced, purchased some Adirondack land, and built a log cabin that lacked electricity and a telephone and indoor plumbing, and, in fact, even a road. To get to her cabin, LaBastille had to boat or walk or ride a snowmobile across Black Bear Lake. On July 4, 1965, she moved in, 120 years after Thoreau moved into his Walden Pond cabin. LaBastille lived alone at her cabin on and off for a decade. She painted her aluminum canoe to look like birch bark.

Woodswoman was a sensation. It landed in a moment of cultural convergence: the back-to-the-land movement, the rise of environmentalism, and a branch of feminism that embraced the outdoors for recreation, spirituality, and freedom. The popularity of LaBastille—almost a real-life, female Grizzly Adams on the East Coast—elevated the Adirondacks in American culture. From a bookseller on Amazon, I purchased a used copy of *Woodswoman*. Inside the front cover, an inscription reads: *Dear Dorothy, I have given this book to every important woman in my life for the past 20 years. When you told us about your upcoming Vision Quest, I knew you were next!*

Chapter 4

FISH CREEK POND PINCHES in at a sandy point of tall pines and then opens wide into Square Pond. Three hundred or so campsites ring the shore of Fish Creek and Square, three hundred or so campsites packed in tight like teeth. Fish Creek Pond Campground could be called The Pursuit of Adirondack Waterfront on a Budget. Nearly every campsite sits on the waterfront and is only twenty-two dollars per night. On a summer weekend, twelve hundred campers might stand on the shore of the two lakes to watch the sun set.

Arriving at Fish Creek, campers stop at the registration booth. A ranger hands them a permit, a map, and reads them the rules: Quiet hours start at ten. Bears are active. Secure your coolers and food. The bathrooms are here, here, here. Here's the shower building. Here's the recycling center. Do not cut trees for firewood.

The roof of the registration booth overhangs the entrance road. Ding, scrape, chip, dent are all things that RVs do to the corner of the roof each summer. Antsy campers are in a rush to see the water. Speed bumps slow them down. Most speed bumps at Fish Creek are fortuitous: where a pine root buckled asphalt, someone nailed a yellow sign to the trunk.

On my first visit, I checked in at the booth and then drove slowly around the lake on the rough road. Campsites ticked by, each one numbered consecutively on small wooden signs. Kids riding bicycles, parents pushing strollers, packs of teenagers playing Frisbee or football. I thought I must be almost to my site. I was only at site 32. More than a hundred to go.

Motorboats, paddleboats, jet skis, kayaks, and canoes; RVs, travel trailers, pop-up campers, silver Airstreams, beefed-up SUVs with knobby tires, KC lights, and rooftop sleeping platforms; tents, screen-tents, and playpens; coolers loaded with meat and milk and beer and cheese; coffeemakers and plastic bins of dry goods; inflatable floats, chairs, tables; tarps blue, tarps green, tarps silver; bicycles, grills, and hammocks—things and things and things packed the waterfront forest full. Lit by campfires and paper lanterns and Tiki torches, televisions and headlights and camera flashes, the evening woods felt energized. The lights, the crowd, the noise: Fish Creek buzzed like a big-time, small-town county fair.

Distracted, I dropped my left rear wheel into a pothole and spent the rest of the summer listening to my car wail like a banshee in the pines.

Into site 152 I backed my car, the exhaust pipe vibrating like it might crack in half. An elderly husband and wife, my neighbors for the night, stared. They had maneuvered their forty-foot, chrome-accented RV snug between some pines to get a perfect view of the water and then unrolled the RV's striped awning to face the lake, a mobile front porch. I had never before and have never since wanted to own an RV. In that moment, though, my envy was fierce. Their rig had probably cost them two hundred thousand dollars. All evening the couple sat in beach chairs and watched the sky and water through the pines, sipping bargain bourbon from plastic tumblers. On a damp picnic bench nearby, I sat on a waterproof map and cooked dinner hunched over a tiny, sputtering butane stove.

Hours later, Square Pond all quiet water and stars and campfire coals, a few campers on the far side of the pond partied at a tropical-themed bar. Half-empty liquor bottles lined up in a long row. Violet and teal spotlights glinting on gold foil fronds. A disco ball. Top 50 Country. Ten o'clock sharp: lights out, fronds dark. They knew the rules.

NEW YORK OWNS FISH CREEK, and it also owns thirty-five or so other Adirondack campgrounds. A few are on islands. Most sit roadside. Almost every summer night I spent in the Adirondacks I slept at a state campground.

Beginning in the 1920s, cars and slightly smoother roads made it easier for more Americans to take vacations. In the East, many tourists went to the Adirondacks. Some slept in rental cabins or in one of the old, bulky hotels that hadn't yet gone bankrupt or burned down. Looking for an adventure, looking for a bargain, some tourists slept along the road. At a scenic spot in some spruce, a tourist would pull over in a Model T, set up a tent and a striped awning, and spend the evening cooking dinner over a campfire and looking at the stars, and a few other tourists might show up, too, and set up tents and light more campfires, and by Labor Day, The Exodus, that scenic spot was bare and muddy, littered with tin cans and glass bottles and heaps of ash, Forever Wild trees chopped down, nearby water rank.

New York began to regulate and build roadside campsites. At first the campsites were simple, a few stone fireplaces strung along a road, patrolled by a roving ranger on a motorcycle. By the 1930s, the state was building larger campgrounds that had privies and clean water piped from a spring. Rather than being for the campers' convenience, the idea was control: clustered campsites were easier to monitor and maintain.

Building new campgrounds required the state to cut Forever Wild trees. A 1930 court case, which ruled that bobsled runs and golf courses violated Forever Wild, also ruled that cutting down a few trees to permit campgrounds respected the intent of Forever Wild. The case gave New York a green light. During the Depression, the Civilian Conservation Corps built campgrounds with amenities such as log amphitheaters and boat launches and beaches. After World War II, campers swarmed. During the summer of 1954, almost 83,000 people were turned away at the gates: No Vacancy. The next summer, that number almost doubled. To keep up with increasing demand, the state built campgrounds with even more campsites, campsite after campsite in the woods or around a lake, campgrounds that had a staff and infrastructure comparable to a small city's. This basic model hasn't changed.

In meanders, arcs, loops, and cul-de-sacs, a road structures each campground. Along these roads, some campgrounds sprinkle campsites; each campsite feels isolated, as if you've driven down a long gravel lane to a private clearing in the woods. Most campgrounds cram sites together. There, when your neighbors have a late-night debate over whether the historical range of the grizzly bear once included what is now the Adirondacks, or when your neighbor's five-year-old throws a tantrum because there's melted cheese on his pasta, you overhear.

Traffic, noise, and things: Fish Creek is the superlative. There are so many things at Fish Creek that you can spot them before they even arrive. Flatlanders drive to Fish Creek in convoys. An RV, three kayaks lashed to the top, followed by a Tahoe pulling an aluminum fishing boat stuffed with coolers and a grill, followed by a minivan packed with the entire extended family and their luggage. Or an F-150 towing a white travel trailer, followed by a second F-150 towing a jet ski, followed by a third

F-150 towing a second jet ski. You can identify Fish Creek convoys driving through the Adirondacks by the incredible volume of things they tow and haul. On Sunday mornings in the summer, the dumpsters at Fish Creek are heaped with things the weekend wore out.

In most other Adirondack campgrounds, mildewed pop-up campers outnumber $200,000 RVs, and rusty, put-put outboard fishing boats and canoes outnumber jet skis. One campground sits across a four-lane road from a convenience store. The day I walked by, the store offered two slices of pizza and a soda for $3.99. A few campgrounds front lakes where motors are banned. Those campgrounds feel like outposts in the wilderness.

Each campsite at every campground is roughly the same: a cozy clearing in the woods with at least one level spot, a fireplace (once stone, now pre-cast concrete), a wooden picnic table, a nearby water spigot, a bathroom within walking distance (flush, usually; sometimes pit), all surrounded by some arrangement of Adirondack scenery (sugar maples, pine stumps, spruce, hemlocks, a sandy beach, rocks, and roots), which gives all the campsites a similar feel—except, really, they're not the same at all, and if you think that any site will do, you give yourself away as green. Most campsites are dry, in the forest. Campers prize waterfront. If you mention certain site numbers at certain campgrounds to veteran campers, their eyes light up. That sandy beach at 57! That mountain view from 82! That morning sunshine at 113! Fish Creek, with nearly every site right on the water, is so busy that you have to make a reservation many months in advance. Before there was a reservation system, families spent the night camped out along the road, hoping to snag a waterfront vacancy the next morning.

Another way to think of Adirondack campgrounds is as scenic, long-term parking lots. Drive on up, stack your things in this tidy clearing for the duration of your stay.

Today, campers reserve campsites on a website and get slapped with a nine-dollar reservation fee. I often spotted seasoned campers walking around campgrounds to take notes for their next visit, trying to find the site with the best view or the site that looks most like the Adirondacks. They walked around, site to site, like science fair judges. For newcomers, selecting a campsite on the website is risky. The map is clunky: blue for water, green for land—a binary the Adirondacks refutes. What looks like waterfront on the map might be swampfront: malodorous, sunbaked, and buggy.

There are roadside campgrounds elsewhere, of course, in national parks and other state parks, at exits along interstates, in small towns. I don't normally enjoy sleeping there. Camping in the Adirondacks feels different.

You're not just sleeping out, you're sleeping out in the Adirondacks. That elevates the experience, somehow, in a way I don't quite understand.

CAMPGROUND SCENES:

A kid singing a song about multiplication tables abruptly stopped to comment on my tent: "That's a *really* small tent." Her gaze was pity. Her family's tent had four rooms arranged in a crucifix. It even had a front porch.

THE INTERIOR OF A campground bathroom: yellow concrete-block walls, gray concrete floor (clean), cotton candy–pink soap in the sink-side dispenser, a cold-water tap stamped "H."

AT A REGISTRATION BOOTH, a ranger said to me, "Ah, site 156. You're down in Bear Country." I laughed, thinking it a tale rangers tell flatlanders to make them feel like they've reached the wilderness. An hour later, mama black bear and her two cubs lolled through my site. All three plopped with a grunt into a nearby mud hole. I panicked, fled to my neighbors' site. That family looked at me as though I'd been spooked by a house spider.

Later, a crowd of campers flustered mama bear. She bolted. Her cubs scampered up a tall pine. No one could figure out which one. Mayhem in the night: rangers lobbing noisemakers, kids wailing, campers slashing trees with spotlights and shrieking—"There it is! There it is! God-*damnit* there it is!"

A FATHER AND HIS FIVE children rode bicycles around the campground, a speaker on one of the bikes blasting "Play That Funky Music." A bit later, an ice cream truck rumbled down the road. It chirped a digital keyboard rendition of "I'm a Little Teapot."

A HUSBAND AND WIFE, my neighbors, could never find anything in their car's trunk. The trunk had a creaky hinge. In one hour, it creaked twenty-seven times.

AT EIGHTH LAKE CAMPGROUND, campsite 35, waterfront, during one of my first trips up there after college with Erin, a wail tore the night. Wolf, I thought, now concerned about our tent's thin walls. Coyote. Fox. Some canine hybrid, all bristle and fangs, some stout carnivore with sharp teeth, short legs, and good lungs, that creature galloping after limping prey it already knew it could pull down and shred but wanting to strike fear deeper, as if a glut of fear might make the meat taste better, maybe a lynx or a cougar or a wolverine had returned, hungry, spiteful. Maybe a serpent or some peculiar bony Ice Age fish hailed by the night sky. That wail collapsed the wilderness tight to our tiny tent. Pine to pine, the wail echoed. A second wail from down the lake cut in, escalated into a chuckling, layered tremolo.

A loon is a big, water-loving bird. Black head, black beak, white chest. Eyes blood red, but the color is hard to see unless you catch the light just right. On its black back and black wings, white feathers splay in a surrealist checkerboard of dabs and streaks and blotches, a pattern that seems to be undergoing a subtle, momentous change that you can't quite catch at a glance. Think: stars in the night sky, appropriate since on windless, clear summer nights, loons float on the reflection of the Milky Way.

Loons are clunky on land. Slow walkers, they're champion swimmers. Loons' bones are thick and dense, making it easy for them to stay under, snoop around for fish. Chasing after a perch or a sunfish, loons dart, and they are known to make abrupt, flipping underwater turns to track that fish down. Feet wide and webbed, legs powerful, bodies sleek, loons swim far and fast, and often they'll pop up across the lake from where they dove. Watching them through binoculars requires spending most of your time trying to figure out where the hell that loon went.

Hunters and sportsmen in the nineteenth century shot at loons. They were good sport, hard to hit. You never quite knew where or when they might pop up. Even into the 1970s, after loons were federally protected, fishermen who couldn't catch fish sometimes called them "that damned fish eater" and shot them, leaving their big bodies to rot.

Some people call loon song—chips and hoots, yodels and tremolos, wail after wail in the night—the "Song of the Adirondack Wilderness," a marker of the solitude and repose flatlanders seek. That's what loons are to me. Some people call loons noisy neighbors. A campground alarm clock might be someone who at 5 a.m. drags a metal fishing boat across asphalt to the water. More often it's a loon.

One surfaced in calm, dark water a few feet to the left of my canoe on a summer evening. The sun had just set on a hot day. Every spruce exhaled a cool breath of relief. Wisps of fog crept across the water. The loon glanced at me. It huffed, almost sneezed. Metallic beads of water trailed down its face. It shook its feathers, beak to tail, with a sound like shuffling brittle paper. The bird's iridescent collar flickered from black to teal to deep purple and back to black, its red eyes flitting about, nervous or curious or miffed at my intrusion. The loon tucked its head back, sprung, almost as if to say, *Here we go!* It dove. A moment later it popped up a few hundred yards away. That's usually all I saw: a distant silhouette half sunk in the water, wings folded, a slight hump of its back over which a low wave might easily wash, head erect, alert, twitchy, beak tapered to a lance, sometimes a pinched fish squirming.

ADIRONDACK LOONS ARE common loons, *Gavia immer*. The species winters along North America's Pacific and Atlantic coasts and along northeastern Europe, and then breeds during summer on lakes in a broad belt across Alaska, Canada, the Upper Midwest, the Northeast, and the coast of Greenland. Most Adirondack loons winter off the New England and Mid-Atlantic coasts. At least one has flown to Florida. In the spring, they fly back to Adirondack lakes, where they spend the warm months raising one or two chicks, if they're lucky, and then migrate back to the ocean before deep freeze. On an evening in early fall, I ate dinner at Tony Harper's Pizza and Clam Shack, a local landmark near a lake where loons nest. Dusk fell inky through windows framed in lacquered knotty pine. The next day the restaurant would be closing for the season. The waitress said, wistfully, that in a few days she'd be flying to Florida to spend the winter. Listening to loons call on a different lake later that night, I thought about how the waitress and the loons had similar seasonal schedules. They'd both fly back up in the spring after the thaw.

Loons require a good-sized lake in order to breed and raise chicks. Most Adirondack lakes of this size have some shoreline development, camps or a village. Only a few big lakes have forest all around. Most permit motorboats. Loons build their nests at water's edge. Jet ski and motorboat wakes swamp loon nests, which might cause a mating pair of loons to give up altogether on nesting there, and curious canoeists can spook a loon from its nest and cause the loon to abandon an egg. Memorial Day and Canada's celebration of Victoria Day bring flocks of recreation seekers just after loons have established their nests, when loons are most likely to be scared away. If a breeding pair of loons abandons their eggs, they take some time to get settled back in. By then school is out. Summer. Tourist season. More boats. More wake. More noise. Then it's July Fourth. Another rush of tourists, and then it's too late in the season for loons to try again.

There are further threats. One of the lakes with the highest population of loons is Stillwater Reservoir, the lake I crossed to get to Beaver River. A rapid water level rise or drop can wipe out all the loon nests. Most lakes receive enough mercury particulate deposition from coal power plants that the fish loons snag are rife with mercury, a neurotoxin, and by eating those fish loons might act funny and abandon their nest or not give their chicks the food or attention they require. Many lakes are still acidic from acid rain, despite a few decades of slow recovery and restoration, and some lakes still don't support adequate fish populations for loons to survive. Even on lakes loaded with fish, abandoned fishhooks and lead sinkers can kill a loon.

Despite these threats, between 600 and 850 breeding pairs of loons summer on Adirondack lakes. For the past few decades, a yearly loon census (a citizen science project) has tracked a stable population. During the early months of the pandemic, when many flatlanders put off travel plans, locals watched loons raise chicks on lakes that hadn't seen a successful hatch for decades.

You can see common loons in plenty of other lakes across their breeding range. Towns in Wisconsin and Minnesota have festivals dedicated to loons. Virginia, Minnesota, claims to have the world's largest floating loon sculpture, which is something I'd really like to see someday. In terms of geographic distribution, there's nothing particularly Adirondack about loons. But loons hold special significance there. The Adirondacks likes to claim loons as its own.

Multiple real estate agents feature loon silhouettes on their signs. The lawns of some camps are decorated with fabric loons, wings spinning blurry in a breeze. I've seen a camp's mailbox decorated with a flower box cut and painted to look like a loon. Pink geraniums spilled out. Booking a motel room for your vacation, you might hear loon song playing on the motel's website. At souvenir shops, you can purchase carved wooden loon figures, loon postcards, loon drawer pulls, birch lampshades on which an artist has painted a loon, loon Christmas ornaments, sterling silver loon earrings, loon shot glasses, loon magnets, loon napkin holders, loon mouse pads, and white insulated mugs painted with a loon. Names of camps include Camp Loon, The Red Loon, Loon's Echo, The Tranquil Loon, Camp Loony, Loonacy, 3 Loons, Loon Loft, Loon's Call, Loon Haven, Over the Loon, Loon Landing, Loonsome Landing, Loonatic Landing (painted on a crosscut saw), Loonatic Lodge, Loon Lodge, Looney Bear Lodge, Loon Dance, Loon Bay, Loon Channel, Loon Point, Loon Lair, Loon Island, The Loon's Nest, Camp Loon Song. My wife, who likes loons as much as I do, maybe more, thought up the best loon-related name for an Adirondack camp. I can't say what it is, on the unlikely chance we can ever afford to buy one.

Here's my take: The Adirondacks is near the southern edge of the loons' breeding range, so the sight of a loon brings the North south, and most visitors have already driven north. Loons hold such resonance because they represent the stranger, wilder realm most flatlanders want the Adirondacks to be. That's a powerful position for a bird: to represent wildness in a landscape loved by so many people.

JUST BEFORE FULL DARK, I enjoyed strolling campground roads: meanders, arcs, loops, cul-de-sacs. It felt like walking through a few dozen backyards. Families and couples and groups of friends sat in chairs, on inflatable couches, or on picnic tables, and gazed into campfires. Almost every campsite had one, roaring, wood smoke thick and low, embers trailing to ash against a sky the shade of blue that's not quite black, a few early stars here and there. Fire-lit, the dark woods danced. Each campfire cast its watchers a molten orange, each person's form flickering hot against the forest. Most days, I had been driving or hiking or paddling by myself, and it felt comforting to be surrounded by people after all that solitude. Occasionally I'd chat with neighbors. More often I was silently grateful that so many people had gone out of their way to enjoy this place, that so many people felt an urge to drive up there with their things and things and things.

After returning from my evening stroll, I'd wash and dry my dishes, try to organize the gear in my car, and then settle into my tent for the night. Bathroom doors stopped squeaking, trunks slammed less frequently. The rhythmic cracking and snapping of campfires pervaded the campground. A loon would call. Usually a camper would be inflating an air mattress with a tinny electric motor: a whine in the woods that just wouldn't stop.

This is when I'd listen for cars.

I'd nestle into my down sleeping bag, head on my pillow, a pine root nudging me in my right kidney, and listen to the iron quiet of the woods. It was an exercise in trying to feel the scale of the forested silence, an exercise in appreciating absence. I'd imagine myself floating a few hundred feet in the air, looking out over the trees, the flicker of a few campfires, a rolling black void of forest and lakes here and there silvered by the moon—some round, some long, some serrated with nooks and coves—the distant, lurid glow of flatland cities beyond the horizon.

I'd inhabit that expansive stillness until I heard the murmur of tires on asphalt, still many miles away, the murmur rising and falling, and then a hum that wavered when the car slipped behind a hill or a thick stand of spruce, and then, as the car drove on the main road a few hundred feet away, the sound ramped up to a buzz and then a deep drone, thumping with an arrhythmic imbalance.

Cars and campgrounds democratized the Adirondacks. Anyone with access to a car, enough money for a tank of gas and the campground fee, and $36.91 for a Coleman Sundome two-person dome tent at Walmart, and $15.00 for a trunkful of firewood purchased roadside, and a good tolerance for adventure and bugs and sinks that only dispense cold water can drive up to the Adirondacks, secure a waterfront site for a few nights.

Adirondack campgrounds can be noisy, choked by wood smoke and lighter fluid fumes, befouled by RV generator exhaust, crammed with neighbors who listen to music too loud and drink too much cheap beer. The state doesn't provide sufficient funding, the bathrooms are sometimes not quite clean, the line for the showers too long, the roads too rough, the campsites too small, too close together, too wet, too steep, too malodorous, sunbaked, and buggy. I first stayed at them because they were a bargain. They're now some of my favorite places in the Adirondacks. I think they're wonderful, campsite after campsite packed with people who drove up with their things and things and things to take an Adirondack adventure. The campgrounds are reminders that this experiment in forest preservation and recreation, this experiment for setting something aside from industrial exploitation for everyone, has worked, that more than a century later this environment is well protected and still snares the imaginations of many people who might not necessarily call themselves outdoorsy, people who prefer Tiki torches and golden foil fronds to a backpack and a freeze-dried meal.

It's easy to think of the Adirondacks of today as inevitable. It could have been otherwise. Before campgrounds, before cars, the region was the exclusive retreat of the wealthy. Forever Wild land was public, technically open to anyone who could get there. But tourists had to have money to stay at a hotel or to hire a guide to see the woods. This could have been the future of the Adirondacks: public land tacitly locked up, a forest that few people other than the rich would ever see.

NOTICE! THIS IS A PRIVATE PARK.

Starting in the 1920s, when more flatlanders showed up in cars to look at the scenery, to boat, to camp, the state responded. It built campgrounds and trails, boat launches and trailhead parking lots—which helped make the Adirondacks what it is today: a Vacation Wonderland for all classes. The emblem of the Adirondacks shouldn't be a guide boat; it should be an automobile parked at a campground. That's why camping there feels different. You're participating in the story of how the region became what it is today.

When I listened to a car at night as it passed the campground and rolled further away, silence clamping the woods back down, I tried to keep all of this in mind.

106

Waiting for his colleagues to finish hacking a tree trunk into a dugout canoe, a surveyor spotted a loon, picked up his gun, and pulled the trigger. The gun backfired, burst. Splinters and shrapnel zinged in every direction except toward the loon. No one got hurt. The surveyors named the lake Good Luck.

107–11

In the decades before sports overran the woods, a hunter sat in a boat on Woodhull Lake. His name was Bisby. Bisby heard the call of a loon from beyond a ridge to the east. Bisby knew it was the type of call a loon makes when it's on the water, not the type of call it makes when it's flying. Curious, he went to check it out. He discovered a chain of lakes that later got his name.

112–23

NOTICE

In late July through early August, you may see crews in boats using spotlights during the night. These crews are conducting a

study for the Adirondack Cooperative Loon program to examine the
health of the Common Loon population. Researchers use spotlights
and taped loon calls to capture adult and juvenile loons. Colored
and numbered tags are placed on the legs of the birds, and a small
amount of blood is drawn to examine the levels of mercury and other
contaminants in loons.

Reading the sign, I heard a loon yodel from one of the nearby ponds.
I pictured a scientist out there in a boat, a boombox held high above
her head—like John Cusack in that scene from *Say Anything*—blasting
loon calls.

124 & 125

Driving along South Lake, I stopped at a roadside primitive campsite. Zero
dollars per night. I heard a loon wail, and then another, and then I thought
I heard a third. The loons turned out to be three kids screaming, splashing
playfully on the far shore.

I drove to nearby North Lake and spotted two loons, two fuzzy loon
chicks trailing. I pulled over and grabbed my binoculars. One after the
other, the parents dove without a splash. The two chicks frantically surveyed the lake, panicked over the abrupt absence of their parents. A minute later they calmed down and stretched their legs straight behind them,
one at a time, slow and deliberate, pointing their big webbed feet. Loon
yoga. A minute later, one of the parents popped up, a small silver fish limp
in its beak. The two chicks perked up, dashed over. In my head, the two
chicks went, *Weeeeeee!*

126

Fragments of a loon egg littered the shore of a pond. Oblong, the size of
a fist, olive green with brown specks, the inside the color of cream. All
around the broken egg, bunchberry grew, clusters of four bright green
leaves as fresh as mint and small white flowers with four petals.

127–33

So far that afternoon I had hiked to Deer Pond, Catamount Pond, Round
Pond, Long Pond, Horseshoe Pond, and Boottree Pond. As I arrived at
each, I juggled the shape of the others in my head. On the shore of Town

Line Pond, I took a break, sat on a carpet of pine needles, reclined against a white pine, the sun sharp in my eyes. On the far side of the lake, two guys paddled solo canoes. A loon floated nearby. Everyone was fishing.

One guy said to the other, "Do you see all of those things out on the water?" He wasn't yelling, but his words carried. The loon let out a sharp chuckle. After a pause and no response, the same guy said, "They're loon feathers!" He exaggerated "loon," like it had eight big O's. Still not eliciting a response from the other man, he shouted, "Each one is a white feather from that loon."

Every minute or so the loon reared up out of the water, flapped its wide wings twice, and then shook its head and flapped once more: molting, a costume change from black and white to a stormy gray, the color I ascribe to winter afternoons in the northern Atlantic. Discarded white feathers drifted across the lake. Backlit by the low afternoon sun of October, they were a plume of weightless sparks.

The lake was not good luck that day. "Did you eat all of the damned fish?" the talkative guy asked the loon, his tone swerving toward anger. I expected him to pull out a pistol and shoot the loon, that damned fish eater. But the fishermen gave up, picked up their canoes, and walked to their car.

The loon swam to my side of the lake, still flapping and still losing feathers. It dove. I leaned back against the pine, squinted at the sun. I counted to thirteen before I could no longer see ripples from its dive.

Chapter 5

VERPLANCK COLVIN DIED IN 1920, about ninety years before I first visited the Adirondacks. But everywhere I went, there he was.

For thirty-five years, Colvin explored, wrote about, surveyed, sketched, mapped, and traversed the Adirondacks. Before Colvin, Adirondack maps were incomplete and inaccurate. After Colvin, they still were, but at least they were better. Every lake, pond, swamp, bog, stream, river, peak, ridge, mountain, gorge, pass, settlement, boundary, road, and path within the mysterious and massive entirety of the Adirondacks: Colvin's goal was to make a map that showed them all.

Out in the field, Colvin often froze, ran out of food, and worked his crews until they demanded more money or quit and trudged home. He worked himself just as hard. One August night he camped with his guides in a notch high on a mountain. In the morning there was an inversion, clouds snug in the valley, sun blazing above. The group climbed to the summit. Colvin ordered his guides to cut down the forest that blocked his view, and then he spent the entire day taking observations and measurements and sketching fragments of a map. For lunch they ate bread, dry. Wrapped in blankets, that night Colvin and his crew slept on the ground with roots for pillows. On a low mountain that offered an unexpected but spectacular view over the forest, a guy in his sixties told me that Colvin had ordered his crew to burn the trees off the peak. Colvin: forever frustrated by trees standing in the way. The guy was dressed in camo pants and a camo shirt, and I think he drove a camo pickup truck, because there was one parked at the trailhead. The story seemed a bit over the top. I later looked it up. It's true. The blaze roared out of control, and Colvin and his crew had to flee. I've never found comment on the reactions of locals. You'd think they would have thought Colvin was off his rocker.

Most locals and tourists today have never heard Colvin's name, but a good number mythologize him. That's why he's still around. They do it for a few reasons. The Adirondacks still looks a lot like the sketches and photographs and written descriptions that appeared in Colvin's reports. You can read Colvin's words and get the feeling that he's on an adventure in a forest you just walked through. The Adirondacks also at times gives the impression that it hasn't been mapped yet, and even if you're holding a map in your hands, the forest can feel unknown, which makes Colvin your colleague. You're both trying to figure the place out. Most importantly, Colvin was a flatlander obsessed with the Adirondacks. He wanted to see it all. His desire to see it all stuck to the land. It lingers, somehow. Faint yet pervasive, almost as if it saturated bedrock, mixed inextricably with sand. In the 1990s, when a regional planning agency upgraded to a set of PCs that could crunch geographic information about the Adirondacks and possibly untangle its complexity, someone named one of the computers Colvin.

I felt this lingering obsession. It often hit me as a manic twinge. I'd scour maps and satellite images to find curiously shaped lakes and try to figure out how I could walk there. I'd piece together canoe trips that would keep me away from roads for a week. I'd plan a backpacking trip through miles of trailless forest to a lake I wasn't sure anyone else had ever seen. What does the shore of Metcalf Lake look like? Can a loon take off from Terror Lake? How tall is that pine on a pond with no name? It sneaks up on me, that impulse to see it all. It makes me want to get in my car, strap my canoe to the top, drive north right away. There must have been a hint of this obsession in the exclamation point I saw when I stood next to my backyard cornfield in the limestone valley, as if I had known about Colvin before I had ever heard his name.

Colvin made his first trip up into the Adirondacks in 1865. He was eighteen. Surrounded by development and agricultural valleys, the interior of the Adirondacks was still largely considered unknown by flatlanders. The Haudenosaunee and Algonquian peoples had known their way around for thousands of years, locals of European descent for a few decades. The land hadn't yet been mapped accurately on paper. During his travels, Colvin noticed mountains where maps showed flats, and rivers or lakes where maps placed mountains, and his guide showed him lakes not yet drawn on any paper map. It was as if everyone who had previously tried to map the region had encountered a magical, shape-shifting land that looked different depending on the direction from which you approached it, or as if the topography morphed with the seasons, an idea that when compared to unicorns and volcanoes isn't all that far-fetched. Colvin eventually discovered why: Iron ore in the bedrock distorted compass measurements. Nearly every previous Adirondack survey had been skewed by fickle compass needles pointing here and there to what they thought was magnetic north.

Colvin's solution was to bind the Adirondacks with triangles. On top of a mountain or on a rock along a lake, Colvin sank a copper bolt and secured it with molten lead: one vertex of a triangle. You can still find them on some summits. Aligning a surveying telescope, a theodolite, directly above this bolt, he measured the angles to landmarks. Colvin climbed other mountains, repeated this process. Eventually he could triangulate the distances between copper bolts. He gave each copper bolt an accurate position on a map.

Triangle after triangle after triangle, bolt after bolt after bolt, Colvin and his crews worked east to west across the Adirondacks, from the High Peaks to the central lakes to the low, flat forest of the northwest, pulling that net of triangles taut, each triangle yoked to the ones around it to secure baselines and benchmarks.

THE MAP: TO AVOID distortion, he planned to chart the final product on a single piece of paper. He couldn't settle for knowing fragments. In a single gaze, he wanted to see it all.

MAKING TRIANGLES, COLVIN AND his crew were always up to something: Shouting "Hurrah!" when the top of a mountain emerged from cloud. Gawking at an aurora borealis, "which covered the whole dome of the heavens with a crimson canopy." Fretting endlessly over the clarity of the air so they could see as far as possible. Commencing an expedition immediately, "for should the streams become frozen and provisions fail us, the situation might become disagreeable." (These are Colvin's words. His crew's words were unrecorded and probably unpublishable.) Launching tripod rockets in an attempt to pinpoint unmapped lakes cloaked by forest—a fire hazard, but it sounds like fun. "Gazing out upon a wealth of mountains and valleys spread before us, we regretted that there was not more time"—a line that for some reason unknown to me is not Colvin's epitaph. Getting lost. Getting lost. Getting lost, and then spending the night at a camp they called Camp Somewhere. Talking to trappers and hunters to learn what they knew. Lugging a twenty-inch theodolite that weighed three hundred pounds up mountains. Assembling a list of 184 lakes and ponds never before charted. Navigating through thick clouds by shouting and listening to the echo, "[fighting] the thickets with new ardour, till chill ooze or splintered branch provoked some fresh displeasure."

THE MAP: HE SET the scale at one inch on paper to one mile on the ground. He ordered 154 square feet of heavy paper. Roughly, the map was to be twelve feet by thirteen.

TO MAKE TRIANGLES, COLVIN had to be able to see the precise location of each copper bolt from many miles away. Colvin stationed men with flags or small cones of tin on a copper bolt. That only worked over short distances. Then Colvin tried hand mirrors. Even packed in wool, the mirrors cracked while workers hauled them through untracked terrain. Ultimately, at many copper bolts, Colvin constructed an automatic signal he called a stan-helio.

In its first iteration, a stan-helio was a boxy apparatus of wire and tin. Four arms of tin sheets swooped concave toward the ground, like a flower doing a handstand on its stamens. Suspended loosely in a rickety wooden frame, the stan-helio bounced and swirled and banged and flitted about in any breeze, striking metallic glints in all directions. The contraption had one purpose: to transform the precise position of a copper bolt into a beacon. Colvin could spot it from twenty miles away. Windstorms and curious tourists destroyed the signals. Fed up with sending crews for repairs, Colvin built sturdier signals, and they evolved into twenty- to thirty-foot-tall log pyramids fastened to bedrock. The largest, built on treeless summits in the High Peaks, required guides to haul trees uphill for a week. On top of each signal, Colvin placed a more durable and more compact stan-helio that spun and wobbled about. From thirty or forty miles away, it was visible, a hot white star.

Through gales, thunderstorms, and blizzards, through the acts of vandals and curious mountain climbers (who might have also rolled a few rocks), these improved signals stood, alert, flashing. I like to think about those stan-helios up there on so many peaks, tin parts clanking lonely in the mist, turning and squeaking one after another as a north wind tore across the Adirondacks, raising the ire of crows and ravens. In a downpour, hollow metallic pings. Hushed by hoarfrost in February. When a storm broke in the west late in the day and the low sun cut the clouds, one hot white star up high on a dark mountain, the light shifting across the Adirondacks from west to east—and then another hot white star and then another, all those hot white stars burning against storm clouds, Colvin's copper bolts precisely below.

THE MAP: COLVIN STARTED a draft. As he learned more about the Adirondacks, he'd erase previous lines—erase and erase and erase—and draw them again.

VERPLANCK COLVIN WAS BORN in 1847 to a wealthy, socially connected family in Albany, New York. Verplanck was his paternal grandmother's maiden name. Colvin showed an early devotion to the natural sciences, and he longed to join the military. He agreed, reluctantly, to study law with his father. During the 1860s, when Colvin was in his teens and twenties and when the state of New York lacked comprehensive geographic knowledge of the Adirondacks, he began collecting information. The region snared his attention. It might have been the potential for profit. I like to think it was the myth. Colvin scoured colonial surveyors' records. He wrote letters to writers who had traveled up there. Soon he quit his father's law firm. He made his occupation the Adirondacks.

Colvin is hard to categorize. He abandoned a cushy, profitable career to seek empirical knowledge of what he saw as a wilderness. Yet he wasn't a hermit. He wanted to be a respected professional. He wanted his exploits and expertise to be widely known. I'm tempted to call him an anachronism, a leftover from an earlier era of conquest and exploration, but that's not right. He represented the feelings of the era in his focus on scientific exploration, but he selected a geography that didn't seem impressive enough to many people. Colvin's survey began in earnest just a few years after John Wesley Powell and his crew made the first voyage through the canyons of the Colorado River, one of the last uncharted places in the West. If Colvin had surveyed the Colorado Plateau or the Yukon—really, anywhere in the West—he might today have wider fame.

Colvin wrote annual reports for his survey, and he gave speeches and published accounts of his travels. He rarely wrote about himself. The most descriptive line appears in a third-person autobiographical sketch he wrote in 1882: "He is a young man of thirty-five years of age, and unmarried; is nearly six feet in height, muscular, and erect; in manner quiet, but in spirit and determination indomitable." Colvin never married. He lived in Albany with his mother, until her death at age eighty-eight, and with his childhood friend and survey assistant Mills Blake. During the survey, guides named a mountain in the High Peaks for Colvin. In the 1940s, a historian discovered the effort Blake had invested in the survey alongside Colvin. In the late fall of 1883, Blake had camped for thirty-seven days in the deep freeze and gales of a high summit to take survey measurements. Snow drifted five feet deep. The historian started an effort to name the peak adjacent to Colvin for Blake. Mount Colvin is seventy-four feet higher than Blake Peak.

Colvin funded the early years of the survey, paid his guides, purchased equipment and supplies. He wasn't a lawyer. He was still rich. Friends convinced him that his map would provide a public benefit, so he approached New York's legislature for funding. By this time, Colvin was widely known. He had been a member of a state committee that studied what should be done with the Adirondacks, twice had his writing published in *Harper's New Monthly Magazine*, and was a prominent member of the scientific community in Albany. The state offered minimal funding. In later years, convinced Colvin's work had value, the state offered much more. Colvin expanded his operation. He split his crew into divisions. He delegated tasks to each division, Colvin's survey now almost a military operation trying to know all there was to know about the Adirondacks. He traveled constantly to supervise the work. A map with a line tracing his travels would've been a tangle. At the survey's peak, it employed around 150 men: surveyors, assistants, packers, cooks, and guides.

If insufficient funding, foul weather, or a miasma of correspondence prevented him from being in the field, Colvin seems to have sat morose in his office. By the later years of his survey, Colvin's office was strewn with tents, traps, guns, canoes, animal skins, snowshoes, and precarious stacks of notebooks. I wonder how it smelled. Colvin sat there, in that heap, examining maps, reviewing field notes, and planning the next season's work.

For the first few years, Colvin's survey was a boisterous, threadbare exploration. In his efforts to secure more funding from the state, and maybe personal fame, Colvin played it up, made it sound like he and his crews tromped through an uncharted wilderness. Strenuous mountain climbs. Late-season mad dashes across harsh and miserable terrain. He liked to tell a story about shooting a cougar and then dragging it back to the flatlands to display in the state capitol building. That story fit neatly within the American tale of subduing the wilderness.

Colvin's annual reports from those early years read like adventure tales. *Topographic Survey of the Adirondack Wilderness*—it was a title people couldn't resist. It promised to reveal a wilderness just a few hours up north. There might as well have been an exclamation point at the end. Copies of the reports were printed, bound, sold. Adirondack enthusiasts still collect them. They sell for hundreds of dollars. I look for a bargain in every used bookstore I visit. When I opened one volume in the numb fluorescent flicker of a subbasement special collections library, I caught a whiff of balsam; a loon wailed.

Eventually, the survey lost its verve. Colvin had mapped most of what he thought was unknown or inaccurate. I've never understood this side of Colvin: he seems to have taken great joy in wandering the unknown—yet he spent most of his life pinning it down: triangles, copper bolts, stanhelios, his map. The survey pivoted toward the mundane task of finding and re-marking property boundaries, an urgent task because timber thieves were stealing trees from state land. Forever Wild could only be enforced if that state knew which trees it owned.

Colvin had begun his survey when amateur scientists, surveyors, and engineers were common. By the later years, professionals dominated those fields, and politicians began to question the quality of Colvin's work. State funding proved capricious. A new governor, thinking Colvin's work a rich man's folly, would slash his funding, and Colvin would have to waste time lobbying the legislature, or he'd have to again fund the survey himself. Theodore Roosevelt, then governor of New York, ended Colvin's survey in 1900. The Adirondacks was changing, too. Colvin had shown up to a blank spot on official maps. It soon turned into a fashionable resort and one of the nation's largest suppliers of timber. Even in 1872, the first year Colvin filed an official survey report, a journalist claimed the Adirondack wilderness was extinct: "The desert has blossomed with parasols, and the waste places are filled with picnic parties reveling in lemonade and sardines"—which was true, but only in parts.

Mostly, no one could understand why after almost two decades of exploring and surveying and consuming funds Colvin had not yet produced a map.

BARBARA MCMARTIN DIED IN 2005, a few years before I first visited the Adirondacks. But she was my Adirondack guide.

Beginning in 1972, the year she finished a PhD in mathematics at the City University of New York, McMartin published a series of eleven Adirondack guidebooks. The series methodically covers the Adirondacks, one region at a time. Doing research and fieldwork with her coauthors, McMartin walked nearly every trail in the Adirondacks. By her calculation, she walked about 450 miles each summer. Titles such as *Discover the Adirondack High Peaks* or *Discover the West Central Adirondacks: A Guide to the Western Wildernesses and the Moose River Plains* caught my eye. I read every one I could find.

There were newly printed glossy editions, crisp corners still square, but I most enjoyed finding used copies, all dog-eared and muddy, covers torn, stars scrawled next to hikes that someone had hoped to complete. Those stars were everything to me, adventures someone longed to take. I imagined those people, sitting at home with their guidebooks open, dreaming about the Adirondacks up there, each star an echo of Colvin's obsession.

McMartin grew up a flatlander but spent summers at her family's Adirondack camp. She and her husband later split their time between Croton-on-Hudson and the Adirondacks before moving north full-time. In the 1980s McMartin was diagnosed with cancer. From this point forward she directed her energy toward researching and writing about the history and bureaucracy of the Adirondacks. *The Great Forest of the Adirondacks* is her masterpiece. Before *The Great Forest*, it was thought that the majority of the Adirondack forest had been logged at some point, leaving a young forest where scraps of old growth remained. McMartin, wise and meticulous, parsed the region's logging history. She considered when various tracts had been logged, what logging technologies were available at those times, and which species of trees loggers could transport to market. What she discovered was unexpected: vast tracts of the forest had never been logged, and much of what had been logged before Colvin's time had only the largest spruce removed and only in areas adjacent to streams, which had allowed loggers to float trees to distant sawmills. McMartin's conclusion: there might actually be a few hundred thousand acres of forest in the Adirondacks that is old growth or is approaching old growth since it has been state-owned and Forever Wild for over a century. It was a fairly significant argument when it was published in 1994, and in the years since it has permeated the way people talk about the region, propping it up, correctly, as a globally important temperate forest, rather than some provincial, cutover back 40.

On a whim, I purchased a copy of *The Great Forest* at a hardware store during one of my trips. The title sparked some excitement in me. Sitting in my tent that night, by the light of my headlamp I read the book through right away, my neck cramped from the hard ground.

McMartin's guidebooks are an extended plea for people to explore more of the Adirondacks than the top ten most popular hikes. She seems to have loved places that most people ignore. She lobbied the state to build short, scenic trails every few miles along Adirondack roads, a plan that would have turned them into interpretive journeys through the region's natural and cultural history and immersed tourists in the swamps and bogs and pine forests that they now zip right past without seeing.

As far as I know, no landscape feature has yet been officially named for McMartin. When this changes, I hope McMartin _____ is some place unpopular, some place beautiful but quietly so.

IN HIS REPORTS AND WRITINGS, Colvin expressed values that now sound ecological, such as protecting watersheds and halting reckless logging, and he wrote poetically about the mystical wildness of the Adirondacks. At times he sounds like John Muir. Some scholars credit Colvin with first suggesting the idea of making the Adirondacks a park. Yet Colvin also believed in cutting canals across the wilderness, in building aqueducts to deliver Adirondack drinking water to New York City, and in a private landowner's right to clear-cut forests to maximize profit. After state politicians slashed his survey's funding for good, refused to give him his back pay, and kicked him out of his office, Colvin spent the last few decades of his life advocating for a railroad that would have sliced through the Adirondacks, resulting in more logging and more development. He never felt the need to resolve what we might see as his ambivalence about what the region should become.

In 1916, when he was sixty-nine, he ran to catch a trolley car in Albany, slipped on some ice, and hit his head. He never fully recovered. His neighbors later called the police to report gunshots at Colvin's home. Police closed in, surrounded it. Colvin was inside testing his guns. Diagnosed with some variety of cognitive decline, Colvin was committed to the mental ward of Albany Hospital until his death in 1920.

On his deathbed, Colvin autographed a boat paddle once owned or carved by well-known Adirondack guide Mitchel Sabattis. Colvin handed it to Mills Blake. The story goes that in one year the long wooden paddle, the wood worn smooth and dark by mud and sweat and sand, was dipped into 250 Adirondack lakes.

Two hundred fifty: I kept that number in my head, almost as if it's some timeless geographic measure to assay the character of the Adirondacks.

THE MAP: FOR A WHILE I thought it was a shame Colvin never finished it. What might a map displaying all of his experience and ambition and curiosity, and the knowledge locals shared with him, have revealed? Maybe it was for the best he never finished it. No map, regardless of size, could have contained what Colvin had learned and felt about the Adirondacks. Even a completed map would have been quickly outdated, archived, forgotten. He might have become just another nineteenth-century surveyor. That Colvin made the Adirondacks his occupation, that he explored it for decades but never saw it all, that he wanted more than anything to plot it all on paper and yet never did—that tale of obsession and adventure, that tale of a new mystery always just beyond, still influences how we look at the Adirondacks today.

I have to wonder, though, if it should. Am I celebrating an attitude that I should approach more critically? That obsession with the unknown, with desiring to be somewhere uncharted, props up the myth of the Adirondacks and fits neatly within that American story of overcoming and conquering an unknown, empty land that's neither unknown nor empty.

That wooden paddle, I keep coming back to it. Perhaps the story is apocryphal. Two hundred fifty lakes—it sounds almost too tidy to be true. And would someone languishing in a hospital with a variety of cognitive decline, someone approaching the brink of death, have his wits about him to make a last grasp at cementing his legacy by autographing an artifact? But I appreciate the lives the autographed paddle (or the story about the autographed paddle) brings together: Sabattis, an Abenaki well-versed in his homeland; and Colvin, the wealthy White flatlander who wouldn't have been able to attempt a survey of what he called a wilderness without the knowledge and expertise of Sabattis and his other guides. There's an opportunity in that paddle to think beyond Colvin's lingering obsession for knowing all of the unknown Adirondacks, and also an opportunity to reconsider how we think about the place of Indigenous people in the past and present of the Adirondacks.

When I was thirteen and thought about the Adirondacks from that limestone valley, when I stood at that highway rest stop in college, and even for the first few years I traveled to work on this book, I completely accepted the tale that Indigenous peoples had never lived there. The common story, repeated in brochures and books and in stories told by locals, is that the land was too cold and too harsh, that it was only a hunting territory, and thus always a remote wilderness without people. The problem is: that's not true.

As the glaciers melted, as the tundra sprouted on bedrock that had been scraped clean by ice, as the land rebounded and inland seas began to retreat, the Algonquian and Haudenosaunee peoples and their predecessors moved in. Their presence precedes the current iteration of the Adirondack forest. They lived there for many thousands of years until Europeans showed up, and then they adapted to the violence and displacement of the fur trade after Europeans arrived, adapted to their homeland being wedged violently in the borderland between European colonial powers, adapted to mining and logging by seasonally taking wage work, adapted to wilderness tourism by being guides and hosting sports, adapted to the arrival of the automobile and middle-class tourists by offering goods and services or by performing the type of stereotypical Indian role—usually a Great Plains Indian with a headdress—that Americans thought was authentic along roadsides or at theme parks. They've never left, and they continue to assert their cultures and histories as individuals and as communities. More accurately, the Adirondacks is a homeland.

Early Adirondack adventurers acknowledged their presence. A few books written in the early and mid-nineteenth century noted the presence of Indigenous people evidenced by clues such as settled clearings and stone tools waiting on a sandy shore for their owners to return. Those books mention sites of cornfields or encounters with skilled Natives. There's a string of place names that date to this era that start with Indian. It's easy to look at those names today and think the people who named those spots were lost in their imaginations. But they were often responding to the presence or material evidence of occupancy by Indigenous peoples.

Later accounts changed. In the early twentieth century an amateur historian, Alfred Lee Donaldson, wrote the first comprehensive history of the Adirondacks. Throughout much of the twentieth century, it was the go-to book for anyone who wanted to learn about the Adirondacks. Donaldson's book argued that Native Americans had never lived there. This exclusion has rippled through the twentieth century, gaining undeserved authenticity with each iteration. It's a convenient exclusion because it allowed the history of the Adirondacks to be written around the idea of an empty wilderness. And it meant the history of the Adirondacks could easily be lumped into the popular American tale of subduing the wilderness and then enjoying it as carefree tourists. That empty wilderness meant that the people who lived there had to be forgotten. This amnesia was essential to the myth.

Mitchel Sabattis died at the age of eighty-four in 1906. He had been dead for over a decade when Colvin signed that wooden paddle. Born just to the north of what's now the Adirondacks, Sabattis arrived in the central Adirondacks with his father in 1830. They spent their summers trapping, moving around to find the most lucrative spots, and then they'd spend their winters nestled down in a log cabin and probably still trapping when the arctic weather gave them a break. The earliest European settlers arrived in the area at about the same time, though Sabattis's father had apparently worked and maybe lived in the region during earlier decades. Sabattis became friends with many of the settlers' children who were his age.

Sabattis later settled in the interior with his wife, Betsy, possibly in the late 1840s. They had fifteen children together, though not all lived to be adults. Betsy was White. Indigenous people and Europeans intermingled their lives in this remote area. Sabattis would have dressed just like any other settler of the era. It's strange that I even need to say that. Of course he did. But invented images, like the headdress-wearing Indian on the brochure for Okara Lakes, have skewed our view of the past. While Sabattis faced discrimination at times—and possibly always did in a more subtle, grinding way that no European noticed or documented—most European settlers treated him like a friend and neighbor. Sabattis was marked as an Indian on census records. So were his sons. Their European wives were marked White. From reading what few documents and stories survive, I get the impression that the family recognized and deftly navigated the indeterminacy of these racial lines.

The Sabattis family hunted and fished and farmed, and later on they offered lodging for flatlanders who traveled up to look around—just as pretty much everyone else in the area, regardless of race, did to survive. Sabattis also offered his services as a guide when more sports showed up in the woods in the 1840s and 1850s looking to hunt and fish and have adventures. He was always in high demand, partly because flatlanders wanted to live the myth by having an Indian guide take them out into the woods for a few weeks of hunting and fishing. I imagine that made for more dramatic dinner party tales once the flatlanders got home, in that era of James Fenimore Cooper. But it was also because Sabattis was exceptionally skilled and knowledgeable. Typically, guides could work in only one region. Sabattis could roam the entire Adirondacks and know right where he was—or at least have the confidence and skills to not let anyone else know he was lost. From accounts of sports he guided—if you can overlook their tendencies to romanticize him—Sabattis was sensitive to the land in a way that flatlanders completely overlooked. He recognized traces of game and indicators of weather and signs of the changing seasons that nearly everyone else couldn't see. This was his homeland. He'd been immersed within its rhythms and sounds and smells and sights for most of his life, and he had learned from other family members and friends who also knew the area well.

What's missing from any surviving archive or any flatlander's account of Sabattis's life is how he viewed his Indigenous family history and how he felt about adapting his skills and his family's history to a land that he had watched transition from his homeland to a place of timber extraction and wage work to a place of wilderness tourism for rich flatlanders. What practices and ideas from his history and culture did he cherish? How did he view his own identity? How did he hope to position himself within an economy that was rapidly changing? How did he feel about settling down on a farm and improving the land when he and his father had spent many years roaming the land freely? What did he feel he needed to hide about his beliefs and views of the world to avoid further discrimination in a small town where he occasionally had to rely on his neighbors in moments of need? In what ways would his views of the land have differed from those of his European neighbors? Did he consider ways to support his family by exploiting his fame as a guide? How did he feel about the strictures and opportunities of his race? We'll never know. Thinking about these questions leads to speculation that Sabattis probably had more agency in his life than we'd expect.

That's what the paddle ends up representing to me—a moment when the life of Sabattis, who had to deal with all these questions and navigate his heritage in a land that was intimately familiar to him and yet changing, overlapped with the life of Colvin, who had set out to explore what he called a wilderness and draw it all on a single piece of paper, every last detail. And we can shift beyond these two lives, Sabattis's and Colvin's, to Sabattis's family history and the lives of all his ancestors who for thousands of years had considered the region part of their homeland, and to the American colonial approach to the land that Colvin worked within, a mindset that I—and all other non-Indigenous people who visit the Adirondacks—live within today. That wooden paddle (maybe) carved by Sabattis and then (maybe) signed by Colvin on his deathbed presents an opportunity to frame Adirondack history within this wider span of lives and ideas.

All I can add is that we need to better recognize and acknowledge this larger history, not just in books and museums but on the land itself and how all of us act there. I wish Native Americans haunted this landscape. I want to paddle a lake in the Adirondacks that has a sign with a name I can't correctly pronounce without intensive language lessons. I want to see road signs and lake names in at least three languages. I don't mean haunt in that false way of using stereotypical notions of Indians to invent an imagined past or to make us believe we're having a more authentic experience: neon motel signs with a Native American's face outlined in blue glowing tubes or a camp named after a fictional warrior so the owners felt a shiver of the primeval each time they arrived. We've done enough of that. By haunt, I mean that as a White flatlander I want to feel uncomfortable in some places in the Adirondacks. I want to feel that I'm treading some place I shouldn't approach carelessly. In parts of New Zealand, Alaska, and Utah I've felt that way, in areas where Indigenous histories and their challenges and complexities are foregrounded. It's not feeling uncomfortable as in I should feel excluded entirely. It's uncomfortable as in being made aware beyond any doubt that where I am hiking or paddling or sightseeing or staying in a motel has a deep, complex, living history that's outside my perception, and that it deserves recognition and respect.

134

During the summer of 1877, a guide noticed a brilliant light shining from the depths of Meacham Lake. He rowed toward the light. It slid away, disappeared. Other people in the boat saw it, and I imagine this caused some excitement: a lake with a light on the bottom, the light flitting about, darting away.

Only later did someone realize that the light on the bottom of the lake was a reflection from the top of a mountain, ten or twelve miles away. One of Colvin's stan-helios, one of his hot white stars.

135

Mitchel Sabattis said Long Lake was called Kwĕnōgā'māk by the Abenaki. Which also meant long lake.

136

A group of history buffs, average age approaching retirement, occasionally assembles to locate artifacts from Colvin's survey. They look for copper bolts or an important point on the map Colvin never made. Founded in 1997, the group calls itself the Colvin Crew. According to their website, they are "an honorable organization formed for the purpose of perpetuating the Adirondack doings and dreams of that pioneer surveyor Verplanck Colvin." For a one-time fee of twenty-five dollars, you can join. Membership entitles you to a membership card and a metal pin that features one of Colvin's stan-helios. I hope to someday become a member.

On May 9, 2015, the Crew found bolt number 180, located on the shore of Upper Preston Pond. One hundred seventeen years earlier Colvin had stood right there.

137

Sabattis called Tupper Lake—not the village, the nearby lake—Pāskāngā'māk, which meant "side" or "branch lake." Before industrialists built a dam, the lake was more obviously a branch of the Raquette River.

138–40

During a survey expedition, Colvin discovered three lakes not noted on previous maps. The first he named Yellow Lake. Sunlight shined to the bottom. The second he named Cold Lake because guides told him the water felt frigid year-round. The third he named Lake Sunshine. Colvin and his guides lucked out with the weather.

141

On May 13, 1974, the probability of Adirondack road signs displaying three languages increased greatly.

That day forty armed individuals from the Mohawk Nation overtook a tract of Forever Wild land owned by the state around Moss Lake. The armed individuals would have argued they were reclaiming what was rightfully theirs. The 612 acres was a small part of a larger territory stretching across northern New York and northern Vermont that the Mohawk Nation claimed had been sold illegally in 1797. Moss Lake was a start.

Approximately two hundred individuals from the Mohawk Nation moved onto the land, and they planted crops like corn and beans and rhubarb, and kept horses, chickens, ducks, geese, and dairy and beef cattle. No White people were permitted to enter. "We lost the whole continent to the Europeans," said a spokesperson, "and in trying to make a new start we want a minimum of outside influence." They intentionally made this new start on public land to avoid seizing private property.

This all took place within a national movement of Native Americans striving to reclaim land that had been stolen from earlier generations; members of the American Indian Movement had recently occupied the site of the Wounded Knee massacre in South Dakota. Adirondack locals were not supportive. Some even called the Mohawks terrorists. Locals formed a group called the Concerned Persons of the Central Adirondacks that then hired a PR person. He believed that the Mohawks should be removed by force. Locals were primarily concerned that the situation would sink tourism. Native Americans taking back their land—it was a hard story for locals to sell to flatlanders.

When tensions flared, State Police manned checkpoints along a nearby road, the road you'd have to drive to get to the nearest car wash from Beaver River. Each side accused the other of firing guns, and one night a nine-year-old girl and a twenty-two-year-old man, both White, were shot as they drove by in a car. Police never learned who had fired the shots.

The group stayed on the property for three years, only vacating it when New York offered them the use of a 5,000-acre tract just outside the Blue Line. At the entrance to the new parcel they posted a sign: REPOSSESSED AREA OF GANIENKEH TERRITORY, EST 50,000 B.C.

142

Trekking around in the High Peaks, Colvin and his guide stopped for a drink. They cupped their hands. The water was tepid, not icy. Colvin knew this meant the source was a pond, not a spring. They yelled "Hurrah!" when they saw the pond, "a minute unpretending tear of the clouds—as it were—a lonely pool, shivering in the breezes of the mountains." Colvin identified the pond as the highest source of the Hudson River. He called it Summit Water. Later he had a poetic turn: Lake Tear of the Clouds. Local guides had always called it Lake Perkins. I wonder what they thought when Colvin, a flatlander, stumbled upon it and thought it needed a new name.

Chapter 6

A LINE THAT'S BLUE is the official boundary of the Adirondacks. It's blue because a cartographer, not Colvin, drew it that color on a map in 1892. The first Blue Line, as it's called, bounded an Adirondacks about half its current size. Iron forges, sawmills, tanneries, and farm fields withdrew from the first Blue Line shortly after, like a waning tide. Trees grew back. New York has expanded the Blue Line several times, most recently in 1971. Areas within the expansions were not in the Adirondacks—and then, like that, they were, a boon to real estate developers (overnight, a parcel of land became a parcel of Adirondack land, sold at a premium) but probably unsettling for residents (a bunch of flatlanders woke up one morning and were Adirondackers).

Now that it seems the Adirondacks is as large as it will ever be, I wish New York would construct a physical blue line. Powder-coated steel or some UV-resistant polymer, it would slice through last year's pale beech leaves, float across lakes and bogs of sphagnum moss, and stripe a camp right down the middle like the fifty-yard line—a land art sculpture delineating a region, the scale making it difficult to know where to site the small black rectangle stamped with artist, media, and the year it was built. I imagine the blue line ten feet wide, wide enough so that in November, from a low-flying airplane, you could trace the jagged shape of the Adirondacks through bare trees, the line snaking along the east bank of a creek, crossing a road, cutting southwest along the surveyed line of a nineteenth-century patent, jogging abruptly north to follow a county boundary. It would give the Blue Line a visual presence. No longer would it be just a line on a map.

Wooden signs cut to the shape of the Blue Line mark where the Blue Line strikes most main roads. I've never seen a family posed in front of one for a photograph, a common scene at national parks. Tires don't wear ruts in the roadside grass. A physical Blue Line would make arrival an event, would create a threshold. Before 1970, often there wasn't even a sign to tell you that you had arrived—a good reminder that an absolute, bounded sense of Adirondack geography is a tale of the past fifty years.

It's no great divide, the Blue Line, and more often than not, the first thing I saw after crossing it was another tree of the same species I had just seen on the other side. In fact, the Blue Line encloses quite a bit that doesn't even look like the Adirondacks. An oblong core of rolling mountains and lakes with pine-studded shores best matches the Adirondack scenic ideal. This scenic core is approximately coterminous with the first Blue Line. I wonder if New York got it right the first time and then took it too far. On calendars and postcards, this area defines the Adirondack look. The rest tags along.

That Adirondack look: it's tall pines that lean at just the right angle, a serrated line of spruce, rusty pine needles carpeting the ground, boulders with medallions of lichen; there's a lake nearby with calm, dark water and at least one shield of rock that slopes to shore; rolling blue ridges stack into the distance.

Many Adirondack lakes have this look, in an almost uncanny way that makes you do a double take because you're sure you've seen this one before. Other lakes don't, but flatlanders pretend they do, because that lake happens to fall within the Blue Line. The Adirondack look and the Adirondack myth are closely related, in that often-unacknowledged way that the texture of scenery permeates culture. I've noticed that more of what's within the Blue Line looks like the Adirondacks when it's foggy, somehow, as if the look expands or contracts in extent depending on the weather. Some areas looked like the Adirondacks when I was driving up, but then driving home that same spot gave me the feeling that I was already in the flatlands.

What's the origin of this scenic ideal? Much of the Adirondacks is higher in elevation and is geologically distinct from the surrounding region. The look has material foundations: rocks, topography, flora and fauna, the color of the water. It's easy to think of the Adirondack look as natural, preexisting, a category made by applying a label to what was already there. That's not the case. These particulars have been selected as Adirondack through a two-century-long string of sketches, etchings, paintings, postcards, vacation snapshots, scenic calendars, and tourism brochures. Each one captioned ADIRONDACKS further entrenches the ideal.

Rather than an ecological boundary, or a cultural boundary, or even a political one, the Blue Line is a container people have been trying to fill with the Adirondacks since 1892. They're still working on it.

Crossing the Blue Line, many times I only knew I was in the Adirondacks because the color of street signs had changed, suddenly, from green with white words—the street signs you see everywhere—to brown with yellow words: rustic street signs. Among actions taken by a committee to make parts of the Adirondacks look more like the Adirondacks, another one was to suggest standardized, rustic business signage: *Signs in hamlets should meet Park-wide standards. Business signs should be fixed to buildings, be made from natural materials, avoid back lighting, and use color schemes harmonious with natural environments.*

Another action was to replace the guide rails along major roads within the Blue Line. Rather than the galvanized guide rails you see most everywhere else, silver and shiny, Adirondack guide rails are made of a metal that oxidizes to a dull brown. That is, Adirondack guide rails are rustic.

I'm the world's foremost flatlander expert on rustic guide rails. I've spent enough time looking at them that I know which parts, such as bolts and flanges and bridge anchors, are available in rust and which shiny parts must be painted brown to match.

Unfortunately, rustic guide rails suffer from a material defect: they're rusting right through. Highway departments are replacing them with ones that shine. I'm sad to see them go. When I drove past highway maintenance facilities within the Blue Line, I'd often look for a discarded segment of guide rail I could take home. I'm not sure what I'd do with it. Lawn ornament? Wall sculpture? Garden fence? It would probably sit in my garage beneath my canoe. A piece of rustic guide rail seems like an ideal souvenir. It's an object so easy to overlook, so easy to dismiss as utilitarian, and yet if you look closely it plunges through Adirondack history, back through automobiles and guideboats and sports and Indians and unicorns, to merge the Adirondack look and the myth and the everyday.

All of this is more than a question of aesthetics. Towns in areas that look like the Adirondacks—by grace of scenery or by mandated rustic materials—receive a boost from tourism. The choice to make the Adirondacks look more like the Adirondacks is partially about identity. It's more about money. Tourists drive right through the parts of the Adirondacks that don't look like the Adirondacks.

Places like AuSable Forks, where in the early nineteenth century loggers cut down every tree in sight to make charcoal to feed an iron forge. When the forge went bust in the 1880s, the owners turned to making paper, resulting in even wider clear-cutting. Downstream from the paper mill, the AuSable River ran a different color each week.

Places like Essex, a quaint village on the shore of Lake Champlain with a district of big, bright stone homes from the early nineteenth century. It feels more New England coastal than Adirondack.

Places like Lyon Mountain, once a company town for an iron ore mine. Gray heaped hills of mine tailings rise like sand dunes above the village, a village of house after house that look just about the same. Driving through Lyon Mountain on a summer afternoon, I saw a group of children sledding down the bare gray slopes on a bright orange plastic snow sled, a rooster tail of dust rising behind. It looked like fun, zipping down the steep slopes, but it struck me as a bit depressing, those kids playing on industrial spoil in a park cherished for its wilderness character. No one has ever printed that scene on a postcard. Adirondack postcard racks are all autumn sugar maples and sunset lake scenes. Those kids on that orange sled made me want to open my own souvenir shop. On one of those postcard racks that's six feet tall and squeaks and wobbles when you spin it, I could curate my own vision of what the Adirondacks looks like. Those kids on the orange sled reminded me of the power and durability of such commonplace representations.

Places like Lake George. But with Lake George there's a split opinion. Some tourists love it and can't wait to go back. Some wouldn't stop there if you paid them fifty bucks. I stood in the village of Lake George one stormy summer evening and watched sunset. The streets, the sidewalks, the water: everything wet glowed yellow and then orange and then purple. Under lingering storm light that felt cataclysmic, the neon signs in town looked resplendent, a few dozen electric sunsets brilliant in the puddles on wet asphalt. *Business signs should be fixed to buildings, be made from natural materials, avoid back lighting, and use color schemes harmonious with natural environments.*

TWO DAYS EARLIER I had left home and driven north toward Lake George. I wasn't thrilled to go. So far I had mostly ignored the southeastern Adirondacks. It's the part of the Adirondacks that looks least like the Adirondacks. It's the only part that made me shrug. I had a reservation at a lakefront motel in Lake George for the next night. According to the booking website, my room had a queen-sized bed and a mini-fridge, and the motel had a pool and a sand beach.

I crossed the Blue Line, somewhere, and then drove north and then east through the day's oppressive heat, driving through what wasn't in the Adirondacks until the state expanded the Blue Line in 1931. The lakes and trees and small towns I saw didn't look like the Adirondacks. It was too hot to feel like the North, not enough fog, too many homes and too few camps, too many Dollar General stores, too much traffic, too many lawns, too much vinyl siding. When I thought—the Adirondacks!—I didn't picture this.

The blazing afternoon dimmed to a golden, dense evening. The pine shade radiated a lulling heat. I drove aimlessly, road after road without a map, heading roughly north. In most of the Adirondacks, you can stop almost anywhere and get out and look around at Forever Wild land. Here it was nearly all private land; there was nowhere to stop. It made me realize how much I appreciated how open much of the Adirondacks felt. In most of the United States, you can't stop almost anywhere along the road and go for a walk. There's so much public land in the Adirondacks that you can frequently stop, go for a walk, and connect with the land. Once someone told me that the Adirondacks was a place where things happen. It seemed like a flippant comment at the time. Things happen everywhere. Now I get it. He meant, more specifically, that in the Adirondacks you have access to the land, and when you have access to the land you have the opportunity to ramble about and with that investment of your time you encounter wild animals and the details of flowers and trees and you find moments of peace and you feel the texture of the land. Locals sometimes told me there's space up there. They don't mean it's big. They mean it's accessible, that you can park almost anywhere and roam. Nearly everywhere else in the United States, public land you can roam is a destination. Within much of the Blue Line, it's the fabric.

Tired of driving, I parked my car and wandered the quiet streets of the village of Lake Luzerne. Children's wet footprints trailed to dry down the sidewalk near the village beach. The Lake Luzerne Motel's neon sign crackled in the humid air. A sinuous blue neon tube arrow pointed toward the asphalt parking lot and the lake beyond. I stopped frequently to read historical markers that mentioned hotels and tanneries. Topping tall poles, the markers were installed a few feet too high. I looked like I was gazing up at something rare roosting in the tallest pines. Passing drivers slowed down in hopes of seeing the rare bird they thought I had spotted.

Besides now falling within the Blue Line, what made this village a part of the Adirondacks? I wondered if the history of the village could be called Adirondack even though for much of the village's history it wasn't. I guess the same could be said for the entire Adirondacks. Compared to 50,000 BCE, the label "Adirondack" is newfangled. This made me think about what the Blue Line and the creation of the Park had accomplished in the 1890s: a clustering of various regions under one name and a line drawn around the whole thing, an act which granted those regions the power to achieve national significance. That process of bounding and naming was more important to the region's history than I had before realized. The Blue Line had made the Adirondacks a definable object we could celebrate, control, commercialize, consume. I had always thought of the Blue Line as just a line on a map.

LAKE GEORGE HAS BEEN a tourist destination since the 1820s, the decade when being a tourist first became a popular thing for Americans to do. It was located in the most accessible portion of the wilderness. That's why tourists have flocked there ever since. Lake George now has more in common with the Jersey Shore than it does with the rest of the Adirondacks. In the 1960s, when a debate raged over whether the Adirondacks required some sort of regional plan to curb development—to keep the Adirondacks looking like the Adirondacks—supporters held up Lake George as the example of what the entire region might soon become if nothing were done.

The best way to get a feel for the texture and attitude of Lake George is to survey the places where tourists have spent the night during the past century. Think of these establishments strung out along a bright strip of a road near the head of a massive lake, forested mountains tight all around. It's dusk, traffic is bumper to bumper, the neon signs are ablaze.

There's:

Blue Moon Motel, Blue Moon in blue neon script.

Seven Dwarfs Motor Court, seven small white cabins with knotty pine panel walls.

The fifty Ultra Modern units at King George Motel, where a guest sits under a yellow umbrella and sips a gin fizz.

Capri Village. The Flamingo. Sand'N Surf Motel. Tiki Motor Inn, now Tiki Resort in an age when Motor Inn might as well say Low-Class, where artificial palm trees line the parking lot, and the motel's roofline resembles a series of peaked huts on a Polynesian island.

A four-story Courtyard by Marriott, one of the few chain hotels in the

Adirondacks. To make it look like the Adirondacks, the architects included rustic flair on the exterior, log beams and twig work, even though Lake George has almost no history of rustic structures.

Fort William Henry Motor Inn, built next door to a re-creation of an eighteenth-century fort, where you could see Red Coats, Indians, cannons, muskets, and a stockade, and in the gift shop you could buy a bumper sticker or a felt pennant.

Mohican Motel, which at one time had the face of an Indian centered on a blue diamond sign. The neon feathers attached to his head blinked on and off, as if the feathers billowed in a breeze. But not a lake breeze; the Mohican Motel isn't even close.

Pinebrook Motel, where the rooms had dark wood-panel walls and the view through the windows revealed the asphalt parking lot, not a pine brook.

Sisson Motor Court, a U-shaped block of rooms built in 1926. Some call it the first motel built in the Adirondacks. Lake George wasn't within the Blue Line until 1931—a fact that in my mind raises questions about the Adirondack provenance of Sisson Motor Court.

Lake Crest Motel, a neon sign with a curled, cresting wave and MOTEL in big letters—every bulb, every bar, every twirl of neon reflecting in the chrome of passing cars.

Doray Motel, a modest, single-story block of motel rooms, wood paneling on the walls, and along the road, there's a neon sign that suggests, in its lack of decoration, that you can stay at Doray Motel on the cheap: a white shield on a short pole, an orange neon arrow pointing toward the parking lot and DORAY MOTEL spelled out in two horizontal rows of neon letters in different colors. When the sign is lit up, tourists driving through town stop to take photos. Tires wear ruts in the roadside grass. The Doray Motel's neon sign is one of the few original Adirondack neon signs that hasn't yet rusted through, or been knocked down by a drunk driver, or been torn down and scrapped because a new owner thought it looked too dated and decided to replace neon tubes with translucent plastic panels backlit by fluorescent bulbs or LEDs, a substitution akin to replacing a fireplace with a YouTube video of a fireplace.

When the last neon sign in the Adirondacks is turned off for good, one last neon flicker and a whiff of overheated, uninsulated wires will mark the end of an important but often overlooked era in Adirondack history. Even though there are plenty of neon signs in the Adirondacks, and I think they're an important part of the Adirondack story, the Adirondack look of today excludes them—neon being the antithesis of rustic—which means they're not often a target for historic preservation. Same with roadside motels. Which raises a larger question: How does the Adirondack scenic ideal dictate the way we think about and preserve the Adirondacks?

At O'Sullivan's Motel and Lakefront Cottages I had booked a room. On the hotel's website, the motel appeared clean. It was located right in town, yet it had a lake breeze. More importantly, the motel offered a midweek special. It was still the most expensive night I spent in the Adirondacks, a fact I greatly regretted at three a.m. when my neighbors returned from a night of drinking and proceeded to scream and bicker and slam doors for the next hour.

I checked into Room #45, cranked up the air-conditioning to blast away the stale, oversanitized scent. I had always avoided Lake George. You couldn't have paid me fifty bucks to stop. I had bought into the idea that Lake George was a canker on the real Adirondacks. When I left my room to go for a walk, I was feeling cynical, annoyed. I wished I had just driven through, checked Lake George off my list, and slept in my tent somewhere quiet and dark where I could hear loons wail.

Crowds swarmed the sidewalks and the waterfront promenade. Antsy tourists scrounged for something cheap but sensational to occupy their time. Historic steamboats plied Lake George. When one of the steamboats tooted its horn, tourists who had been in town for less than twenty-four hours jumped, something I noticed only because I jumped and then realized a quarter of the crowd looked equally startled.

I bought an ice cream cone, twist with rainbow sprinkles. In the heat, it dripped down my hand and arm. Then without warning it rained. Fat drops bounced on the road like marbles. Everyone fled to the motels. I ducked beneath an awning in front of a strip of tourist shops. The clerk at the Shirt Shack stepped outside, looked at the empty sidewalk, and shrugged. Dingy water cascaded down street gutters. I pulled up my jacket hood, cinched it tight, walked down to the lake. Oily plumes slithered across the water. Low, writhing clouds cloaked the camps and motels along the shores. For fifteen minutes it looked like the Adirondacks.

The rain stopped. The crowds returned. Asphalt steaming, town smelling like wet worms. A frantic family pushed past me as they rushed to get to a pasta dinner cruise aboard a steamboat. The storm had triggered some change in the village, or had at least improved my mood, and I was starting to enjoy Lake George. I spent the whole evening eagerly walking around to see the sights, trying to get some sense of the whole frenzy. At the tourist information center, a room packed with racks of brochures, I overheard an employee suggest that two French tourists should go parasailing. A man wearing a cowboy hat and a bolo tie drove laps around town in a black pickup truck. The truck towed a trailer, and on the trailer stood a giant bull statue, something about a rodeo and Texas BBQ painted on the bull's flanks. A loon wailed. I heard it again and stood on the sidewalk and scanned the stormy sky. Each time someone opened the door to a souvenir shop, a blip of a loon recording snuck out. The CD was $18.99. If the CD player in my car had been working that week, I would've bought it.

A feathery sunset flared up the lake, as if the employee at the tourist information center had pressed a big red button. From the foot of the lake, the neon-pink, prow-like roof of the Pink Roof ice cream shop pointed up the lake at the sunset like a cosmic directional beacon. Two waitresses on a smoke break tilted their heads back. Traffic slowed. Tourists filled balconies and rushed to the lakeshore to take photographs. Everyone stared at the sky. It was one of those lovely moments when some ephemeral natural phenomenon snaps a whole town's attention beyond the human world.

A few hours later, headed back to my hotel for the night, I was feeling better about Lake George. It's a nostalgic remnant of midcentury roadside Americana, and surrounded by all of that whimsy and neon and noise, I could feel the whole of the Adirondacks up north bearing down, the weight of those quiet, wild lakes, the weight of those miles of forest. Lake George felt like one last desperate gasp before the world went dark. That feeling—of standing on the verge of the wilderness—is what has made Lake George such a popular destination for so long. Lake George would be just another resort town if it weren't within the Blue Line, and somehow the Adirondacks would be diminished or incomplete—maybe even slightly boring—without the spectacle of Lake George.

I LEFT THE NEXT MORNING, groggy because of my drunk neighbors, and drove north through the eastern fringe of the Adirondacks, more of what wasn't within the Blue Line until 1931.

In front of the Penfield Homestead Museum in Ironville, I slowed down, looked at the big white house but kept driving. A few miles down the road I pulled a U-turn and drove back. I spent a pleasant afternoon talking to a volunteer docent in her seventies or eighties. She told me how the area I had driven through that morning had once been stripped of trees to feed charcoal to iron forges. She mentioned vistas along the roads I had driven that morning and would drive later that afternoon, giving me a list of specific landmarks so I could find my way to each view. I never found any of them. I only found trees. Her memory took in a time before the trees had grown back, when you could still see the shape of the cutover land, back when the area had only been within the Blue Line for a few decades. It was like talking to someone with X-ray vision who mistakenly thought her ability was universal. I didn't ask her if she felt Ironville was a part of the Adirondacks. I was worried what she might say. Locals in the parts of the Adirondacks that don't look like the Adirondacks seem to view the Adirondacks as something frivolous that happens elsewhere.

I drove through small towns and past dozens of farms abandoned a few decades ago, forest growing back brushy, and then some farms that looked like they had once been abandoned but were again productive: CSA signs, hoop houses, and chicken tractors in the weeds. The land had a big sky and rows of trees between fields like the limestone valley where I grew up. Later I'd read that cheap land attracts young, landless farmers to the region, not unlike the first settlers who had ventured here from New England. Could these young farmers sway the Adirondack scenic ideal somewhat toward fields and cows? Fields and cows had been scattered around the Adirondacks in the nineteenth century when the scenic ideal had been established, but most flatlanders had left them out of written accounts to make the wilderness appear more wild. Would that happen again? Was the look of the Adirondacks malleable? Who determines what is authentically Adirondack? It made me realize the making of the Adirondacks is a process that will never end—and glad for it. What we think we want the Adirondacks to be will guide what it becomes. I don't say that to be fatalistic. I say that to offer hope.

Later I stood on the shore of Lake Champlain, the eastern boundary. I looked east to where the Blue Line splits the lake, Vermont beyond. There, in the middle of what felt like an inland sea, the blue line would float, made out of that pool noodle foam, gulls landing: a flutter, a squawk, a few downy feathers.

Chapter 7

▟▖

AMONG THE MEDLEY OF materials that might skew an Adirondack camp rustic—ranging from stone to birch bark, moose antlers to corrugated steel, logs to vinyl siding molded to look like logs—my favorite, without a doubt, is brainstorm.

At first glance, brainstorm siding looks like clapboard siding: long, horizontal planks, plank after plank up a wall, each plank overlapping the one below it. A wall of clapboard is a wall of straight, horizontal lines. Square and smooth on all sides, clapboard siding allows you to forget the board was formerly a tree. Brainstorm flaunts what it once was, plank after plank up a building, one edge of a tree slightly overlapping another edge of a tree. From clapboard's bottom edge cut square, brainstorm strays. Knots, warbling bows, rippling waves that curl, a kink here, a kink there, a stub where a windstorm snapped a branch, brainstorm has them all, and more, too, any quirk or deviation from plumb you might see in a hundred acres of pines.

The popular origin story of brainstorm: In 1907, architect William Massarene, a flatlander, designed a lavish, sprawling Adirondack camp for Archibald and Olive White. White Pine Camp topped a sandy point of pines on the shore of Osgood Pond. You had to board a boat and cross the pond to get there. Massarene's plan specified clapboard siding. Ben Muncil, self-taught, master builder of Adirondack camps for the wealthy and a local, had a fit when he saw Massarene's plan. Muncil and a local millwright, the story goes, invented brainstorm to make Massarene's design look more Adirondack.

That story probably isn't true. Massarene had traveled widely. Most likely he saw buildings with the material when he toured England, where its use might date to the sixteenth century. Whatever the source of his inspiration, he specified the material on blueprints for White Pine Camp. In England, the material is often called waney-edge. It's not clear who changed it to brainstorm. In 1907, the term "brainstorm" was hot in the news. The defendant in a notorious murder trial had claimed that a temporary episode of insanity, a brainstorm, had caused him to commit the crime.

White Pine Camp was a brainstorm brainstorm. Painted dark green, brainstorm clad the boathouse, the two-lane bowling alley, and the dining hall; it clad the tennis house adjacent to the English clay court; it clad the gardener's residence; it clad all of the guest cabins and the owner's cabin, too, and the long block of rooms where the servants slept.

A widower, Archibald had made his money in utilities and salt before he remarried. Much younger than her husband, Olive was a socialite and occasional actress. The Whites did not venture up north for wilderness reverie. New York City papers printed blurbs about White Pine Camp parties. A play performed in 1909 at the camp's open-air theater included fire bursting red and green, and electric lights strung through the woods, pine to pine. One character wore leopard skins. The play concluded when actors torched a dragon "on a funeral pyre amid an elaborate pyrotechnic display."

Archibald and Olive once invited twenty-five guests to visit White Pine Camp. They rode in a stagecoach from the train station. Speedier modes of travel were available, but the Whites wanted to give their guests a taste of the past. A short joyride. Lakes, trees, the smell of pines. Then in the sand road there was a man flat on his face. Drunk, injured, ill, maybe dead. The driver stopped, climbed down to find out what was going on. The man in the road snapped to his feet, a gun hot on the driver. Masked men and Indians in war paint leaped out of the woods, all firing pistols in the air and "whooping." The bandits tied the male passengers' hands above their heads and seized all valuables. One bandit's mustache fell off, and a hostage recognized the bandit as Archibald White—White and his friends playing the role of bandits and Indians because that, to them, was the myth of the place. The passengers probably gasped, appalled, and then laughed and rolled on up to the brainstorm brainstorm for a few days of loud, bright fun on Osgood Pond.

Parts of the Adirondacks at this time were sites of labor for loggers and miners and farmers and their families who struggled to get by. Parts of the Adirondacks at this time were fun-sized versions of the West for rich flatlanders, made possible by copious amounts of cash and the knowledge, ingenuity, and energy of locals. I'm amazed more flatlanders weren't accidentally shot. These parts could've been a stage show called Frontierland—coincidentally, the name of an Adirondack theme park that opened a few decades later.

The Whites weren't alone. Beginning in the 1880s and ending, abruptly, in 1929, owning an opulent, rustic retreat in the Adirondacks was a status symbol for the nation's ultrawealthy. Many of these retreats were compounds that included a dozen buildings (everything from an icehouse to a blacksmith's shop to a root cellar to a collection of cottages or tent platforms for guests, even a building where a carpenter could repair a birch twig rocking chair), sometimes a farm to supply fresh vegetables and milk, and even a second retreat to escape to when the first was too crowded. Sprawling rooms radiant with birch bark on the ceiling and oiled hardwood wainscot on the walls, fawn hides and Japanese fans and snowshoes above the granite hearth, massive logs with the bark still on holding up the roof of the front porch that, of course, had a spectacular view across the water, a herd of deer mixed with a few gazelles mounted to a wall of peeled spruce bark, eyebrow dormers and octagon dining rooms right on the water and peaked roofs that looked like a pagoda, a bedframe that had a two-story branched snag for one post and a stuffed owl perched high in the branches, grand staircases of tree trunks and branches, twig work spelling out the camp's name on the boathouse—regardless, they were still called camps. When the Whites purchased their property, it lacked one Adirondack element that every wealthy family desired: an island. They hired a contractor to dig a ditch to isolate the tip of a sandy spit. Some of these camps were built for society, clustered on lakes ringed by camps of equal size, and some sat on preserves that sprawled for thousands of acres: a getaway from society. I don't think there's ever been an example of such concentrated wealth connected to appreciation of wildness and natural beauty.

Then the Depression cut luxury spending, and even before that the passing of a federal income tax had already slowed new construction of these camps, and both world wars interrupted the availability of funds and materials and workers. For the rich, part of the appeal of the Adirondacks was that it had been hard to get there. That exclusivity faded, and then in the 1960s airline travel and the interstate highway system robbed the

Adirondacks of some of its luster: the rich could now easily travel to more exclusive, exotic destinations just as quickly. The Adirondacks has been called America's Switzerland. It's not quite. The camps also demanded constant maintenance. Rustic materials liked to rot and leak and burn. Later generations either didn't want to or couldn't afford to pay for repairs. How would you track someone down to rebuild a baroque porch railing constructed of woven birch sticks?

No one quite knew what to do with the camps. A few burned or rotted or were knocked down, and others limped along in various states of decay. No one paid them much attention until historians in the 1970s started calling the camps, collectively, the Great Camps.

As a category, Great Camps share little other than size and an expression of some sense of what the owners and architects thought the Adirondacks should be. Depending on how you decide to set boundaries between which camps are great and which aren't, there are between fifty and seventy-five Great Camps. They're scattered around the region. Clusters stand on the lakes that look most like the Adirondacks and were once not too far from a train station. Conceptually, they range from hunting lodges to castles, country estates to Swiss chalets. The Great Camps that haven't been torched or bulldozed or given up to rot have been converted into tourist attractions, resorts, off-campus learning opportunities for regional colleges, historic sites, or remain in private hands and occasionally pop up on the real estate market, and people who love them *ooh* and *ahh* and then drive to the gas station to buy a Powerball ticket.

Even though Great Camps are remnants of extreme concentration in wealth and a reminder of the economic inequality between locals and part-time Adirondackers, the Great Camp aesthetic has become iconic. Stone, wooden beams, birch bark on the walls: Great Camps have influenced Adirondack rustic style, even for practical, contemporary buildings. Commenting on the opening of a new Rite Aid in the village of Lake Placid, a popular Adirondack magazine wrote, "it looked more like an Adirondack Great Camp than a chain drug store." Like rustic guide rails, the aesthetic of Great Camps has become one more way to make the Adirondacks look more like the Adirondacks. The popularity of the Adirondacks when many other national and local parks were established, and the coverage many Great Camps received in newspapers and magazines because of their rich, well-known owners, account for the notes of Adirondack rustic you see in many of the buildings built there. That rustic look has even filtered down to the materials you see on high-end suburban homes today. That guy who had the Adirondack ceiling fan on the bottom rack of his shopping cart at the Big Box home improvement store in Ithaca most certainly didn't own a Great Camp. I find it fascinating that this style has so infiltrated the nation that he was nonetheless buying a fan inspired by Great Camps. It's part of our national style.

MOST ADIRONDACK SCHOLARS CONSIDER Pine Knot to be the first Great Camp. Pine Knot was William West Durant's laboratory. In the 1870s, it began modestly, a single-story chalet, a few one-room cabins, pavilions for cooking and dining. Working with local carpenters and masons, Durant expanded Pine Knot into a complex of buildings clustered informally around the sunny shore of a point on Raquette Lake: a two-story Swiss cottage, an icehouse, a kitchen, guest cottages, a telegraph office, a blacksmith's shop and a carpenter's shop, a recreation room, the servants' quarters, and boathouses, and there were stone chimneys, and rotting pine stumps with flowers planted in a chopped divot, and stairs made out of logs, and a hand railing capped with a carved finial that looked like a multi-stem mushroom, and some buildings had wooden frames but were clad in logs, and some were covered in sheets of bark and some buildings had tree trunk porch posts that climbed straight up, most of the way, before the limbs branched to hold up the roof, and vines climbed exterior walls—all of which made Pine Knot look like the forest was trying to reclaim it. That was the exact look Durant hoped to achieve.

A photograph of Durant at Pine Knot shows him descending a wooden staircase from a wooden porch. He's wearing a derby hat and a dark suit. Two birch trees crowd the stairs. It seems that Durant placed the building just in that spot, just at that angle, to have the stairs descend between the bark of those two birches. To Durant, Pine Knot was a type of model home, a way for him to show wealthy acquaintances what the Adirondacks might be made into with money. He hoped to sell them camps and property. Some days, when I'm feeling cynical, I think most Adirondack history since Pine Knot should be treated as a sales pitch.

Durant spent more than a decade of his childhood touring Europe with his mother and sister. His father, Thomas Durant, remained in the United States to manage the construction of the eastern half of the first transcontinental railroad and to build a railroad through the Adirondacks. The Union Pacific made it. The Adirondack Railroad stopped short. But for a few decades it was the fastest way to get to the wilderness, and it was better than a buckboard wagon, though tourists still had to ride in one of those for the better part of a day after they got off the train. At that time, the elder Durant controlled a larger percentage of Adirondack land than the state of New York. From Europe, the younger Durant voyaged to Egypt to participate in an archeological dig, and he was trophy hunting in Sudan or Ethiopia in 1874 when his father, spooked by a financial panic, requested his family's prompt return to New York. William presented his father with a lion cub, a trophy immediately conveyed to the Central Park Zoo. Durant was twenty-four. He took a job on Wall Street.

Durant ventured into the Adirondacks for the first time in 1876. That year Colvin was working twenty miles to the west. Durant traveled up his father's railroad, then bounced in a wagon on a mountain road for thirty miles before getting into a boat and then another boat to get to Raquette Lake. The only signs of habitation were a few camps owned by guides and trappers and settlers. In the scenery and in the railroad that stopped a bit short, Durant sensed an opportunity. He spent the next twenty-five years working to make his family's vast wilderness estate into a world-famous resort, building and planning camps, hotels, roads, steamboat lines, and railroads, an effort aided by his family fortune. He understood that a reliable way to get there was essential to attract buyers. One of the railroads was built to convey tourists from one lake to another. It was only three-quarters of a mile long, the shortest standard-gauge railroad in the world. Along with people, it hauled guideboats, tied to the top. An optimist, Durant thought the Adirondacks would be "the resort of the future." He only stopped trying to build that resort of the future when he had exhausted his family fortune—even the half he had stolen from his sister—and his creditors wouldn't loan him another cent.

To sell land at a profit was Durant's scheme. But he wasn't a philistine huckster. He occupied himself with a concept of what leisure in the Adirondacks might look like. Stealing elements from gardens he had seen in Europe and in Central Park and Prospect Park, and from the chalets he had seen in the Alps, and merging that collage of ideas, forms, patterns, and aspirations with the Adirondack vernacular use of wood, bark, and sticks found in hunting shanties and logging camps, he fostered a rustic aesthetic of luxury. It's going too far to give Durant all the credit. Other designers were building rustic structures at about the same time, and there was a growing national movement toward handcrafted construction. Durant was so influential because he promoted his projects with photographs and made sure people with power and influence visited them.

When I see rusting guide rails, when I see birchbark lampshades, when I see the Swiss chalet railing at the Red Top Inn, when I see Adirondack fans at Big Box stores in the flatlands, when I see wood and stone details on Adirondack gas stations, when I see brainstorm, when I see roadside

signs with yellow words on a brown sign (not the stock green and white)—
I like to think through the lineage of Adirondack rustic that leads back to
Durant, the son of a railroad tycoon who had the money to make the resort
of the future look any way he wanted it to. Imagine if Durant had held a
fascination for Romanesque Revival, and that had caught on, and that was
today the style associated with the region. That rustic today dominates the
look of the Adirondacks makes only marginally more sense.

Even after Durant spent all his money and fled the Adirondacks and
struggled to find a steady job, wealthy landowners continued to copy his
ideas. They still do. At least they try to, though it usually doesn't quite work
out. Durant, his fellow designers, and the skilled workers who built the
camps—their rustic aesthetic had grace and a bit of whimsy, and they understood the necessity of restraint and moderation, the value of mingling
complexity and simplicity in a way that gave you a sense of the texture of
the region but not a headache, and they appreciated the value of situating a
camp to embrace the shape of the land and cutting as few trees as possible.
Newly built rustic buildings in the Adirondacks tend to blare, massive
structures decorated with big logs and too much stone veneer, birch bark
walls for the sake of birch bark walls, and the camps end up looking like a
joke about a joke that was never meant to be one.

IN 1918, WHITE PINE Camp was sold when the Whites divorced. It was
Calvin Coolidge's summer White House in 1926. It sold again, was donated
to a school, was abandoned and then sold to several investors interested
in historic preservation. They renovated the dilapidated buildings. It's now
a resort. You can book a room and spend the night surrounded by brainstorm. I've done that twice, off-season and midweek and in the smallest
room available—once part of the building where the servants slept—which
made the nightly rate reasonably affordable, more so than the night I spent
in Lake George. I went because I wanted to have some sense of what
staying at a Great Camp felt like.

There's a long entrance road, and at one point, you have to get out of
your car and open a rustic gate of twigs and branches and copper tacks. The
point is to say: you've arrived. When I was a kid, I saved aluminum cans,
smashed them with a sledgehammer, and then stored them in black plastic
bags. Eventually my parents bought me this plastic hand lever crusher
that we mounted to the wall by our basement door. Every few months I'd
sell the heavy black bags of crushed cans as bulk aluminum scrap to a guy
down the valley so I had some extra money to spend. Stopping to open
the gate to enter the former estate of a rich family was the most out of my

element I felt anywhere in the Adirondacks. I questioned whether I should put on a sport coat. I almost lost my nerve, almost turned back to find a campground where I could sleep in my tent. White Pine Camp ended up not being pretentious at all, but that pause I took at the gate stuck with me.

At White Pine Camp, I've seen loons on Osgood Pond, and I've seen coyotes scamper across the ice. At dawn on a crisp morning, a skim of fog on the water, I paddled my canoe from the lake into the Osgood River, a wiry, mucky creek stitched tight with stunted spruce, a place a moose might live without complaint. I paddled around a tight curve. A sandbar snagged my boat. Something large but unseen barreled through the forest toward me, cracking spruce branches. I braced myself for something big and furry and mad. I waited for a hoof to plunge through the floor of my canoe. Whatever it was, it stopped short and trotted the other way, snorting. This must have been something else the rich treasured about Great Camps: they could vacation in opulence and yet quickly row—or, more likely, be rowed by a guide—to someplace that felt wild.

The brainstorm bowling alley at White Pine Camp is a few feet from the lake, pines so close to one wall that the builder had to notch the eaves around the trunks. I liked to walk down to the lake at night, when the whole place was quiet and dark. Tendrils of fog. Moonlit pines reflected on flat water. I liked to pretend I had been born a century earlier—and rich, my family's money coming from oil or copper or international trade, and that this money supported the whole compound, and that a few miles away my private railroad car waited in a siding to whisk me back to the city. I'd sit there and think about guests bowling late some night in the summer of 1911. On the electric shore of that dark lake up in the wilderness: tumblers of whiskey and a few beers; hoots and laughter, a glass broken, a door slammed; the thud of the ball on the wooden lane; the smooth, ascendant roll; the splintering crash of the pins. Outside, it was all stars and tendrils of fog and moonlit pines on flat water, two loons hooting back. Too often the way we've written the history of the Adirondacks pushes us to imagine ourselves wealthy.

ELSEWHERE IN THE ADIRONDACKS, I've seen brainstorm:
   On Marty's Chili Nights, a Mexican restaurant in the hamlet of Indian Lake, the sight of which caused me to swerve and skid to a stop in the gravel lot across the street. On a gas pump canopy and on the gables of a car wash. On a front yard wishing well. On a baseball dugout. On the registration booth and the bathrooms at Fish Creek. On a mock tavern (Willie's) at Pirate's Cove Mini Golf in Lake George. On a newly built camp adver-

tised as having "New Adirondack Style." On a roadside produce stand just within the Blue Line. I took a break from writing this book to visit Alaska with my dad. In the town of Talkeetna, on an ice cream stand that sold a fireweed flavor, I saw brainstorm.

Driving around the Adirondacks, I became a brainstorm connoisseur. The edge of high-quality brainstorm has the mellifluous flow of a white pine that has grown through the forest for decades, even centuries. These boards have an organic edge with subtle variation that's pleasing to the eye. Tracing that edge of brainstorm, you trace time, the storms and seasons, the droughts and sharp gusts of wind that made each mark. Low-quality brainstorm is a hack job, looks like someone bungled a square board with a dull axe, and someone else tried to make the board curve and flow with a jigsaw, rusty blade bent.

THE WHITES BOUGHT LAND to build White Pine Camp from Paul Smith. Paul Smith's was the place to be. When he got the chance, Paul Smith liked to buy vast tracts of Adirondack land, thousands of acres at a time, and then sell choice building lots to wealthy clients who then built camps. Paul Smith often cleared enough profit from those sales to pay for the whole tract. He once said to a reporter, "I tell you, if there's a spot on the face of the earth where millionaires go to play at house keeping in log cabins and tents as they do here I have it yet to hear about." He had more perspective on the absurdity of this influx of wealth than Durant. But Paul Smith played along.

Paul Smith also owned the sawmill that cut the first brainstorm board. Likely he owned the pine from which his workers cut it. Paul Smith's land was known for big pines. It still is. For the Columbian Exposition World's Fair in 1892, Paul Smith donated a specimen of white pine thirty-one inches in diameter. It was 226 years old. Paul Smith also owned a world-famous hotel known by everyone as Paul Smith's. A settlement, Paul Smiths, sprung up around the hotel so workers and guides had a place to live. Paul Smith's guides lived on Easy Street. Other Adirondack hotels had to advertise their features and the advantages of their location. Paul Smith's just had to print PAUL SMITH'S, ADIRONDACKS, and guests mobbed the place, though Paul Smith's wasn't above boasting: *Here is a forest park of more than 30,000 acres, being the largest hotel holding in the State of New York. This magnificent playground of Nature is free to every guest at Paul Smith's Hotel to fish in, to hunt in, to row in, to drive in, to walk in, to camp in, to breathe the Adirondack air in, and to use for every benefit stored among the life-giving recesses of the North Woods.*

Paul Smith himself became so closely associated with the Adirondack air that tourists went out of their way to have a photograph taken with him, with good old Uncle Paul, and his likeness and his name were so iconic and well regarded that he used them to sell Paul Smith's Pure Spring Water. What I most like about Paul Smith is that he used the myth of the Adirondacks to cut a profit, to draw flatlanders up there, but then he became tangled up in the myth himself. He once filed a lawsuit to stop a man from advertising a brand of whiskey, without authorization, as Paul Smith's, a picture of Paul Smith on the label. For damages, Smith sought one thousand dollars. He won an injunction but only got a hundred bucks.

Born in Vermont in 1825, the son of a logger, Paul Smith arrived in the Adirondacks in the 1840s. In 1912, he died wealthy and respected at the age of eighty-seven. One of his obituaries noted, "When he went to the Adirondacks many years ago the woods were full of Indians; when he died they were full of millionaires." That's nonsense. When Paul Smith died there were still Native Americans, and millionaires, and millionaires playing Indian, which complicates the simple frontier process ascribed to Paul Smith's life.

Even today there's a romance about the span of time through which Paul Smith lived, and thus there's also a romance about Paul Smith. He showed up to a wilderness largely unknown to flatlanders, twenty years before Colvin, and then more flatlanders showed up to hunt and have a good time and sleep in backwoods log hotels, and then even more crowds showed up and hotels were built and the wilderness became fashionable and the hotels got fancier and bigger. Paul Smith had a strong Vermont face and sharp blue eyes. He liked to tell jokes at his friends' expense. He spoke to both millionaires and his workers as equals. He was a good shot with a rifle. He limped a bit because he had once fallen off a building under construction. He drew a crowd when he told a story. He worked hard but thought himself lazy, in that self-effacing Yankee way. He liked to walk around his vegetable garden with his thumbs hooked in the armholes of his vest. A tall blue-eyed man who limped a bit and hooked his thumbs in his vest: Paul Smith gives literal body to the rise of the Adirondacks from the backwoods to a millionaires' retreat, even more so because he happened to die before automobiles overran the woods, and then Paul Smith's burned to the ground and what some now see as the Golden Age of the Adirondacks went bust.

That's not how I see it. I don't think Paul Smith would have seen it that way either, automobiles marking the end of the good years. I think he would have seen the automobile as the next way to haul more tourists to his hotel's front door. To get to Paul Smith's, early guests endured a forty-two-mile stagecoach ride. Later, railroad tracks were built closer and the stagecoach ride dropped to fourteen miles and then to seven, and in 1906, The Paul Smith Hotel Company built Paul Smith's Electric Railway. It carried passengers in an electric trolley car six and a half miles from the railroad to the hotel's front door. Paul Smith was there to make a buck, not define a style like Durant. When automobiles arrived in the woods, Paul Smith would have seen an opportunity. He would have built an enormous parking lot. He would have wanted to see his name roadside, PAUL SMITH'S in red neon tubes, flanked by a copse of electric green, wind-bent pines, the pines blinking on and off, swaying in the lake breeze.

HIS GIVEN NAME WAS Apollos Austin Smith, which was shortened to Poll, pronounced Paul, and then finally just written that way. Paul Smith left Vermont to work on a canal boat. After hearing stories about the wilderness, he ventured up into the Adirondacks as an assistant to a hunter. He probably scraped deer hides and hauled traps. He might have rented a boardinghouse for a year or two, sheltering sports and guiding them on trips to find trout and deer. In the early 1850s, he purchased land. He built a small hotel called Hunter's Home. No one ever called it Paul Smith's. He brought his mother and his father along to help out. Paul guided, his mother cooked, his father tended to the animals and the garden. Hunter's Home was modest. A kitchen with a dining table, space for ten or so sports to bunk, the bar a barrel of rye whiskey and a dipper in the corner: place your four coppers on the flat top and serve yourself. A sport sitting on the front porch looked out to a view of charred pine stumps, spindly potatoes planted between, some girdled, grotesque pines in the distance, a scene that didn't match the Adirondack scenic ideal. Most guests were lawyers and doctors from eastern cities.

Due to the lack of individual bedrooms, only men could visit Hunter's Home. One day Paul Smith was guiding a repeat guest. The guest had become Paul Smith's good friend. Lake to lake they went, looking for trout and deer. The two men stopped at a particularly scenic spot. I've been there. It looks exactly like the Adirondacks. Paul Smith's friend commented that here was an ideal location to build a larger, more refined hotel where his wife and children could also spend the summer. Paul Smith agreed, but he didn't have the cash. He secured a loan and purchased fifty acres of land at six dollars per acre. He began building a hotel with seventeen rooms, the St. Regis Lake House, officially. No one ever called it that. From a mound of sand, the white hotel with three dormers looked across the lake. It opened in 1859. To build the hotel, Paul Smith kicked out an encampment of Native Americans.

That year Paul Smith married Lydia Helen Martin, his wife, his business partner, his writer of contracts, and possibly the wise and prescient mind that commanded the entire operation of Paul Smith's. I think she was the one who convinced, nudged, or even shoved Paul Smith to leap from guide to land baron. Lydia attended what is now known as the Emma Willard School, located in Troy, New York, an unusual opportunity at that time for a woman from a rural family. Her ambition boosted Paul Smith's. Before he met her, he wanted to build his seventeen-room hotel, wanted to guide, wanted to be comfortable and maybe have some money to buy more land. Together they built an empire.

During the hotel's early years, Paul and Lydia served as the staff, Paul guiding, Lydia cooking. Soon they hired maids and cooks and waiters and guides. After the Civil War, business boomed. The Smiths expanded the white hotel on the mound of sand, built an addition and then another and another and a new porch and then tacked on an annex out back, until the white hotel on the mound of sand was a conglomeration of structures, styles, wings, windows, and rooflines, a building that kinked and turned, ran a little ways and kinked again, all yoked together with porches and wooden walkways. Paul Smith's could hold five hundred guests for the night. Some in tents. Some in cottages. Some on couches. Someone sprawled out on the pool table. All those people packed into that bright hotel against the pines. When the hotel was booked, visitors joked that the Smiths glued guests to the walls. I bet Lydia and Paul would have charged those guests the full rate. With good reason. The Smiths owned one of the most popular hotels in one of the nation's most famous Vacationlands. Besides, Paul Smith liked to say that if you planned to rob his guests, you'd better do it on their way up.

A telegraph machine, women wearing silk dresses, sports from Boston or New York holding fishing poles that had never been wet, seasoned hunters returning muddied and cold, a dead deer with a crowd gathered around, multicolored ribbons flickering in the breeze, trout nailed in a row to a wooden rack, a vase of pond-lilies picked during a scenic tour, rifles, stacks of Saratoga trunks, poodles and hounds and mutts, guides lounging on the grass, music and dancing and cards and bright lights in the parlor, clear glass bottles of seltzer, chairs with red and gold upholstery and brass tacks, Brussels carpeting, cowhide boots, high-class cuisine that rivaled any found in the Big City, a barbershop, private dining rooms, guideboats, a bowling alley: all of this was Paul Smith's at its peak, the hoopla made more outlandish—and, to me, lovely—by its location in the middle of nowhere.

Decades later, after Lydia died, Paul and his two surviving sons managed the electric railroad, a telephone company, and a series of hydro-electric dams that powered the hotel and nearby towns, and years after Paul Smith died and Paul Smith's burned, the fortune and assets of the business empire were willed to found a college in Paul Smith's honor, Paul Smith's College, built where the hotel once stood. Its primary majors were forestry and hotel management. It's still known for both and is today the only four-year college within the Blue Line. On my first visit to Fish Creek, the college-aged woman who sat in the booth and read me the campground rules wore a sweatshirt that said Paul Smith's.

Chapter 8

THE GREAT CAMPS THAT survive are sequestered; you have to go out of your way to see them. More modest camps are the most ubiquitous object in the Adirondacks. Along roads, along rivers, dry in the forest, and especially fronting lakes, camps are everywhere. They annoyed me at first, all these buildings I thought were encroaching on the wilderness. Now I find them fascinating. In style, location, materials, and name, each camp is someone's idea of what the Adirondacks should be.

They add up to the greatest collection of rustic structures in the world:

A TOW-BEHIND CAMPER with two rims, no tires, jacked up on concrete blocks sometime in the 1970s. Two broad teal stripes wrap the mildewed aluminum body. Off in the woods, a brainstorm outhouse, door ajar.

ONE ROOM AND A PORCH marooned on a boulder in the middle of a lake.

AN A-FRAME, TRIANGULAR window at the peak, a railing on the deck that makes the whole structure look like a chalet nestled in the Swiss Alps.

A WOODEN STRUCTURE BALANCED on a floating platform powered by two outboard motors. The platform is moored to a rock in a lake and registered as a motorboat. Or at least it was moored to a rock in a lake and registered as a motorboat until the state declared the camp lacked necessary permits and ordered the owner to remove it.

In response, the owner said, "Am I going to sue the bastards? That's a real possibility."

NESTLED IN THE PINES on a broad island, a hundred-year-old two-room camp. Above the fireplace, there's a buck mounted on a board with a neatly routed edge, the oak board stained to look like walnut by someone who had never before stained wood: splotchy. Driving to camp one day, the camp's owner spotted a plaid couch on the side of the road—FREE—and picked it up. He barged the couch broadside across the lake on two motorboats.

A STEAMBOAT, FROM DURANT'S era, beached and converted into a camp with a waterfront view.

IN A STAND OF MATURE maples that flares red and orange in October, a house trailer with a fresh coat of bright-red paint.

BOLTED TO A CLIFF, a boxy modern structure with a sprawling ipê deck. The deck's railing is stainless steel wire instead of boards, so the railing doesn't obscure the camp's view of the High Peaks.

MIGHT BE SO HARD for guests to find, hidden down one of a few dozen gravel roads in miles of forest, that it requires a flashy roadside object to catch guests' attention: Seven pieces of pink surveyor's tape knotted on a maple branch. A plywood cutout of a moose. A Colonial-style three-bulb streetlamp. A boulder painted white. A lobster pot buoy. A wagon wheel. A circle of orange spray paint on a dead tree. Seven circular red reflectors screwed to a pine in the shape of an H.

LOG LODGE. SUNNY COVE. Mosquito Camp. Camp Chaos. Elk Horn Shanty. The Otter Banks. Fern Rock. Mountain Home. Grandma's Holiday Inn, and right down the road, Pontiac Chief, and then next door, Thundershack. Or named Ideal Rest and then sold and renamed Belle Aire. I tallied forty-two camp names that included "Pine." One had brainstorm and can be rented on VRBO. My five favorites: Porch in the Pines, Underpines, Lone Pine, Seven Pines, Pine Not (the only Durant pun I've ever encountered).

$120,000—GREAT HUNTING CAMP on +/− 80 hillside acres that has been lightly logged. Includes a 360 sq. ft. cabin that sleeps 6 at the top of the hill which can be reached by foot or 4-wheeler. Off the grid but has solar panels & generator.

$189,000—A TRUE ADIRONDACK Chalet ~ 3 BR and 2 Baths ~ 2100 Sq Ft. ~ Open concept floor plan ~ Wood stove ~ Sunroom ~ Knotty Pine and Beam Interior ~ Sky lights ~ Master with separate balcony ~ Large deck, Gazebo & Detached 2-car Garage.

$375,000—LOG CABIN LOCATED on the Stillwater Reservoir w/ 4,000 ft of road frontage, and over 600 feet of water frontage. Nice sandy beach area, and a 60' floating dock, gazebo & hot tub. Cabin has one bedroom, loft area, full bathroom, eat-in kitchen & enclosed porch. Sits on 32 secluded acres.

$795,000—SPECTACULAR!—CUSTOM-BUILT 4,000 SF four bedroom, 3½ bath home on a point with expansive water views. Five heated garage spaces. The Hexagon dining room maximizes the stunning waterfront views.

ALGONQUIN WHISPERS. BEARHURST. Adirondack Zen. Camp Woodsmoke. River House. Kookaburra. Camp Boulder Over. Chickadee Hill. Happy Hour. O-So-Co-Z. Beaver Stump.

CAMP RUN-A-MUK. A slogan on its sign: "Snipe Hunting, Bear Wrestling, Skinny Dipping."

CAMP RUN-A-MUK (a different one). A slogan on its sign: "It Doesn't Get Any Better."

THE OWLS NEST. LAKEFRONT, screened by hemlocks, a mid-century ranch, the interior updated to give the impression of an upscale condo, the T-111 siding recently painted a middling, modern gray. (It's pronounced TEE-one-eleven, and is coarse plywood with a vertical gouge every eight inches or so. It can be purchased at any home improvement store in four-by-eight sheets: Adirondack rustic on a budget.)

IT'LL DO.
This Is It.
Both one-room T-111 cabins far from any lake.

ONE LAST GREAT CAMP story that's too good to ignore: In 1923, Marjorie Merriweather Post, daughter of C. W. Post of the cereal empire, purchased an existing camp on Upper St. Regis Lake, not far from Paul Smith's:

Topridge. She had it renovated and expanded into what many researchers consider the grandest of all Great Camps. The apogee of Adirondack rustic tops an esker.

During Post's ownership, the main lodge stood imposing and broad, low rooflines and bulky stone chimneys. From the outside it appeared to be moderately rustic. It was a geode. Inside, the great room sprawled, eighty feet by one hundred, roughhewn wooden beams rising to the thirty-foot-high peak of the ceiling, walls clad with split logs. Two antler chandeliers, a guideboat, and a birch bark canoe hung from the ceiling. Craftsmen bent saplings into handrails and used tree trunks for posts. Taxidermy specimens included a polar bear cub, an African antelope head, a buffalo head, opossums, foxes, a caribou head, and a big white owl. Fabric for chairs and rugs included floral, zebra hide, polyester cheetah fur, and cowhide. Post's second husband was an ambassador to the Soviet Union. One of the sixty-three other buildings in the Topridge complex was a Russian dacha topped with onion domes. To give the great room a better view of a mountain, Post requested a larger window. A ten-and-a-half-foot-tall plate glass window arrived via train. Workers barged the glass across the lake, just like that guy's plaid couch.

By boat or by floatplane, guests arrived at the boathouse, a whimsical, contorted structure of tree trunks and branches that looked as though the most eccentric lines and curves found in a square mile of forest had been coerced into holding up a roof. A funicular lifted guests to the great room. Servants hauled the luggage. In July and August, when Post was in residence—usually once every few years—eighty-five servants were on staff. Among them: guides, a boatman, a naturalist, a tennis pro, a hairdresser, and a dance instructor, and guards, cooks, and maids, and one dedicated maid and one dedicated footman to attend to each of the eighteen guest cottages. Two maids spent four hours each day dusting the great room, all those twigs and curios. In 1973, when Post died, three moving vans hauled Native American artifacts to the Smithsonian.

Post willed the property to the state of New York, but upkeep was too expensive, so the state sold the camp. Here's where the story gets really good. Roger Jakubowski of New Jersey bought it in 1985 for $911,000. At the time, Jakubowski called himself a "hot dog salesman." He owned nine Wendy's fast-food restaurants, two motels, a handful of arcades and hot dog stands, and a supermarket downstate. Since the 1890s, the era of Paul Smith, Upper St. Regis Lake has been the home of the St. Regis Yacht Club. Twelve thirty-two-foot-long identical sailboats, called Idems, were built to race. Eleven still float; the other one is in a museum. When

Jakubowski purchased Topridge, the camp included an Idem. He renamed the boat *Hot Dog* and to the stern attached a wooden hot dog, a gesture that strikes me as a middle finger wagging at the old money all around the lake.

Jakubowski went on an Adirondack bender. More Land. More schemes. He was quoted as saying, "I should own the entire Adirondack Park, that's what I think." Paul Smith never went that far. A few years later, creditors of Jakubowski sold Topridge to a real estate developer from Texas.

143

Then, almost as by magic, we were encompassed by a huge black ring. The surface of the lake, when we had reached the centre, was slightly luminous from the starlight, and the dark, even forest-line that surrounded us, doubled by reflection in the water, presenting a broad, unbroken belt of utter blackness. The effect was quite startling, like some huge conjurer's trick. It seemed as if we had crossed the boundary-line between the real and the imaginary, and this was indeed the land of shadows and of spectres.

—John Burroughs, in the 1860s, on a pond mundanely named Nate's

Chapter 9

∎∎∎

THE HIGH PEAKS ARE the type of terrain hikers pine to climb: steep and craggy, cut by streams that leap and bound, pure water tumbling into pools of jade. The High Peaks are laced with challenging trails. Some with chains or ropes or ladders to ascend cliffs. Some with log bridges that float on bogs. Some with wooden planks bolted to rock slabs. The High Peaks are famous for summits that deliver fifty-mile views. The High Peaks are frequently featured in tourism ads, calendars, postcards, magazine articles, and social media posts. The High Peaks are within a six-hour drive of most major cities in the Northeast, a fast four lanes almost the whole way. All of which means that during the summer and on weekends when the weather is grand, in the High Peaks it's hard to find a place to park.

Six parking lots dot the fringe of the High Peaks. The busiest is at the Adirondack Loj, owned by the Adirondack Mountain Club. Gravel lobes splay into the forest. There's space for about two hundred cars. As parking lots go, it's picturesque. Boulders and trees, no light poles, no painted lines. Early on a Monday morning in July, I drove up to the lot. At the entrance, a parking attendant sat in a booth. I paid ten dollars and hung an orange parking permit from my rearview mirror. The lot wasn't full, but it was getting there. Jackets and backpacks, camp stoves and boots, fleece hats and sleeping bags, the lot looked like backstage at an L.L.Bean catalog photo shoot.

Sky clear, sun already hot, the day looked like it was about to be grand.

I tied the laces of my hiking boots and packed two granola bars and an almond butter sandwich and a water bottle in my backpack. I walked behind a long row of parked cars—plates from six states—and signed in at the trail register. I climbed four miles up a steep trail and had a good time at it on that day turning grand, climbing up the trail that snuck through a pine forest, crossing a mossy stream, and then scrambling up a steep slab of wet rock. I passed a group of summer camp kids who shouted *Mud!* or *Rock!* each time someone in the group spotted either. They were bound to go hoarse before lunch. An older man wearing corduroy pants and a plaid shirt stood to the side of the trail, resting. He was winded but smiled at me as I walked by. A hundred feet up the trail, I turned and looked back. He leaned over his wooden cane, slung a felt canteen over his shoulder, and slogged on up.

As I climbed, the forest changed, from sugar maples and beech to spruce and balsam that smelled tangy in the sun. A million drops of sunlit dew were stars in a night of spruce shadows, the soil in the shade damp and cool to the touch. I scuttled up yet another slope and saw hobblebush berries that looked like bouquets of lime-green Skittles. The trees—now fir and balsam, paper birch and mountain ash—were shorter the farther I climbed, and then the tops, mangled by gales, only reached my waist, then my knees. At treeline, 2,500 vertical feet above the parking lot, the balsams hit the deck, growing in gnarled, tangled clumps on the ground: krummholz. Then the trees were gone. Up a broad snub nose of rock and tufts of grass and sun glare, the trail curled to the top of Algonquin.

FOR AN ADIRONDACK PEAK to be a High Peak, it must be taller than 4,000 feet. I guess you have to draw the line somewhere. Forty-three peaks meet this criterion, clustered in the northeast quadrant of the Adirondacks. The Mountain or Peak or Mount is usually dropped so that in conversation the peaks have a one-word name. Two of the forty-three peaks are taller than 5,000 feet, just barely: the highest peak in New York, Marcy, and the second-highest, Algonquin.

Forty-three High Peaks and there's a group of hikers who have hiked them all, and then some. They call themselves the Adirondack 46ers. To become a 46er, you must hike to the summit of forty-six peaks. It's not for me, but some people find great joy in the quest. Four of the peaks on the official list are shorter than 4,000 feet (but were once thought to be taller) and there's one peak, exactly 4,000 feet high, that doesn't officially count because it was once thought to be a few feet shorter. Many 46ers climb it anyway. A restaurant in a town near the High Peaks serves forty-six types of sandwiches. The Algonquin has roast turkey, applewood smoked bacon, avocado, sprouts, and Russian dressing.

The first recorded 46ers were Bob Marshall, who later helped found the Wilderness Society, George Marshall, and Herb Clark, a friend and guide. All three finished in 1925. They thought they had finished a few years earlier when they had climbed the last of the forty-two peaks on their list. A historian conducting research for a book about the High Peaks pointed out the few peaks the trio had missed. Bob Marshall might have been inspired to hike the peaks by reading Verplanck Colvin's adventures. Marshall wrote a short book about hiking the High Peaks. It includes brief directions on how to reach each summit and also ranks each peak's view. Many of the High Peaks that have vaunted views today ranked low in Marshall's opinion. In the 1920s, loggers were still active in the area, leaving an unsightly clutter of branches and treetops, which often caught fire and scorched nearby forests. Although guides and tourists had been climbing some High Peaks regularly since the 1850s, and there are even speculative reports that Indigenous people climbed the High Peaks to find medicinal plants, Marshall's book is what finally brought the peaks together. Published in 1922, his book is the founding document of the High Peaks.

The story of the 46ers begins a few years later. In the 1930s, a group of parishioners from Grace Methodist Church in Troy, New York, began climbing in the High Peaks. A few members were inspired by Marshall's book and by another book about the High Peaks, *Peaks and People of the Adirondacks*, written by Russell Carson, the historian who had alerted the Marshall brothers to their four-peak oversight. Sunday was the only day the church members could get away to make the drive north. Some Sundays, they skipped church, climbed a peak, and worshiped on the summit. Grace Hudowalski, Edward Hudowalski, and Reverend Ernest Ryder were the club's founders.

The founders didn't set out to hike all forty-six. A peak one weekend and then another peak the next, before too long the founders were halfway there and thought they might as well hike them all. The trio founded the club in 1937.

Forty-two, forty-three, or forty-six, the High Peaks are crowded into about 200,000 acres. The most popular peaks, those that are overrun on a grand day, are packed into about 50,000 acres, split between a few Wilderness Areas. Six million acres: on any given day, the majority of Adirondack hikers walk trails that lace those 50,000.

During the first thirty years that followed the creation of the Adirondack

Steamboat (*Killoquah*) docked on Raquette Lake, ca. 1890. Photographer: Seneca Ray Stoddard. Courtesy of Adirondack Experience.

Moose head, perhaps imported from a place where moose still lived, mounted above an Adirondack hotel's fireplace, ca. 1902. Photographer: P. H. Riddle. Courtesy of Adirondack Experience.

Automobile camping at Fish Creek Pond in the 1930s. Eastern Illustrating Co. Courtesy of Adirondack Experience.

Gathering of sports and guides around a guideboat at an Adirondack hotel in 1886. Mitchel Sabattis is near the middle, between the two trees. Photographer: J. F. Holley. Courtesy of Adirondack Experience.

Restored neon motel sign at Northwood Cabins, near Tupper Lake, 2017. Photograph by author.

Verplanck Colvin and Mills Blake surrounded by survey equipment, ca. 1880. Courtesy of Adirondack Experience.

Mitchel Sabattis standing in front of a guideboat, 1886. Photographer: J. F. Holley. Courtesy of Adirondack Experience.

Brainstorm siding at White Pine Camp, 2018. Photograph by author.

William West Durant at Pine Knot Camp, ca. 1890. Photographer: Seneca Ray Stoddard. Courtesy of Adirondack Experience.

Grace Hudowalski at the summit of Mt. Phelps, a High Peak. Courtesy of Adirondack Experience.

Noah John Rondeau seated outside town hall, ca. 1950. Courtesy of Adirondack Experience.

The entrance to Knapp's Trading Post, 2016. Photograph by author.

Park, from the 1890s until the 1920s, New York didn't make much of an effort to promote recreation. To encourage High Peaks tourists to stroll the mountains, to walk up high to see a good view, hotel owners and private organizations blazed routes. Local guides were hired to do the work; sometimes guides found the routes themselves to attract clients. Over the years, rough routes turned into well-worn trails, with signs indicating destinations and distances, and groups published guidebooks with maps. Guides became redundant. When the state finally got around to building more trails in the park, many of those additional miles were cut in the High Peaks.

This High Peaks cluster of well-marked, scenic, and adventurous trails turned into a liability in the 1960s and 1970s. With mass-produced, lightweight camping gear and the rise of environmental awareness, interest in adventurous outdoor recreation spiked. Hikers overran the High Peaks— pounded footpaths into gullies, littered the forest around campsites and lean-tos, slept on top of summits, and left behind scorched fire rings.

Each 46er is awarded a number. The number is the cumulative total of people who have climbed all forty-six peaks. (You're not officially a 46er unless you join the club and pay dues.) The Marshall brothers and Herb Clark are one two three, even though the club didn't yet exist when they climbed. (The 46ers is a historically minded organization. To many members, Verplanck Colvin would've been a narratively satisfying #1, but he never climbed them all.) Between 1925 and 1935, two more people hiked all forty-six. Ed Hudowalski was #6. Reverend Ryder was #7. Grace Hudowalski, #9, was the first female 46er. By 1950, the club had issued eighty-seven numbers, which must have seemed like quite a few. The last 46er of 1980 was #1,662. In 2000 it was #4,784. Today, the number of 46ers is just above 13,000. A few thousand more aspiring 46ers chip away at a few peaks each year.

Only 46ers can order patches and other gear festooned with the 46er logo. On the summit of a high peak, a 46er patch on a hiker's backpack usually brings her a few silent nods of awe and a flurry of unwanted questions, like, What's your favorite peak? Most hikers attach their number to their name the way you would a PhD.

From the top, many high peaks grant incredible views. Many don't. Those peaks are thickets of wiry balsam and hobblebush that hikers reach by plodding through long muddy ruts where they slide and trip and curse and get wet feet and blisters and get eaten alive by bugs and drop their water bottles and lose their phones and get scratched by branches and bruised by rocks. An aspiring 46er climbs those peaks anyway. If the 46ers didn't exist, most viewless peaks would see only a few people every decade or so. Hikers visit those peaks only because they're on the list, like a scavenger hunt that requires you to visit the childhood home of an obscure public figure. When the Marshall brothers and Herb Clark climbed the peaks in the 1920s, the trio logged the first recorded visit to a few summits. Twenty-eight didn't have trails cut to the top. Today, many peaks are still dubbed trailless but have herd paths worn to the summit by at least 13,000 hikers.

There's a strong correlation between the rise of the 46ers and the increased use of the High Peaks. In the mid-1960s one 46er questioned the ethics of the club placing a pamphlet with information about becoming a 46er in a rack of tourist brochures. The rack included brochures for roadside tourist attractions like the North Pole and Frontiertown. At the North Pole, you could visit Santa and touch a metal pole that was always icy, even in July. At Frontiertown, you could ride a stagecoach and meet cowboys and Indians. The 46ers suffered an existential crisis. They still haven't entirely shaken it off. That 46er had a fair point. The 46ers and theme parks, each a type of Adirondack entertainment, became increasingly popular in the mid-twentieth century as roads to the Adirondacks improved and flatlanders could drive up there faster. The High Peaks have always been adjacent to the fastest routes north: steamboats on Lake Champlain, then railroads along that lake's shore, then Route 9, then the Adirondack Northway, also known as I-89, the Adirondack's only interstate highway, finished in 1967. (Made redundant by the Northway's fast four lanes, Route 9 today offers a tour of the myriad ways in which white pines colonize abandoned motel parking lots.) The High Peaks are a type of roadside wilderness theme park: pay your ten bucks to the guy in the booth, park your car, trek on up to the top to see the view.

Use of the High Peaks has dramatically increased since the 1970s. Because of increased regulations and oversight—including the Leave No Trace campaign—conditions in the High Peaks have improved. It's now illegal to camp on or near summits. Work crews have armored trails with rocks and steps and drains so they don't erode into gullies. Forest Rangers have dispersed heavily used camp sites and fine backpackers who camp illegally. Most hikers carry out what they carry in and are respectful of the land and of other hiker's experiences. Not all. To many flatlanders, the High Peaks Wilderness is the wildest portion of the park. The High Peaks Wilderness Area posts quiet hours, from 10 p.m. to 7 a.m. So does Fish Creek. Some trails in the High Peaks are now so swarmed by inexperienced, inconsiderate, incompetent, indelicate hikers that the state has had to affix new signs to trailside trees in hopes of stemming an unexpected problem. The signs make a simple request, one of those things you'd think you wouldn't have to ask adults of our species: please do not defecate directly on the trail.

New York is doing its best to convince hikers to hike somewhere else in the Adirondacks. It's not working. To flatlanders who place mountains at the top of their scenic hierarchy, most other Adirondack scenery feels monotonous, lakes and trees and trees and trees, and then you walk a few more muddy miles, and there's another lake and more trees, and it all starts to look just about the same. If we have a national scenic ideal, it's not a few more muddy miles. High Peaks scenery is bold and loud and winsome: cliffs, scenic views, crags, peaks, and waterfalls—there's always something to see. It frequently resembles a Hudson River School painting. A hiker can post a photo of the High Peaks to Instagram and the photo compares favorably to the mountains near Ouray, Colorado, that the hiker's friends just climbed. On social media, most of the Adirondacks looks soggy buggy bland.

Without building more trails outside the High Peaks, or without imposing a permit system that curtails visitation—an approach that has been considered on and off since the 1970s and is being kicked around again today—the only hope for the High Peaks is that they fall out of fashion. Given their proximity to so many cities, given the easy-to-reach adventure they provide, given the myth of the Adirondacks of which the High Peaks is a crucial part, that's unlikely to happen anytime soon.

BROAD, GRAY, AND GRIPPY, the summit of Algonquin is a fractured shield of anorthosite, the billion-year-old bedrock bones of the High Peaks. Glaciers scoured the summits and dropped boulders on top, and the ones that remain are too big for hikers to roll. The summit is a perch, slightly convex and mellow until it takes a dive 1,500 feet down—to the cleft of Caribou Pass on one side, to Indian Pass on the other. Leaning away from the wind, I pulled on a sweatshirt and then a light jacket. I pried off my boots and socks, sat in the sun, stretching my bare feet on the warm rock. I had that self-conscious feeling of making myself too much at home in a stranger's house. Everyone up top was in a good mood, chatting pleasantly. I reclined sometimes to look at the sky, a few puffy clouds, and sometimes I stood up and walked around.

At the summit, precisely, there's one of Colvin's copper bolts. Standing near the bolt, I could see in every direction for a distance that seemed to go on just about forever: mountains, a few lakes, and trees to the west; mostly trees to the east but also a few towns, some farms, a towering ski jump built for the 1980 Olympics, said to be the tallest structure between Albany and Montreal. I could cover it with my pinky nail held at arm's length. I stood up there and thought about one of Colvin's stan-helios clanking around, hot white stars on the other peaks.

Every few minutes a new group of hikers crested the summit trail. Surprisingly, only one had a selfie stick. I overheard a teenager say, "This is going to be my new computer background!" Enormous shadows swept across the forest and the lakes and occasionally swamped the summit, as if someone had turned off the lights. A guy sitting a few feet from me had a 46er patch on his backpack. I asked him what had been his favorite peak to climb. I must have been too eager, too earnest. He rolled his eyes—as if he was thinking, *This again?*—and pretended to think about it for a few minutes before saying he couldn't decide. I think he didn't want to tell me. He thought I'd go there next. I wasn't in the club.

Another hiker had a water bottle that listed the High Peaks and a laminated piece of paper that she held up to identify the peaks within sight.

There was Marcy, looming massive a few miles away, named after a New York governor. First climbed in the 1830s, Marcy now attracts so many hikers that the easiest approach, which is still quite demanding, is worn four times as wide as most Adirondack trails. If the High Peaks is a roadside wilderness theme park, Marcy is the marquee. In 1839, a journalist thought Marcy deserved a Native American sobriquet, Tahawus, He Who Splits the Sky, a title by which, apparently, no Indigenous person had ever called that peak. And yet it caught on, and some people still call it that.

There was Colden. I climbed Colden a few months later. On top, no one else around, I spent a few minutes on my hands and knees examining the branching structure of wind-pruned tamaracks that resembled bonsai.

Colvin or Blake, I don't think I could see either.

There was East Dix, I thought. Two hikers swooped in to correct me. One said the mountain was now called Grace Peak, and the other said, actually, I couldn't see Grace Peak at all. Grace Peak is named after Grace Hudowalski. The mountain's name was officially changed in 2014. It's one of only two High Peaks named after a woman. The pale-blue-and-white-checked shorts Hudowalski wore while climbing in the peaks to become #9 are housed in the collection of the same museum that holds Colvin's snowshoes. After cofounding the 46ers, Hudowalski spent decades volunteering in various administrative roles for the club. She is most remembered as club historian. Hudowalski believed that personal reflection enhanced the experience of hiking the High Peaks. She encouraged hikers to write letters to her, to tell her about hiking the peaks, and she wrote back, thousands of letters in some years, offering advice, encouragement, caution, directions, and stories of her own. The other High Peak named after a woman is Esther. Supposedly, it's named after a fifteen-year-old girl, Esther McComb, who tried to climb Whiteface in 1839 but got lost and ended up on a previously unnamed peak. Historians have recently argued that the story isn't true: Esther McComb might never have existed. Aspiring 46ers often plan ahead so that their forty-sixth peak holds personal significance. Number forty-six makes a statement. Hudowalski's forty-sixth peak was Esther.

There was Basin, or at least I think it was Basin, and there was Seward, I think, a trailless peak named after another New York governor, and Donaldson next to it, named after Alfred Donaldson, the historian who argued Native Americans never called the region home. Donaldson had moved to the Adirondacks to recover from tuberculosis. He never did. But he improved enough to spend ten years researching and writing his book, publishing it in 1921. Next to Donaldson, there was Emmons, named after Ebenezer Emmons, the geologist who named the Adirondacks the Adirondacks.

SHADOWS MOVING, THE LIGHTS went on, the lights went off. A while later, the guy with the wooden cane and the corduroy pants and the felt canteen reached the top. He beamed. He was thrilled to tilt his head back and see so much sky after gazing down all day at rock. Wobbly with exhaustion and excitement, he spun around and pointed his cane at each of the mountains, as if knighting each one.

THERE WERE SANTANONI AND Panther and Couchsachraga, which not many people have any idea how to pronounce. When Grace Hudowalski climbed Couchsachraga, she usually stopped at Cold River City, population: one. In a wedge of private land surrounded by the High Peaks, Noah John Rondeau built the city and voted himself mayor. A Town Hall. A Hall of Records. A cluster of wigwams, one called the Beauty Parlor, soap stashed in a bear skull on the dry sink. The doorways were low. Rondeau was only five-two. On a shelf in the Town Hall, Rondeau placed glass jars (salt, flour, grease) and his library, which included books about astronomy and philosophy, a worn Bible, and books by Thoreau (of course) and H. G. Wells. Rondeau maintained a flower garden. An honorary 46er, Rondeau sometimes hung banners welcoming 46ers to Cold River City. Rondeau didn't own the land. A logging company did. Hudowalski and other 46ers carried gifts to him, a birthday cake or a copy of the *New York Times* or a new flannel shirt. In 1946, a reporter wrote that Rondeau "occupied a hole in a woodpile way the hell and gone back in the Adirondack wilderness." I think that was the reporter's way of saying—the Adirondacks!

In 1943 and 1944, Rondeau stayed at Cold River for 381 consecutive days, his record. He played the violin, he cut firewood and wrote poems and wrote letters and wrote in his diary in a secret code that was only decoded in the 1990s, he slept on an air mattress, a bear hide for a blanket, he painted scenery and nailed deer antlers or beaver bones to the Town Hall, he hunted and fished and hauled water, and all the time he looked dignified, his beard shaggy, a big, crooked pipe out the left side of his mouth, his thin spectacles granting his narrow face a look of contemplation, which was a good look on him, fortunately, since he had plenty of time to do that.

In January 1947, a plane flew low over Cold River City. A forest ranger dropped an invitation along with a pound of bacon and a pound of butter: a backwoods bribe, necessary since Rondeau could be skeptical of state officials. The invitation requested that Rondeau appear at a sportsmen's show in New York City. He would be paid one hundred dollars to attend. Rondeau declined. He didn't want to trudge seventeen miles through deep snow to reach town. The plane came back and eventually Rondeau agreed to go, but only after New York committed to flying him out of the woods in a helicopter.

In the city, Rondeau ate three-dollar steaks and was interviewed by radio show hosts and appeared on television. At the sportsmen's show he played the part of the myth of the Adirondacks: furs and pelts and his 46er patch and snowshoes and a bow and arrow. He was the American frontier alive and well in the Atomic Age. He signed thousands of autographs. For the next few years, he gave speeches and attended more sportsmen's shows. The Hermit of Cold River, who occupied a hole in a woodpile way the hell and gone back in the Adirondack wilderness, commanded an appearance fee of up to eight hundred dollars.

A few years later, a violent windstorm battered the Adirondacks. State agencies closed the forest due to the risk of fire. Exiled, Rondeau worked at Frontiertown and also as Santa Claus at the North Pole. His cabin was disassembled and moved to the museum that holds Hudowalski's shorts and Colvin's snowshoes. You can still see it there today. Rondeau died in 1967. He's the most famous Adirondack hermit. I don't know why there isn't a High Peak named after him.

There was Whiteface. Since 1935, a paved toll road has climbed almost to the summit of Whiteface. The road required workers to cut Forever

Wild trees; New York had to amend its constitution to allow construction. Sixty-one thousand people visited the summit during the first year. Today, you drive uphill, past the North Pole, Home of Santa's Workshop, and after turning left and paying a toll, you drive up the smooth, sinuous road to an alpine parking lot. There you have two options: you can hike up a rock and concrete path that sneaks along a knife-edge to the summit; or you can walk into a 424-foot-long tunnel. The tunnel is dim and damp, the rock walls refrigerant. At the end of the tunnel there's a pair of corroded industrial doors. They look not unlike doors to a Bond villain's subterranean lair. The elevator behind those doors lifts you 271 vertical feet to a stone turret that caps the summit. If you drive or ride the elevator, the peak isn't one of your forty-six.

There was Nye. In 1873, a cartographer named it after William Nye, one of Colvin's favorite guides. Nye's early life was peripatetic. Born in Vermont in 1816, he later spent time on a whaler in the Indian Ocean, returned to Vermont to farm, went back to sea for a few years, and then headed west toward St. Louis to join John Frémont's 1848 expedition, which was guided by Kit Carson. Nye got sick along the way and stayed behind, a bit of luck for Nye since many members of Frémont's expedition that winter died frostbitten and starving on a foolhardy push over the Rockies. Nye eventually found his way to the High Peaks, built a sawmill, sold it, and then became a guide.

There was Phelps, named after Orson "Old Mountain" Phelps. His obituary claimed he was "a little man, shaggy as a rough-barked cedar. He gave voice to sage conclusions and whimsical oddities in a high querulous tone, wrote poetry and exhaustive essays upon nature as he saw it, and in the expression of his appreciation of the beauties and sublimities of his region, he monopolized the attention of tourists who came . . . from all parts of the civilized world." In 2015, there was a kegger on the summit of Phelps. A friend of a friend of a recent 46er lugged the keg up to celebrate the hiking achievement. At least two hikers did keg stands. Someone posted pictures to Facebook. Aghast: that would describe how some in the 46er community felt. From the pictures, the keg appears to have held five gallons. If that's true and assuming it was full—and why wouldn't it be?—it would've weighed about sixty pounds. From the Adirondack Loj parking lot to the summit of Phelps, it's four trail miles and 2,000 vertical feet. Hauling that keg is an athletic feat that deserves greater recognition in High Peaks history.

There was Gothics. To get to many of the trails that ascend Gothics, hikers walk a gravel road through the land of a private club, the Adirondack

Mountain Reserve. If hikers make a reservation in advance, they can park in a gravel lot, walk past the club's golf course and the club's tennis courts and the club's four-story hotel (hints of Queen Anne revival and a long porch) and then around a rustic gate that guards the gravel road. Club members and their guests ride a short green bus to the trail. Hikers who aren't members, like me, walk the road, choking on diesel exhaust, a noxious start to a day in the salubrious High Peaks.

There was Cascade. Requiring only a short hike to a spectacular view, Cascade is the most popular High Peak. If someone only hikes one, it's probably Cascade. The morning after I hiked Algonquin, I hiked Cascade. I squeezed my car into a slim parking lot along the shoulder of a busy highway, next to a car with Florida plates. Its owners, a husband and wife in their fifties or sixties, tied their sneakers in triple knots and started up the trail. Heaps of fast food wrappers and empty 64 oz. soda cups and loose items of clothing filled the car's backseat. The High Peaks must have been a stop in the middle of a long drive somewhere else. I started up the trail and soon passed the car's owners. The wife said to her husband, "Well, dear, here we are in the Adirondacks." There was no exclamation point.

Cascade's summit is also gray rock, lime-green and olive-green lichen splattered like paint and one pink splotch of a species I eventually identified after much careful thought as strawberry bubblegum. On the most popular map of the High Peaks, which is printed on loud, crinkly paper, the terrain that a hiker overlooks from Cascade is split between front and back. At least five groups of hikers were up there in the wind, flipping their maps back and forth, trying to figure out which High Peak was which, the maps making a racket.

TWO SUMMIT STEWARDS DRESSED in khaki shirts and khaki shorts stood at the top of Algonquin. During the busy season, Summit Stewards spend all day on the most popular High Peaks. Both stewards on Algonquin were in their twenties. They looked like they could hike to the summit much faster than anyone else who was there. Summit Stewards answer questions, such as What's that mountain over there? and How long does it take to get back to the parking lot? and Where's the bathroom? and they pick up granola bar wrappers before the wind snatches them, and kindly scold people who hog the summit, and use the rule of thirds when requested to take a photograph of five shirtless guys, all hoots and hollers and high fives, and tell stories about campers, like how one guy punched a bear in the face because the bear tried to get into the guy's tent at two in the morning to have a snack, and sometimes have to do strange things, like tell someone that he can't play a bagpipe up here because it's ruining other people's wilderness experience, and occasionally assist with the rescue of a hiker with a compound femur fracture, and when it's foggy and there's no view and no hikers show up, they sit up there in the clouds by themselves and play the harmonica. But they have just one official job: to teach hikers about the plants.

On Algonquin's summit, plants grow in nooks between rocks, in cracks, in shallow scoops in the stone where a bit of wind-blown soil stuck, in serpentine, kidney-looking shapes with stones placed around the edge to form a border—plants like Boott's rattlesnake root, Lapland rosebay, alpine goldenrod, mountain sandwort, and deer's hair sedge. When the wind gusts through deer's hair sedge it sounds like a crumpled plastic bag lost to the wind. Every time I heard it that afternoon, I snapped my head around, outraged, to see who had let a plastic bag tumble tumble tumble—fly—into Caribou Pass.

Twenty-one peaks in the High Peaks harbor summit patches of tundra-like plants, seventy acres overall. They're remnants. When the glaciers melted, lichen and moss colonized the cold sand and rock. Tundra plants moved in. Eventually temperatures rebounded and trees could sprout, survive. The forest migrated back north, and alpine plants, unable to compete, retreated upslope to the highest summits. They are now marooned. Adirondack alpine summits give you the feeling that you've either driven many hundreds of miles north to the tundra or traveled back in time ten thousand years. Similar plant communities can be found elsewhere in the Northeast, too, on a few other mountain ranges, like the Presidentials in New Hampshire and the Chic-Chocs in Québec.

Soil on High Peaks summits is shallow, sodden, and acidic, and the summits are windy and frigid and have a curt and fickle growing season, and alpine plants have a minuscule growth rate and hug the ground. Alpine plants creep. If a hiker strays from a trail to get a better view, he tramples them, and when a boot tramples a plant, a few decades or even a century of growth might be squashed or the plant might just die. Thin soil now exposed, when it rains a torrent plucks away a clod, or a freeze-thaw cycle cracks it, or the soil desiccates and the wind blows it away, and soon there's a gouge that widens with each storm until it's cut to bare rock and no plants can root.

Summits are the social scenes of the High Peaks. In parking lots, hikers rush. They want to get on the trails. Hikers race up the trails to reach the top, to see the view. There they finally take a breather, eat a granola bar, mingle, chat. Up top, when the weather's grand, it's a party, even if the party is dry. In 1964, Edwin Ketchledge noticed that hikers walking and lolling on the summits were damaging the plants. With more hikers making the climb each year, Ketchledge worried that the mangy peaks might soon go bald. Ketchledge devoted a good portion of the rest of his life to finding and then implementing a solution.

A lot of people called Ketchledge Ketch. Ketch fought in the 10th Mountain Division during World War II. He was almost killed by German troops in the Apennine Mountains in Italy. He had to have one of his lungs removed and was discharged with full disability. He later taught botany, plant identification, and forest ecology at SUNY Syracuse, and he ran a summer field school in the western Adirondacks. Even with only one lung he hiked High Peaks faster than most people he dragged along. He climbed many of the peaks dozens of times. He might have climbed Algonquin 180 times. Ketch was #507.

On a High Peak Ketch established test plots to try various methods of restoration. He experimented with different mixtures of common grass seed, fertilizer, and agricultural dolomitic lime. He needed to identify a combination that would rapidly root on exposed alpine soils, cementing everything in place. He found one that worked. As it happened, the successful mixture rooted, survived (barely, and only if fertilized frequently), stabilized the soil for a few years, and then, conveniently, the introduced grasses lost their vigor and died just as mosses and liverworts and lichens colonized the area. These plants created refugia for woody plants and alpine flower seeds and rhizomes to get a fresh start.

Ketch became a gardener. Assistant gardeners did the grunt work. Starting in 1971, Ketch and his assistants lugged hundreds and hundreds of pounds of seed and fertilizer to the summits. The gardeners crawled on hands and knees around the summits to distribute the mixture. Over the next three decades, Ketch and his crews seeded about half of the alpine zone in the Adirondacks.

When there's a party at the top in the High Peaks, it's a garden party.

After his success seeding the summits, Ketch realized wayward hikers still trampled the mosses and young plants colonizing the soil. One proposed solution was to limit or block access to the summits. Ketch didn't like that. He believed everyone deserved an opportunity to experience the beauty and wonder of climbing a High Peak. He wanted hikers to feel the thrill of ascending through the hardwood forest with its sugar maples and beeches, and into the shadows of spruce and balsam, the balsam shorter and shorter until the trail breaks out onto the open summit with a view and a bounty of diminutive alpine plants. I appreciate his vision of plant preservation. He wanted to protect the plants but still let hikers see them. He saw the plants as ecologically significant but also as an important part of a hiker's experience of the High Peaks.

Ketch worked to develop a seed mix that made alpine vegetation more resistant to foot traffic, so everyone could walk around the summits without caution, almost a high-traffic alpine vegetative carpet. He could never quite get that to work. His alternate solution was to educate hikers about the plants and to advise hikers to step only on rocks, as if hopping across a stream. He also advocated for the development of the Summit Steward program. Photographic comparisons between the 1980s and today show that alpine plants on the peaks are making a comeback. Summit Stewards get much of the credit. Since 1989, when the program began, Summit Stewards have had almost 600,000 conversations with hikers.

In mid-June, those alpine plants pop, a confetti of white and yellow and pale pink petals pinched by rock. A few weeks later, just as the busiest mountain climbing season begins, the show's almost over. It's enough to make a Summit Steward curse under her breath. How do you make hikers who are enthralled by the views care about locally rare, fragile plants that now resemble a feral suburban lawn? On Algonquin that afternoon, each time a hiker stepped on a patch of plants, one of the stewards winced and then swooped in to politely ask that person to not do that again. A group of summer camp kids blindly stomped around. Their college-age trip leader sat on a rock and scrolled his phone. (Islands for alpine plants, some of the peaks are also islands of cell service.) Granola bar wrappers and clear plastic sandwich bags tumbled wind-whipped across the summit. The stewards kept their cool. They tried to engage the kids by sharing a fact, something about the ice age, something about the tundra.

Late in the afternoon, after most of the crowd had left, ravens circled and then landed, hopping and flitting and poking about the summit in their mischievous way, searching for granola bar crumbs. The stewards huddled near a boulder and fumed to each other about the oblivious hikers who had trampled alpine plants. Because they spend so much time at the top, the stewards get to know each plant personally. Each trampled alpine plant is a tragedy.

A hiker's careless footfall had torn a fresh clod of moss loose and flipped it onto the rock. It was drying in the sun, but it still had a chance. I picked it up and wandered around to figure out where it had once grown. It was like trying to place a solid green puzzle piece in a thousand-piece puzzle of an Irish field. Eventually I found the spot. I put the moss back, rotated it 90 degrees for a better fit, tamped it with the heel of my right hand, and splashed some water on it, feeling virtuous.

Many hikers on the summit that day had said they were envious that *this*—knighting the peaks all around—was the stewards' office. Just before descending for the day, quitting time, the stewards' complaints about wayward hikers escalated in volume and soured in tone. Grouchy and garrulous, the stewards sounded like disgruntled office workers two beers in at a Thursday night Happy Hour. But they got over it and started exclaiming about the view and the weather and about the summer they had spent in the tundra. Clocking out, they started down the steep trail. The whole way back to the parking lot they were in good cheer.

Chapter 10

IF THERE'S A MONTH to mark when leisure in the wilds became part of American identity and when Americans began celebrating the Adirondacks, it might as well be July 1869. That month flatlanders trampled the Adirondacks. It was a stampede. Women and men, young and old, sick and healthy, rich and not quite so rich but still well off: by steamboat, by train, by carriage, and by stagecoach, they all rushed up there because of a book.

Published in April, the book had revealed a wilderness of health and sport and adventure and leisure not too far from eastern cities. The book was *Adventures in the Wilderness; or, Camp Life in the Adirondacks.* If it had been first published today, in our time of catchy, hyperbolic titles, it might have been *The Northern Wilderness Exposed: How to Have an Epic Time Up There!* William H. H. Murray wrote it. He was a Boston clergyman (at least for a while), a lover of the outdoors, a famed orator, a horse gambler, and a graduate of Yale. After the publication of *Adventures*, his fans and supporters called him Adirondack Murray, the prefix to which all Adirondack writers still aspire. The tourists rushing north were called Murray's Fools. A bestseller, the book brought Murray fame and wealth. The book also brought him accusations of falsehoods and exaggeration and outright, despicable deception.

I can't think of a contemporary book with such abrupt sway over travel plans. The closest comparison might be how the movie adaptations of *The Lord of the Rings* boosted New Zealand tourism. It seemed as though everyone with enough money and time wanted to see Middle Earth. Today, for a book to do what *Adventures* did, it would have to feature a place most people had heard rumors about but didn't expect to actually exist, and that place would have to end up being pleasant and restorative and far enough away to be exotic but not so far away that it was difficult to get there. If Atlantis happened to surface one hundred miles off the coast of New Jersey and someone wrote a book about how to get there and what to do while there, that book might receive a response similar to *Adventures*.

The book is a riot. It's an enjoyable if slightly odd read. There's practical advice on how to get to the Adirondacks and what to do once you're there. There's Murray's testimony about the healthfulness of outdoor recreation in the North Woods, still a fairly radical notion at the time. On what to wear and what supplies to bring, Murray offers his opinion. Bug repellant is essential, a mix of tar and sweet oil. Bring crushed sugar, not powdered: powdered sugar is too difficult to salvage if you spill it in the woods. Most of *Adventures* recalls the Adirondack travels Murray had with his guide, John Plumley. Murray portrays himself as an imperfect wilderness traveler. He doesn't project perfection, as Colvin did. Murray trips, he falls, he fails, he laughs at himself, he gets up and does it again. Murray was up there to have a good time. There's also the chance that I like the book because Murray uses an abundance of exclamation points.

My only grudge against Adirondack Murray is that during a thunderstorm he shot at a loon, again and again, the loon diving at the crack of each shot, and then popping back up, diving and then popping back up until it wore itself out, and Plumley rowing the boat to where he thought the loon might rise, and Murray's bullets plucking the loon's feathers, plucking the flesh off its back, and the rain pouring down, and the lightning cracking, and Murray taking one last shot and leaving the loon to die. Even worse, he wrote about it in *Adventures*, and the Fools thought it was a thing they should do, too.

Buoyant and confident, inexperienced and underprepared, Murray's Fools overwhelmed the few backwoods hotels; proprietors were shocked by the crowds. Many Fools had to wait on the fringe until they could find a guide to take them up to see the wilderness. The fringe didn't look like the Adirondacks Murray had described. Rather than a health-giving wilderness, Fools saw scorched forests and vistas of stumps dotted with charcoal kilns, and they didn't see any deer or any trout bigger than their thumb. Even if a Fool was lucky enough to find a guide, it was probably a farmer who offered his services only for the paycheck and probably didn't know all that much about the woods. In a quirk of literary popularity aligning with environmental abnormality, the summer of 1869 was unusually chilly and wet, the mud knee-deep. Mosquitos and punkies and blackflies hung around all summer, swarming and hungry. Few Fools who rushed north that year found a good time.

Murray caught the blame. Was called a liar, a fraud. Was called a murderer for telling stories of miraculous forest cures that gave consumptives false hope of a snappy recovery. Wealthy sportsmen, who had enjoyed solitude up there for decades, scolded Murray: he had exposed their secret wilderness to the masses. Murray didn't much care. He wanted more people to breathe Adirondack air. At least that's what he claimed. When the masses arrived, Murray moved his camp to a remote lake. I'm not sure if he was a hypocrite or if he truly had no idea how popular his book would become.

I don't blame Murray for the actions of uninformed, frenzied flatlanders. He wrote about both the joys and hardships of the wilderness. The Fools ignored his warnings. There's more to the situation than the book. *Adventures* landed in a post–Civil War New England, where an increasingly affluent urban population was ready to climb onto a train and travel elsewhere to have a good time outdoors. That year, 1869, railroad tracks crossed the continent, iron rails binding the frontier, binding that American tale, East linked to West, and then there's this book, this small maroon leather-bound book, a sport with a gun in gilt on the cover, this book about a lively wilderness just a few hours north, a magical place, full of ghosts and fish and deer and adventure, where you could sleep under the stars and listen to tall tales, this book about a wilderness where for a bit of money and a bit of time you could get back to an America that some people thought used to exist. As much as Murray's words, a longing for an imagined past hauled Murray's Fools north.

ADVENTURES FOREVER ALTERED Adirondack history. Tourists rushed north that year. They haven't yet stopped. There's pre-Murray and post-Murray, and today, in these post-Murray times, any flatlander who travels up to the Adirondacks is still a Fool, whether you own a camp or hike into the backcountry or sit on a hotel porch.

Murray's book changed the fortunes of many interior villages. Settlers had tried mining and farming. Those efforts had mostly failed or were about to by the time Murray wrote his book. There were logging jobs but the work wasn't steady. Some Adirondack towns have had a thriving, tourism-centric economy since July 1869. These post-Murray towns,

mostly in the interior—the part that looks most like the Adirondacks—
have a curious relationship to the myth. They rely on the myth to lure flatlanders and their money, yet the myth is defined by an empty wilderness
without towns, or at least only allows quaint towns with picture-perfect
main streets and no indications of work. The result is that towns support a
myth that excludes them.

One post-Murray town is Long Lake. Settlers from New England
trickled west along a rough road to Long Lake in the 1830s and 1840s,
choosing stony hills with long shadows over the sunny flatlands of Ohio.
They arrived at about the same time as the Sabattis family. When settlers
reached Long Lake, they crossed, the lake too long to walk around but so
narrow that you could swim across, if you had to. On the western shore,
settlers knocked together log cabins, moss for insulation and a spruce bark
roof, and grew crops, cut hay to feed livestock. Long Lake was Long Lake's
Main Street, the small farms strung along the shore. Settlers rowed a boat
or walked on the ice to get around. Long Lake was the largest settlement
in the Adirondack interior. But the growing village stalled, the land too
rocky, the road too rough. Most families cut their losses and left. By 1860,
only a dozen families remained. They soon gave up, too.

Post-Murray, sports and tourists poured into Long Lake. They spent
money on food and guides and a dry place with a bed to spend the night,
tourists sleeping in backwoods boardinghouses and then hotels and then,
decades later, in rental cabins and roadside motels. At dusk on summer
evenings in Long Lake, I liked to stand on the town beach and watch a
rooftop neon sign flicker on: MOTEL in giant red letters, the reflection of
each letter rippling on the water, a range of the High Peaks looming in the
distance. The sign might as well say MURRAY.

Long Lake is close to the geographic center of the Adirondacks. I like
to think that the middle of the Adirondack forest, as precise as one of
Colvin's copper bolts, sits directly beneath a white pine that stands near the
town's main intersection. As it happens, the white pine grows through the
roof of a bulky green building that contains Hoss's Country Corner. More
accurately, the building tries to contain Hoss's Country Corner but doesn't
quite cut it, and an array of buildings and shacks sprawls out back. White
birch bark decorates the eaves and windows. Cedar trunks hold up the
front porch roof. Adding to the rustic character, the pine pokes through
the peak of the shingled roof. Above the roof, branches splay, needles a
silver-green shimmering in the sunlight, the trunk inside lit by fluorescent
tubes. The trunk looks fake in that light, a joke locals might play on flatlanders. Hoss's Country Corner is two full stories and a peaked gable. The

pine is twice that tall. Twig-work signs on the building advertise worms, ice, beer, firewood, groceries, live bait, books, boots, gifts, and maps.

Between some bookshelves and the camping gear aisle, the white pine rises through Hoss's wooden floor. Flanked by a rack of fake raccoon-skin caps, the trunk resembles a rustic structural beam, an echo of the Great Camps. It crooks, straightens out a bit, knocks through the wooden ceiling. Shreds of once-damp fiberglass insulation dangle, as if the pine had punched through. It did not. The pine stood there first. It grew tall outdoors. When Hoss's Country Corner needed more space, the owners moved a building and wrapped it around the pine.

Murray called Long Lake "the best rendezvous of the wilderness." The Long Lake tourism board is always on the hunt for a catchy slogan to attract more tourists. I'm surprised they haven't yet picked up on this one. One recent slogan was "Feelin' Long Lakey"—quaint, but sort of like defining a word by using the word you're trying to define. *The Best Rendezvous of the Wilderness*: it makes Long Lake sound like a flurry of firelight and good food and foot-stomping fiddle tunes, a bright gem in the middle of the big dark woods.

AN HOUR'S DRIVE SOUTHWEST of Long Lake is Old Forge, another post-Murray town. In Murray's time, tourists went from Old Forge to Long Lake by following lakes and rivers. Murray didn't think the scenery around what is now Old Forge was worth a look. He thought it was soggy buggy bland. He encouraged tourists to rush through the area, get to the good parts.

Today, on summer afternoons, Old Forge bustles. I've always liked Old Forge. Driving north, even now, when I reach Old Forge I feel as if I've arrived at the threshold of a six-million-acre wilderness. Carrying white plastic bags full of postcards and scenic calendars, tourists stroll the side-walks, past cafés and real estate offices, past motels and mini-golf courses and ice cream stands. Old Forge is in Herkimer County. Locals call Old Forge Herkimer County's Cash Cow. Houses painted, lawns trimmed, Main Street is trig and square, mostly. In front of one shop, a tuft of tall white pines loiters. When the weather looks fine and traffic is steady, the shop's owners mount the head of a bull moose to one of the pines. From a few blocks away, the moose appears complete, mobile, like it's peering through a pine forest, possibly considering a trip to the school across the road. An index card attached to the pine with a thumbtack lists the price: $2,185. *Please Do Not Touch Moose.*

Past the moose pine, past a bar with one-story brainstorm and the other log, past the Art Deco movie theater, past the arcade with a neon ice cream cone perched on the roof, an amusement park dominates the far side of town. A big sign shouts: ENCHANTED FOREST. The sign greets everyone driving up into the forest. Adirondack theme parks are often criticized for having no connection to the land. I like to think of the sign as a fair assessment of what's ahead.

Across the road, there's a hot dog counter: Pied Piper. I wonder if Jakubowski ever tried to buy it. On the roof of the squat brown building, there's a sign, a jaunty piper painted in crisp colors. The Pied Piper's piper gets pulled down and hauled into storage every winter. I knew tourist season had arrived when I drove through Old Forge and the piper was back on the roof, triumphant. On a summer night when the air smelled like pinesap and sunbaked asphalt, an atomic yellow glow lit Pied Piper. The glow burst, radiant, from the window where customers order ice cream. Out front at the picnic tables, a group of teenagers in shorts and T-shirts ate soft-serve twisted cones. Their grandfather sat there, too, wearing blue jeans and a red flannel shirt. They chatted pleasantly, about waterskiing and a hike to a scenic view. Ten minutes later the group stood up and walked out of the glow. The grandfather's red rusty pickup truck rolled out of the shadows, the teenagers sitting in the truck's bed, the grandfather's arm dangling out the driver's side window. Three honks and the red rusty truck rumbled into the night. For a long while I sat there in the glow and thought of them driving through the woods. Cool breeze. Sound of rubber tires on the road. Spruce and pine and maple treetops a blurry black against the stars. The truck's headlights leaning hard and fast against the heavy dark of a forest that seemed to have no end. To me, Old Forge will forever be that atomic yellow glow in the shadow of a forest enchanted.

Before the first snowstorm, when the Adirondacks is lonely and quiet and gray, the residents of Old Forge string multicolored pennants in loops and lines and squares, which gives town the atmosphere of a used car lot. Surrounded by an expansive system of snowmobile trails, Old Forge calls itself the Snowmobile Capital of the East. Everyone in Old Forge calls snowmobiles sleds. The pennants delineate surfaces where sleds should not go: sidewalks, front yards, flowerbeds, water fountains. On a quiet November morning, summer tourists gone, the piper in storage, and not yet any sleds, I heard snowsqualls approaching from the direction of the moose pine, a briskly rising rustle of sun-brittle plastic.

Then, as it goes: snow fell, lakes froze, herds of sleds arrived. One cracked through thin ice, the rider sodden and numb but otherwise fine. A local made some cash winching the machine up from the bottom. In January, I visited again. From my motel room, I listened to the buzz and rattle of sleds roaming town. They sounded like swarms of metallic bees.

Old Forge felt flush. Motels packed. A forty-five-minute wait for a restaurant table, not even an open seat at the bar. The next morning, temperature around zero, a middle-aged man wearing snow boots and a baby-blue terrycloth robe bolted out of his motel room to start his sled. He bolted back inside, let the sled idle. A blue cloud of exhaust climbed the pines. All across town, snowmobilers gathered by motel room doors to plan their route for the day through the Enchanted Forest. Neon pink, neon blue, and neon green, striped with reflective tape and wrapped with logos, their insulated snowsuits were confetti against the snow.

Much of the Adirondacks sits quiet and empty during the winter. The western region, which receives the most snow because of lake effect from Lake Ontario, is almost as hectic in the winter as in the summer. Sleds offer Old Forge a second high season Murray never could have predicted.

I HAVEN'T YET MENTIONED something important: the most remote spot in the Adirondacks is 5.3 miles from a road. It's tucked among the High Peaks, not far from where Cold River City, population: one, once stood. Six million acres: subtract what's within three miles of a road and subtract what's within two miles of a lake where motorboats roar—scraps remain. They total less than 3 percent of the Adirondacks. This is another fact I try to overlook. It undercuts what I want the region to be. It makes my exclamation point sound flip.

Sometimes I take that view, to see the Adirondacks as laced with roads. Sometimes I'm more upbeat. Not all Adirondack roads are the same. Most are gated dirt roads that lead to remote estates, private inholdings on state land, or are used to haul timber. Only occasionally does a car or a truck pass. As for paved, public roads, there are many on the fringe, but in the interior, there are just a few.

Expansive forests remain between these paved roads. Walking north to south across the Adirondacks, it's possible to trek through eighty miles of forest and cross only two paved roads. East to west, it's possible to walk seventy miles and cross only one. These distances are cut straight through. If you didn't want to swim or lug along an inflatable raft or climb dozens of cliffs or get sued for trespass, you'd need to walk quite a bit farther. These are not the endless spaces of the West. Forty miles without a paved road:

that's an Adirondack boast that would make a resident of Escalante, Utah, chuckle. But for the East, the Adirondack forest is vast. Ithaca, New York, where I live, is surrounded by rural land with some paved roads but not more than average for most of the rural East. If I walked out my front door and kept going for seventy miles, I'd cross ninety-four paved roads.

Despite these chunks of forest, The Roadside is the most frequently viewed landscape in the Adirondacks: a long double yellow line that curls and drops and climbs through the forest, asphalt, white line, gravel berm, a strip of grass and milkweed and golden rod, maybe a big rock. Darting from town to town or just passing through, most tourists don't see much else. At sixty miles per hour—at least seventy-five if you're a local—the forest that fronts The Roadside is a long windshield blur: green, green, and more green. It's easy to forget that beyond the blur there's often a forest that could absorb a week of walking.

Driving Adirondack roads, I like to think I'm on the bottom of a canyon sliced deep and slender through a broad, leafy plateau. The forest beyond my windshield blur pushes back with an intractable heft; the forest pushes back on both sides like thick stone, and there I am, down deep in the guts, strata to my flanks, hands at ten and two, leaning over my steering wheel and looking up to try to see the sky.

The Roadside isn't only trees. The pine that pops the top of the green building, the moose pine, the Enchanted Forest sign: these are a few of the quirky, kitschy, flashy objects you see along The Roadside in Adirondack towns. They stand out from the long green blur. Each object highlights some part of Adirondack history or some archetypal element of the Adirondack environment or some idea of what someone wants the place to be. Most of them exist to attract the attention of passing flatlanders. They're mostly commercial, trying to make a flatlander laugh or at least make a flatlander curious enough to stop and spend some money. But they go beyond this. The objects grant a lively rhythm to The Roadside, making it something other than a long green blur. They are whimsical and fun and don't take the Adirondacks too seriously. There's something enjoyable about driving through the forest for miles and miles, and then seeing, say, a neon sign that says Northwood Cabins (HEATED, NO VACANCY), two happy trees outlined in green and blue tubes on top, or the roof of a diner that's curled to look like a giant toboggan. I think of them as post-Murray artifacts in the automobile age, all the Fools still driving by.

Those quirky roadside objects are starting to disappear. Bureaucratic and popular ideals of what the Adirondacks should look like no longer accommodate them, veering toward a blandly austere rustic, objects and signs that blend in with the trees, that mass-produced Great Camp look. I'm concerned that one by one old signs and objects will rot or crumble or get knocked down by drunk drivers, and newer regulations will limit what can be built. The Roadside might turn into a bland rustic cliché, a forest theme park with rustic signage.

Chapter 11

SIREX WOOD WASPS. ASIAN long-horned beetles. Hemlock woolly adel-gids. Pine shoot beetles. Emerald ash borers. Brown spruce long-horned beetles. Spotted lanternflies. Any of these exotic pests, or any of a dozen or so other imported bugs or blights, might ride up to the Adirondacks on a camper's firewood stash, and once up there, inflict ruin, death, and decay on what might be the largest intact temperate forest left in the world.

By state quarantine law, untreated firewood may only be hauled fifty miles from where it's cut. They're coming soon anyway. No need to give them a ride. This puts flatlanders in a pinch. They can't haul firewood from home (where it's free when you chop down that backyard maple that's shading out your tomatoes). And on Forever Wild land—well, you know. Adirondack locals sell firewood to campers. It's a traditional cottage in-dustry, a quick way for locals to bank some cash. In the last few decades, business has boomed.

Homemade racks loaded with firewood crowd The Roadside, a se-quence of images and words as you drive:

Two rows of bundled logs, each bundle knotted with purple string. $6 per bundle. Three round, red reflectors to snag your attention.

A grid of solar-powered LED lights to ease late-night transactions. Slide the money into a locked ammo box chained nearby.

A wooden rack, 2.00 a cube, the square grid now shifted askew to parallelograms. *Please* deposit payment in the coffee can. INTEGRITY:

WHO YOU ARE WHEN NO ONE IS WATCHING! THANK YOU FOR YOUR BUSINESS.

Red spray paint on a bare board nailed to a dead spruce: CAMPWOOD and a long, squiggly arrow pointing *that* way.

A heap of loose logs, twenty logs for $5.00.

GOT WOOD?

Four dollars per box. Five dollars per rook. Six dollars per bin.

PREMIUM DRY FIREWOOD. Twine-bound sticks, like someone cleaned up her yard after a windstorm, $2.00.

A two-sided rack of cubbies under a gabled roof, structure sanded smooth and stained. It's on wheels. If one roadside spot goes bust, the rack can be hauled elsewhere.

SMILE FOR THE CAMERA! A grainy, black-and-white security photo of two firewood thieves.

At the end of a driveway, a wheelbarrow full of dry wood, 10.00$.

A rack built of diamond-plated steel, $4.00 per rack, and just down the road, ADK FIREWOOD, $5. DRY-DRY-DRY.

Gas stations and hardware stores also sell it, kiln dried and prepackaged in plastic wrap, cut somewhere outside the Blue Line. That's as bad as buying August sweet corn from a grocery store.

I found the firewood trade fascinating. Judging by the quality, size, and stocking frequency of roadside racks, vendors seemed to have made varying levels of commitment to their enterprise, some small-time, some saving for college or a new sled, some with hopes of expansion, franchise, an Adirondack firewood empire, the Paul Smith's of roadside firewood.

Over the few years I researched this book, I watched as some proprietors expanded, added a new rack or a new sign, and I watched other racks rot. About margins, about schedules, about marketing strategy, I wanted to know more. In the Adirondack climate, what's the expected life span of a hand painted sign? Does posting a UV-resistant plastic sign typeset in Comic Sans *and* Helvetica increase sales? Does red spray paint boost your authenticity? How many hours per week does it take to cut, chop, and stack enough to supply one stand? Are security camera threats a bluff? How many cords can one business sell in a summer? Which day of the week is the busiest? Do solar LED lights increase sales? Looking for answers, I loitered at firewood racks, hopeful someone from a nearby house would storm out the front door. When that didn't work, I sent letters to vendors, I left notes, I made calls.

No one ever got back to me.

Chapter 12

THE SMALL WHITE PLANE carved a wide, low loop over the water, made a second, lower pass near the treetops, and then landed on Blue Mountain Lake with a gentle whoosh like polite applause. Jostled by the waves, the plane taxied toward the beach where I stood waiting with my boat. The pilot cut the engine, nudged a pontoon onto the sand, and opened the plane's small door and stuck his head out, his face all big mirror sunglasses and a broad smile. Tom Payne stepped out of the cabin and onto one of the pontoons with that swagger of a pilot who had just made a tricky landing in front of an audience. He wore sandals, shorts, and a short-sleeve khaki button-down shirt. The shirt looked like he had buttoned it up the whole way once or twice but not anytime recently.

I had never stood next to a plane so small, especially not one I had summoned. Cautious, intimidated, I stood back. Tom waved me over, told me to hop in. I waded into the shin-deep water and climbed into the cramped cabin with my bag and paddle. One of my friends used to own a 1992 Honda Civic. Stepping into the plane felt like stepping into that 1992 Honda Civic shrunk to three-quarters size: reliable, trustworthy, cramped, bare-bones, flimsier than you might hope it to be. I squeezed into the back but Tom said I could sit in one of the two seats up front. Tom plucked my canoe out of the water and leaned it on the plane's left pontoon and tied it on. The rope he had was too long. He laced it back and forth along my canoe to take up slack, then tied it off with a knot I couldn't follow.

I wanted to ask him to take a photograph of my canoe tied to the plane, but I was trying to play it cool.

Tom pushed the plane away from the beach, hopped onto a pontoon, climbed into the cabin, slammed the door. There was a nonchalance to his motions. He was a taxi driver who had just thrown my luggage into the trunk and then pulled into traffic without signaling or bothering to check his mirrors. Metallic and hollow, sounding like a tin can noisy with clicks and beeps and shudders, the plane bobbed on the choppy lake. That morning I had left Raquette Lake when the water was calm. The fog had cleared, eventually, and toward noon, as I paddled through the tamarack swamps that flanked a serpentine river, the wind had picked up: another storm pushing in from the west. The three-day trip that had begun on the tail end of a storm was now ending just before another one. I had lucked out. I could've named each of the thirteen lakes I paddled over those three days Sunshine.

Tom started the engine. I don't remember if he pushed a button or turned a key. The plane coughed and fluttered, settled into a punchy, chugging rhythm. He tacked the plane into the wind out toward the middle of the lake and then looked at me, smiled a smile that looked sinister because of his big mirror eyes—steady, unchanging—and said, *Are you ready?*

Levers. Switches. Three buttons in a row: tap tap tap. The engine roared and whined, the plane reared back, zipped down the lake, skipping on the chop, smacking, bouncing, nicking the crest of the highest waves: tin can flying. Sucked back into my seat, I looked out the window to my right, looked way down to massive boulders the glaciers had tossed on the bottom of Blue Mountain Lake. Pale, monstrous, oddly animate, they looked like whales rising to breach. The plane fluttered and knocked in the wind. We cleared the trees and kept climbing. Forested, rolling mountains unfurled on all sides, dozens of lakes glinting in the September sun.

My first thought: Colvin would've killed for this view.

TWO DAYS EARLIER I had driven up Route 28 to Old Forge, my canoe strapped to my car. Route 28 is my favorite Adirondack drive. I'd normally stop in Old Forge to see the moose pine and then drive Route 28 east to Blue Mountain Lake. It's the only road between the two. Forest, forest, forest: Route 28 cuts and turns and weaves through forest. Tall pines, pointy spruce, birch bark falling in papery sheets, hobblebush tangled below. I'd go out of my way to drive the road at dusk, when silhouetted branches flowed tight around my car, high beams hot on the trunks, the double yellow line lit up reflective, slicing the middle. Forest and branches and a wedge of dusk sky down the road. Someone had unofficially modified a yellow diamond road sign to read ROUGH ROAD NEXT 163 MILES. Hyperbole, without a doubt, that extra 3, but sometimes driving Route 28 I felt the sentiment was spot on.

In 1860, the dirt path precursor to Route 28 dead-ended near what is now Old Forge. Sports climbed into guideboats, guides at the oars. A few decades later, post-Murray, sports and tourists stepped off a train. The new arrivals bought a steamboat ticket and climbed aboard. It was a highway of water: Old Forge Pond, First Lake, Second Lake, Third Lake, Fourth, Fifth, Sixth, Seventh, Eighth; Brown's Tract Inlet, Raquette Lake, Marion River, Utowana Lake, Eagle Lake—crossing all that water, lake to lake with a few walks in between, to get to Blue Mountain Lake. The series of lakes, the first eight known as the Fulton Chain, arcs from the west toward the middle of the Adirondacks. It has been a travel route since the glaciers melted. In 1929, Route 28 was completed to Blue Mountain Lake, putting the steamboats out of business for good.

My plan for this trip was to avoid the road, to stick to the water route.

That morning Old Forge felt conspicuously empty, as if it had been crowded a few hours ago, tourists wedged into every nook, and something had spooked everyone into flight. That was correct, in a way. It was mid-September now. The flatlanders were mostly back in the flatlands, missing out on a typically glorious time of warm days, cool nights, no bugs. But that morning there was rain. Wind-torn clouds snagged in the tops of the tallest pines. The sky looked too heavy to stay aloft. I parked near Pied Piper and sheltered under my car's rear hatch. I fumbled with my phone to get my radar app to refresh. No luck. The screen showed no rain anywhere east of Ohio, a lie. I sat there wallowing in that pre-trip regret that always makes the whole thing seem like a horrible idea.

Old Forge to Blue Mountain Lake, I would paddle thirty-six miles over the next three days. I could've driven it in forty-five minutes, right up Route 28, which passes fifteen feet from the beach where I'd stand waiting for the plane. I wasn't in the wilderness. A sleeping bag, a tent, I carried neither. My days I spent on the water or walking the carries between, and each night I slept in a hotel. What did I pack? Some food, a phone charger, and a pair of jeans, the jeans folded and kept dry in a rubber bag so I looked presentable in the evenings. I forgot extra shoes. For the entire trip I smelled like damp Tevas. Both hotels had a bar where I could order dinner. The second night, at the Raquette Lake Tap Room—on the lake where Durant built Pine Knot—I sipped my beer for a long while so I could eavesdrop while one local told another about repairing a floatplane. I asked the bartender what there was to do in town. She said I could go see the beaver dam. I had recently read a brochure for a popular nineteenth-century hotel on Raquette Lake. For tourists, it had had the same advice.

A few weeks before my trip I called around to hire an outfitter to shuttle me and my boat west from Blue Mountain Lake back to Old Forge. After paddling one direction, I would need to get back to my car somehow. No one would do it. With regional colleges back in session, outfitters were all understaffed. Discouraged, I almost bailed, stayed home. Driving up, I had always seen a billboard advertising scenic flights in a floatplane. I enjoyed seeing that sign. It made the Adirondacks feel wilder and more expansive than it really is. Floatplanes made me think of Alaska. Last ditch, I gave the company a call. The man who answered the phone at Payne's Air Service said he would be happy to pick me up, fly me back to my car. I thought I was making a ridiculous request. He didn't seem to think so. He quoted me a price, a fairly reasonable one, about as much as the night I spent in the motel at Lake George. I read him my credit card number. He told me to call when I was in Blue Mountain Lake and ready for a ride. I wrote the phone number on a scrap of paper, tucked it into my wallet. It's still there, creased, torn edges now fuzzy. Pulling cash out of my wallet, more than once I've dropped the scrap of paper on the filthy floor of a checkout line and have picked it up and put it back.

TIRED OF WAITING OUT the rain, I made myself get on the water. After the long drive up, it felt good to be out of my car, felt good to stand shin-deep in the water to load my boat. I launched, paddled a few slow strokes out onto the pond. The sandy shore dropped beneath me. On cue, the clouds parted, the sun broke through, the lake sparkled without restraint. Float-ing on a lake I had looked across so many times from town felt strange, disorienting, as if I had overrun the edge of a cliff, my legs spinning blurry to defy the abyss.

A channel snuck toward First Lake, a crenulated shore sharp with pines and maples, a few spruce. The channel felt like a prelude. Camps lined both sides, one after another, a gallery of camps, a boathouse or a dock in front of each, sometimes a waterslide or a floating trampoline or a FOR SALE sign pounded into the sandy soil. Looking sideways at so many camps, I got a crick in my neck. Most camps were vacant, chairs empty on docks, umbrellas cranked closed. The channel turned slightly, water smooth and glossy. Hills pulled up from the waterline on both sides, reds and oranges just starting to show through the green. A pontoon boat raced by, its wake slapping both shores. Camps lined the shore of First Lake and then Second. A shallow channel, gold sand in the sun on the bottom, curled into Third Lake. I settled into a rhythm of paddling lake to lake and steering a wide berth around the few jet skis and pontoon boats while still enjoying the scenery.

And then over there on the north shore of Third Lake was Bald Mountain Colony. I had never seen it before. Instantly I knew what it was. In the forest along Route 28 there's a sign at the beginning of a gravel lane that drops to the lake. The word "colony" on the sign had always caught my eye. A commune of artists or a back-to-the-land gathering that had decided to never end, that's what I had thought might be down there on the water.

The lake narrowed. Docks and pontoon boats studded the shore. A few dozen house trailers and pull-behind campers occupied the gaps between the pines, the structures close enough to each other that you'd hear any of your neighbors sneeze. It seemed that pine roots had grown tight, bound everything exactly where it would always be. Pines, trailers, campers, plastic Adirondack chairs, lawn orbs, jet skis, kayaks—all would rot in place right there. This rot: on a few camps the process had started some time ago.

At the foot of a broad lawn stood a high arched sign that said BALD MOUNTAIN HOUSE, letters toward the lake, toward where steamboats had once docked. A concrete path led between the sign's two supports and then uphill through the lawn to where the hotel used to be.

Charles M. Barrett built the Bald Mountain House in the 1890s, a long three-story white building, front to the lake. One-hundred thirty-five guests could spend the night. Dressed in suits or in gowns and floral hats, guests sat in a row of rocking chairs on the porch to gaze across the lawn and the high arched sign with backward letters. Gaslights lit the pines. Spring water flowed down a pipe from a nearby mountain. Trophy bucks and black-and-white photographs of Adirondack scenery hung on the dining room walls. A pressed tin ceiling and a harlequin tile floor, wooden tables draped in white tablecloths, white cloth napkins curled into cones and placed in stemware at each seat. The property had tennis courts and a croquet lawn, a bowling alley and a dance hall where a four-piece orchestra played.

After World War II, the hotel began to fail, just like the few other big hotels that had survived the Depression. Wealthy guests who had once spent a month or two each summer at the hotels now preferred to build their own private camps or travel to more exotic resorts. Tourist season was too short for hotel owners to recoup the expense of maintaining old wooden structures that preferred to rot and splinter and burn. Most of the hotels had been built simple and cheap. They had never looked like Great Camps. They were objects of speculation and profit. Failed hotels were demolished or torched, the empty properties chopped into lots. Upper-middle-class flatlanders bought lots, built camps. Lower-middle-class residents of the booming industrial cities of central New York also wanted a getaway. They preferred the freedom of darting around in automobiles over the stuffy hotel social scene, with its rules, with its scheduled activities, with its cloth napkins curled into cones and placed in stemware. This group wanted an affordable spot in the Adirondacks, a spot to sleep beneath the pines, a spot with a sand beach and a good view of the water, a spot to have a good time up in the wilderness.

Dick Barrett, Charles's grandson, transformed the Bald Mountain House property into Bald Mountain Colony. A few years later he demolished the shuttered hotel. At first, the colony was a place to spend a few nights or a week in a tent or a camper, a campground like any other. Families returned to the same campsite at the same time each year. A community developed, and eventually the Barretts began offering leases. A family could sign an annual lease for a lot, and up Route 28—forest, forest, forest—that family hauled a house trailer or a camper, parked it in the pines. If a lease was terminated or not renewed, any structure that wasn't mobile became the Barretts's property. This provision kept colony camps modest. No one built a structure they wouldn't be willing to leave behind. Each January, a renewal letter arrived in the mail. Leases are heirlooms. More than one divorce settlement has hinged on which party will get the lot lease at Bald Mountain Colony.

Most camps at Bald Mountain Colony could now only be rolled elsewhere by abandoning vital appendages. Campers and house trailers are the cores around which residents have pieced together camps by assembling parts. A roof over a trailer, like a hat, brainstorm in the gables. A rustic deck with tree trunk posts that could be attached to a Great Camp. A shallow, slanting roof to create an outdoor dining and living room twice the size of the original camper, storage space for life jackets and paddles up in the rafters, all that good spider habitat: stale air and cobwebs. A second camper cozy against the first and a roof over both to make a single dwelling, brainstorm tacked on here and there to give it that Adirondack look.

I kept close to the shore near Bald Mountain Colony. I felt drawn to the place. A thin blanket of clouds had turned the sun hazy, almost iridescent. The light felt soft, the air humid, tacky. Damp campfire ashes, a charcoal grill the day after a cookout, a smell like that hung over the water, mixed with the astringency of pine sap and a hint of gasoline from one of the docked pontoon boats: summer stale and musty, about to drop cold.

One end of a pale-yellow house trailer with a red front porch sat a few feet from the water. A good wave might've wet it. Slightly convex, the rear of the trailer almost touched a pine that leaned over Third Lake, a small rectangular window with rounded corners tilted open to let in the lake breeze. Someone at the camp had anchored a satellite dish to the base of the pine, trying to catch a signal. An aluminum canoe was stowed on shore, and a purple jet ski sat dry on a metal rack. The soft light made the scene idyllic. The yellow trailer with the red front porch was the perfect complement to the plush gray-green light of the pines.

For Bald Mountain Colony, I felt a sudden rush of appreciation, to the attachment residents had to this getaway in the pines, to this mode of leisure. I wanted to add the scene to the postcard rack in my souvenir shop, "THE ADIRONDACKS!" superimposed in bold letters outlined in white, typeset at an ascendant angle from lower left to upper right, the card sitting one slot above the kids sledding down the gray spoil dune.

Anywhere else I would have overlooked these trailers. Up there, they were a collection of modest camps that bucked the trend of Adirondack camps as trophies of isolation and wealth. They seemed to be more social, more of a community. It reminded me of how I had felt at Beaver River watching that family unload supplies from their pontoon boat. (Add that to the postcard rack, while we're at it.) Here, at Bald Mountain Colony, was yet another way to enjoy the Adirondacks that didn't fit the stories of solitude and wilderness and money often told about this place. Our national expectations of the outdoors are so often rooted in isolation and escape and wealth—the rugged individual in the wilderness. Here was a community that offered something different about what it meant to be an American outdoors.

The channel to Fourth Lake narrowed again, twisted, a pinch point where passing steamboats had once swapped paint. On the Bald Mountain Colony side, one camp displayed statues of the Blues Brothers, Jake and Elwood leaning back in their chairs, sedate, enjoying the waterfront view. Each camp had a concrete block firepit. I thought about the smoky glow of a July evening, campfires burning low in the pines, a radio blasting the Eagles. This all sounded good. Kitschy but good. This was a place where I wanted to spend some time.

On the opposite shore, just a few feet away, several steep wooden staircases slanted up from docks to the top of a ridge. I caught a glimpse of a few large, well-spaced camps up there, peaked roofs scraped clean of moss, gutters cleared of pine needles, expansive windows with the spectral sheen of triple-pane Low-E glass. The camps up there looked down.

Most developed shores on the lakes I paddled that day have gentrified. New owners demolish older, smaller camps to build bigger ones. The price of waterfront lots is beyond the reach of all but the wealthy. In Old Forge, it's flatlanders who get the waterfront views, not locals, a source of understandable bitterness. On the most desirable lakes, that's happening all over the Adirondacks. Bald Mountain Colony remains one of the few places where for a modest investment you can secure a waterfront camp. If you're lucky enough to find one for sale.

One day, scouring Craigslist for firewood vendors to contact, I spotted a listing for a trailer in Bald Mountain Colony. It was $34,900. Two bedrooms, one bath, a peaked metal roof on poles to shelter the trailer, and a dock on Third Lake. Site rent was $200 per month. In the listing photographs, the trailer looked cramped, smothered in an eternal pine dusk, lamps clicked on inside at noon. Like most camps in Bald Mountain Colony, the trailer wasn't the selling point. No one really cared about the trailer. If it was somewhat clean and usually dry, and the mildew on the outside could be blasted off with a pressure washer, if it had a bed or two and a foldout couch, if most of the windows had screens to keep out the horseflies and mosquitos, the trailer was just fine. The trailer was just a way to join the community—that's what was really for sale.

A year later I would return to Bald Mountain Colony, drive up Route 28, drop down the steep gravel road to Third Lake. I parked my car next to a truck owned by a guy who was unloading a brand-new garden gnome. He placed it next to a tall pine, and then his girlfriend, recently divorced, asked him to move it a few feet to the right. I spent a few hours with the flatlanders who rented lots, one person introducing me to the next. I interrupted meals of baked chicken and potato salad and low-stakes poker games. No one complained or asked me to leave. Most people I talked to lived in Rust Belt areas of central or western New York, and everyone was cheerful and talkative, all enjoying the pleasant summer day. They all loved this place, loved how it brought together friends and let everyone have fun in the woods. To them, that sign along Route 28 read Paradise.

But each conversation slid into worry, a simmering uncertainty. No one wanted to talk specifics. Here's what I pieced together: Someone in the family who owned Bald Mountain Colony had recently died. The management of the place was in flux. For years—for decades—the rates and rules had been predictable. They had recently turned fickle, skewed by favoritism. Everyone worried that someone in the family would sell

Bald Mountain Colony, cash in by selling the scenic spot to a real estate developer who would build condos or six-figure camps with triple-pane Low-E glass.

Ever since, when I drive Route 28, I worry that the sign for Bald Mountain Colony will be gone, replaced with a banner: COMING SOON! BALD MOUNTAIN VILLAS *RUSTIC LUXURY ON FOURTH LAKE*. This uncertainty, this impending change: it's part of a trend I sensed everywhere I went. The Adirondacks of today is the product of a particular historical moment: cheap gas and an economy with a rising middle class. This era has already started to wane, and if that's true, and if fewer flatlanders can afford camps, I wonder how it'll change the Adirondacks. It seems like the myth of the Adirondacks and the idea of an empty wilderness and the stagnant middle-class economic conditions of the twenty-first century conspire to erase places like Bald Mountain Colony.

AFTER THE CHANNEL, FOURTH LAKE felt like an inland sea, a sudden immense view beyond, a tremor that signaled wind agitating open water somewhere ahead. Lulled by the pace of moving paddle by paddle, lulled by the unexpected stagnant warmth of the late afternoon, I was getting tired, and suddenly it seemed like I had a long haul to go before I reached Inlet, way up at the head of the lake that swept to my right like a dog-legged fairway. Forested mountains pushed tight against the north shore. Gusts rolled the lake into shimmering swells that picked me up and set me back down smoothly about where I had been before. When I was halfway up the lake, the clouds broke. The sun struck me and then struck the shore, struck the mountains, struck a rocky island to my right, striking camp after camp, dock after dock, like dominoes falling fast, the light racing down both shores to smack the tall pines at the far end. I thought about how there wasn't a forest clearing within twenty miles that could hope to contain the sudden slender shadows of those pines.

At the head of the lake I beached my canoe next to a plastic alligator below the Woods Inn. Butter-yellow with white trim, four stories tall, the hotel sat on a shallow rise above me, a good view back toward sunset. I could hear cars slowing down on Route 28 when they entered Inlet, but I still felt as though I had arrived somewhere inaccessible, somewhere wheels couldn't go, as if Route 28 had never been built.

When Route 28 was built, Inlet did an about-face, lake front to road front, steamboats to automobiles. A few blocks of tidy storefronts hug the road. Gift shops, a hardware store, a post office, a restaurant. A café with a façade that looks like it's from Dodge City. An ice cream stand with a pink neon sign that says Northern Lights. Wedged along an alley is a train caboose that's a restaurant. A rustic furniture store's inventory overflows into a roadside lawn. Inlet feels like it once held a town-wide election to adopt a unifying theme, but everyone voted for their own plan.

I left my boat near the alligator and walked up the rise. It felt strange to approach the hotel from the water: that side of the hotel had been the front but was now the back—steamboats to automobiles—and neither the new front nor the old front now looked much like the front, so the hotel gave the impression of having two back doors.

It's one of the few nineteenth-century Adirondack hotels still open. In fact, it's one of the few that still stands. Fred Hess built the hotel in 1898. He called it Hess Camp. He sold it to someone who then sold it to Philo C. Wood. Wood called it the Wood. Wood remodeled and enlarged the building. Bill Dunay, a fighter pilot during World War II, purchased the hotel in 1946 and ran it for the next forty years. Then it closed and rotted. Fourteen years later, two flatlanders bought it, fixed it up.

I had stayed there before, and I enjoyed walking the halls, pine floors creaking a wonderful creak of Adirondack pines grown tall before the Adirondacks was the Adirondacks. That night my room had a tree trunk mounted floor to ceiling: a coat rack, I eventually realized, and I hung my life jacket to dry. The curtain rods were scavenged branches cut clean on the ends. In that charming way of old hotels rearranged to meet contemporary expectations of amenity, I reached my room's lakeview porch through a screen door in the bathroom.

This trip: I thought I had planned it because all summer I had been driving too much, and I was fed up with the Adirondacks and the crowds, and I felt like I had made too big a deal about the park and its history. Driving and driving and driving, I had convinced myself there was nothing to see, that it was all just a rural forest that didn't really matter. I had been spending too much time thinking about the idea of this place and not spending enough time immersed in the place itself. With more perspective, I realize I planned the trip because I needed a chance to rethink the boundaries we've drawn in the Adirondacks. Nineteenth-century travelers to the Adirondack wilderness didn't mind a night or two in a hotel. Some even looked forward to the opportunity to break up the dark forest with a dry bed and a hot meal. The whole of the Adirondacks was treated as a wilderness because it looked and felt different than the flatlands, not because it met some wilderness ideal: empty and supposedly pristine. That's changed. Flatlanders going to what we now consider wilderness often want nothing to do with towns or hotels. At the very least they consider them separate places. This further skews the focus of the region toward wilderness, or at least creates a divide between what's wild and what's not. On this trip, I wanted something in between. I wanted to paddle, to be out in the weather and smell the balsam, to be immersed in the environment, but at the end of the day I wanted a dry bed, a bar, a good conversation. That sounded like a pleasant way to see the land.

I'm not alone in this approach. There's been a recent effort to curate multiday hiking or paddling trips through the wilds of the Adirondacks. Each night tourists sleep in a lodge or a backwoods hut on private land or in a town. The result is a connection between towns and the lands that surround them. It's called Hamlet to Huts. In some ways, the plan is like hut systems in New Zealand, the White Mountains of New Hampshire, or the San Juan Mountains of Colorado, except that those huts are more often way out in the wilds. The Adirondacks, with its mix of remote forests and small towns, with its mountains and its abundance of lodges, motels, and underused Great Camps, is an ideal place for these types of trips. There are hundreds of trails that could be extended or built to link communities and wild areas into longer trips.

When I first heard about Hamlet to Huts, I dismissed the effort as crassly commercial, another spiffy, branded adventure to bilk money from flatlanders. Now I see it as an effort to use routes of travel to stitch together the various types of places that compose the Adirondacks. The trips aren't only in Wilderness Areas, not only The Roadside, not only in towns. The trips embrace the complexity of the Adirondacks. Trips such as these are an argument that all of the Adirondacks is connected and that we should treat it as such. To see one part—to see wilderness but not neon signs, to see old-growth pines but not a white truck hauling woodchips—is to miss why this place is so valuable to how we think about the environment. That's what I was really after with this trip, why I didn't drive Route 28 to a Wilderness Area: I wanted to start bringing together the whole thing, Blue Line to Blue Line, towns and forests, quiet days and nights spent listening to stories about floatplanes. This trip was a modest act from which I could begin.

THE NEXT MORNING, INLET was quiet and calm. The rising sun cut the fog. I enjoyed being in town when most other tourists had gone home. I had been allowed to stay in the amusement park after the gates had closed for the season. That morning, the sun getting hot, Inlet felt different than it had when I had driven through. I couldn't quite say why. Actually, the entirety of the Adirondacks felt different that morning. I could feel a sense of the scale of six million acres wrapped all around me.

At the village's grocery store—tiny but well stocked—I bought a giant oatmeal-raisin cookie and three Granny Smith apples. The previous evening, I had dropped my wallet in the shallows near the alligator. I handed the clerk damp dollar bills and apologized. She said it happens all the time. The store had a hair dryer to dry wet cash. On one wall the owner had hung photographs of cars racing on frozen Fourth Lake, cars making broad fast loops on the ice. For three or four months each year, I realized, most Adirondack lakes are white fields on which the slender shadows of the tallest pines fall freely.

BAG PACKED, BOAT LOADED, I paddled through the inlet that gave Inlet its name. The inlet led to Fifth Lake, which was a puddle compared to Fourth, and at a shallow, rocky stream, Fifth Lake ended. For the first time since Old Forge, there wasn't immediately another.

I walked up the carry from Fifth Lake to a sidewalk parallel to Route 28. The sidewalk cut in front of a rustic gas station, tree trunk posts and a river cobble veneer wall. A local in a hurry tried to turn from Route 28 to the gas pumps. Long with my twelve-foot boat on my shoulder, I was in the way. The driver nosed her car forward, nudging me to get going. I dragged my feet and smirked. The driver fumed. Later I felt bad about it. She was probably late for work and the low fuel light on her dash lit up, and she was stressed, rushing, and here was this fool of a flatlander blocking her way.

I crossed Route 28 at a painted crosswalk. Here, at the only place between Old Forge and Blue Mountain Lake where my water route intersected Route 28, a wooden sign read:

Guide-boater,
Kayaker, &
Canoeist
Crossing

—or at least that's what I think the sign said before someone stole the last two lines. Maybe a snowplow snapped them off. The sign could've made a similar claim for the past ten thousand years. I crossed the road and launched in Sixth Lake, then paddled into Seventh. Both had some camps but fewer than the earlier lakes. As I was heading farther east toward Blue Mountain Lake, I was entering an area of more Forever Wild land: more trees, fewer camps.

The plane ride I'd take the next day must have been on my mind. All afternoon I was in a daze, as if I was spotting myself unexpectedly from above, the yellow hull of my boat down there. There I am! Pulling my boat onto a sunbaked sand beach at the head of Eighth Lake. There I am! Paddling down tortuous Brown's Tract Inlet, bow pointing at a wall of pines on one side and then bow pointing at a wall of pines on the other side, again and again, tracing a line of black water squirming through frost-killed ferns. There I am, way down there! Balancing on a squishy beaver dam that plugs the route, hauling my boat over the dam, now knee-deep in foul-smelling muck, and trying to crawl back into my boat, yellow hull now Brown's Tract mud—the color this region's guideboat builders once painted their hulls, with good reason.

Safely in my boat downstream from the beaver dam, again following the sinuous creek, I realized why arriving in Inlet by canoe had felt different, why the entire Adirondacks had felt different that morning. Cars and roads have made the Adirondacks less strange. Traveling through the Adirondacks by car changes the environments you see. In a car on Route 28, I never would've seen the golden sand in the sun, never would've seen twisting Brown's Tract Inlet, never would've stepped in that foul-smelling beaver dam muck on the backside of a beaver dam. I guess this is true about any place. Cars get us there faster but insert a degree of abstraction. Ed Abbey told us this in the sixties. From a car in the Adirondacks, you mostly see trees—forest, forest, forest—which are easy to write off as just some more of the green you might see anywhere in the rural East. Roads avoid bogs and twisting streams, avoid rocky edges of lakes. Roads give us the idea that the Adirondacks is predictable, somehow comprehensible, that it's something we can catch at a glimpse, that it's something we can zip right through, check it off our list of places to see and move on to the next, something that doesn't deserve more attention and scrutiny. Roads make us underestimate the beauty and scale of the region, which makes it easier to dismiss.

The past century and a half of Adirondack history has been about how to get flatlanders there faster: stagecoaches, steamboats, trains, cars. What had this progression in speed done to how we see the land? I remembered Barbara McMartin's plan for a series of roadside pull-offs and short trails that would immerse visitors and locals in the various environments of the region. That seemed like a good start. At least it would here and there immerse drivers in the particulars of this place.

From Brown's Tract Inlet I paddled out into broad Raquette Lake. The next morning I'd paddle through another sinuous river to Blue Mountain Lake and call Tom Payne to get a ride. But for tonight I had arrived.

Evening light smoldered in the pines on the far side of the lake. The Raquette Lake Tap Room and Hotel stood on the shore awkwardly, waiting patiently near the water for the rest of town to show up. Thirty minutes later, I would beach my canoe and walk up to the Tap Room. I would wander around Raquette Lake. By my count, Raquette Lake has twelve buildings. Thirteen if you include a caboose that's a souvenir shop. Fourteen if you include a tour boat that in the winter is an icebound bar. Fifteen if you include a shed under which someone parks an orange tractor that pulls a trailer of For Sale firewood. Town felt haphazard, the buildings built here and there, until I learned they were arranged around what used to be a loop of railroad track at the end of a route built to get tourists and Great Camp owners here faster.

I regretted that I would never truly know the Adirondacks as early nineteenth-century travelers had. Route 28 cut a clean, sterile line through the forest. Lakes and streams narrowed and squeezed through a gap with gold sand in the sun on the bottom and then opened into a lake and then twisted and turned before opening up again. In that moment, it seemed that roads had sapped the Adirondacks of some vital experience. The pine in Long Lake, the moose pine in Old Forge, the Northern Lights neon sign in Inlet—as much as I enjoyed seeing them, that evening I had my doubts they were sufficient compensation.

Chapter 13

A FEW MILES FROM PAUL SMITH'S and across the road from Fish Creek is Knapp's Trading Post. Clad with brainstorm painted red, the Trading Post sits along a road that had one hell of a time finding a dry route through a clutter of lakes: sharp turn, shallow turn, double-back, crook—then you see that red brainstorm beacon. Out front there's a haggard white pine stranded in asphalt between a gas pump and a tire filling station, a garbage can stuck in a fake pine stump, and an ice cream trolley that hasn't rolled anywhere for quite some time. Roadside, there's a sign with large, sun-bleached letters. The letters were once orange, maybe yellow. Each letter has tabs on the back. The tabs slide in a series of horizontal grooves, and the letters could be rearranged to change the message to the weekly special. I've never seen the sign say anything other than:

GAS   ICE   WOOD
BEER   SUBS
MEAT   DELI   ATM

Every time I drove past the Trading Post I stopped. Usually I didn't need to buy anything. I stopped because I liked how it felt to arrive, to drive through miles of forest and not see much of anything except trees and then park my car in the gravel lot and walk through the front door: a cramped but lofty wooden interior, a stuffed eagle and a stuffed owl roosting on the exposed beams, the head of a ten-point buck mounted on a wall near a bulbous security mirror, a bear hide stretched above a sign that said

"Health & Beauty Supplies," the short aisles of tall shelves heaped with a rabble of any item you might need on an Adirondack vacation, things like taco shells, hot dogs, hot dog rolls (regular and gluten-free); potatoes wrapped in aluminum foil (ready for campfire coals); beer (in a cooler called the Bear Cave), water (gallon jugs, bottles), soda, milk, organic milk, a variety of cheeses (some in a spray can), energy drinks, juice of all types; toilet bowl cleaner, window cleaner, car batteries, cat food, cat litter, dog treats, dog food; veal, turkey bacon, shrimp, Rhode Island littleneck clams by the half-bushel, lobster, dry-aged beef, lamb racks, hamburger, chicken by the pound; the Trading Post's house-made breakfast sausage, which often sells out on busy weekends, and late-sleepers say *aw, man!* when they get the news; ice, blocked or cubed, a whole freezer stuffed full; the type of pre-made cakes and desserts sold in a paper box with a clear plastic window on the top; various cookies and crackers and chips, and some fruits and vegetables; ant poison; water guns, water balloons, plastic sand castle molds; firewood in plastic-wrapped bundles, lightbulbs, candles, Tiki torches, fire starter logs; folding canvas chairs (green or beige) with two cup holders, one for a drink, one for a bottle of bug spray; a rack of postcards with those Adirondack scenes you see everywhere, sunsets splayed pink and orange on placid lakes; blue formaldehyde-free liquid deodorizer, Fresh Scent, that you squirt into RV and boat holding tanks, an RV sewer hose kit with New Swivel Fittings, rubber gloves, swimming goggles; a net to catch frogs, fishing poles and fishing lures; three or four types of inflatable rafts, one a shark, one a monster truck tire; flip-flops, red-checked vinyl tablecloths; WD-40, motor oil, tarps, ropes, bug spray (quite a few bottles but not as many as I had expected), orange plastic tent stakes, metal tent stakes with orange plastic tabs; a gag cracked cell phone screen decal; an air mattress, a kit to repair an air mattress or to repair a shark raft that a pine branch punctured. The store had that familiar, comforting smell of our mass-produced consumer society: plastic wrap, preservatives, and a whiff of diesel exhaust and damp cardboard. A balsam breeze drifted through the wide-open front door.

When I stopped at the Trading Post one sunny September afternoon, I asked at the front counter if someone could spare a few moments to talk to me about the store. Phil Knapp surveyed the vacant aisles, glanced sideways at the other employee working the register, and said to me, a bit skeptically, "Well, how can I help you?" We walked outside, sat on a bench in the sun.

Comfortably middle-aged with close-cropped dark hair, Phil wore silver sneakers, cargo shorts, and an orange, sleeveless Harley-Davidson

T-shirt. On the back of the shirt was a woman wearing a string bikini. Phil blurted out a risqué joke and then he immediately asked me not to write that down. He told me I could instead describe him as animated. Phil is animated. He worked in the corporate world for twenty-five years, and now that he no longer does that, now that he spends summers in his store and winters somewhere warm, he has the easy composure of someone who retired rich at a young age—except, that is, for the months of July and August when Phil hustles, when he works 110 hours per week, when he's wound tight and is all nerves and is likely to snap at an employee because it's noon and she hasn't yet placed today's newspapers on the rack out front, for goodness' sake.

In the sun, sitting on the bench, Phil was calm and reflective. He enjoyed sharing the store's history. Originally the building had been a barn. Some men tore it down, hauled it ten miles to its current location, and rebuilt it. The grand opening took place in 1948. They timed it just right: more and more flatlanders drove north in the decades that followed. At the time there was another store nearby but this one put that one out of business. Phil's family has run it since 1978. They timed it just right: more and more flatlanders drove north in the decades that followed. Today the shelves contain 11,000 items during peak season. Business booms when a summer is warm and sunny. On a day like that, Phil's customers don't want to make a twenty-five-mile round trip to buy hot dogs from the closest competitor. They'd rather be out cruising in their boat or sitting on their dock or hiking through the woods. Phil went through quite a hassle to get approval to install diesel pumps by the pine out front. There was concern that a spill of diesel fuel would leach rapidly into nearby lakes. Phil has always wanted to put in a laundromat, since the hundreds of campers at Fish Creek can walk or boat to the store. He said there are too many regulations to ever turn a profit. The store sits on sandy soil just upstream from a lake with a very dedicated, organized, and well-funded group of protectors.

Once every few minutes, Phil said it was a beautiful day. Each time he said that he leaned back on the bench and glanced up at the blue sky and the sun in the pines.

The employee who had been working the checkout register with Phil walked out of the store, sat down on a wheeled firewood cart, and then scooted over like a two-legged crab to talk. Phil said Jackson was related to the Rockefellers—who had once owned a Great Camp nearby—and Phil and Jackson both laughed, and I laughed, too, thinking it some old joke. I stopped after what I thought was a reasonable amount of time. They kept going, all chuckles and wheezy gasps in the afternoon sun, and then they calmed down and Phil got a serious look on his face and said, Actually, it's true, which I sort of believed and sort of didn't believe, and looking back at it I think they might have been playing a joke on me.

Phil's customers range from the owner of a million-dollar camp, to the owner of a fifty-thousand-dollar motorhome, to the owner of a ten-dollar tent that was still sealed in its cardboard box on a Walmart shelf the day before. Later, watching customers in the aisles, I tried to figure out if anyone owned a Great Camp. Everyone wore about the same kind of clothes, lots of denim, flannel, and off-brand Gore-Tex, and was buying similar items. Knapp's Trading Post obscures many of the typical American markers of class.

I asked Phil about his store's red brainstorm. His eyes lit up. He looked at the side of the building, tilted his head, brought his right hand to his chin, as if analyzing a perplexing but iconic work of art, and said, "It's very Adirondack." He raised both eyebrows in a high arch. A few years earlier, business was good and Phil needed more cold storage. He added a new cooler onto one side of the building. The cooler is about the size of a large carport. Proudly, Phil called it the largest walk-in cooler in the North Country. I have no reason to doubt that the largest walk-in cooler in the North Country wilderness is clad in brainstorm, and it makes me immensely happy to consider this peculiar Adirondack fact. A tractor trailer of ice arrives every other day during the summer. Out back there's an icehouse that once stored blocks of ice cut from nearby ponds.

During the expansion, Phil tried to buy new brainstorm boards to cover the exterior of the cooler. Being sensitive to the store's aesthetic, he wanted the entire building to match. The brainstorm boards he could buy were all too narrow. The original brainstorm had been cut from pines much larger in diameter than those available to cut today. Phil pried some of the wide-board brainstorm from the side of the building and nailed it back up on the front, so that from the road it looked as though everything matched. In the brainstorm on the unseen side of Knapp's Trading Post, I hadn't expected to find a telling history of the twentieth-century Adirondack forest.

A few months later, lakes frozen, forest gray and white, I drove by the Trading Post. The roadside sign stood blank, a black rectangular void in all that ice and snow. It made the whole place feel desolate and bitter. I sped up, drove away. A few months after that, lakes sloshing, forest green, letters back up on the sign, flatlanders everywhere, I stopped in to ask Phil some more questions.

I caught him on a hectic day. He didn't remember me, but he pretended he did and agreed to talk to me. He hunched impatiently over the stainless steel deli counter and surveyed the aisles packed with customers. I pulled my notebook out of my pocket, flipped through it, trying to find my list of questions, even though I had them all memorized. Phil thumped one of his feet on the floor and tapped the fingernail of his left pointer finger on the counter, over and over, his eyes flitting around the store to see who could be helped or what could be done. Then his eyes cut back to me.

TO FLATLANDERS THE ADIRONDACKS has long been a refuge from the outside world, a vacationland, a realm of repose, a place to get away from the everyday. Maybe Murray deserves partial credit for starting it, his book establishing the Adirondacks as a healthful and adventurous but safe wilderness. But it preceded Murray. The Adirondacks sat there just north of an industrializing East Coast, waiting for us to realize we needed to flee the world we had built.

I felt it, too, this urge to escape, this idea that I should be enjoying myself up there. I started my travels for this book during the rancorous 2016 presidential election, and they continued through the Trump administration. I thought: here was an opportunity to recuperate, to rest, to look at the scenery for the sake of looking at the scenery. Crossing the Blue Line, I felt myself put the problems of the world behind me, as if a clunker of a kayak had just sailed off my car's roof and clonked down the road. *Lean against that pine. Enjoy the sun, the quiet, the clean air.* This sense of escape is why I spent so much time in my car driving. If I was driving, if I was on the move, I thought I wouldn't so easily fall for that Adirondack repose. I worried that if I went for a weeklong canoe trip, or if I backpacked into the most remote spot within the Blue Line, I'd lose any chance of maintaining distance from the myth. Driving, always getting back in my car and getting on the road, somehow gave me the distance I needed to achieve at least some perspective on this place and its myth, as if somehow I could outrun it if I never stayed in one spot for too long. This put me in a strange spot. I wasn't a tourist. I wasn't up there to relax, to get away. I wasn't a traveler passing through. I certainly wasn't a local going about my everyday routine. I was running from what I was also trying to chase.

Driving didn't always work, and I wonder if my inability to completely sever myself from the myth—in fact, at times my lack of interest in even trying to sever myself from the myth—skewed the places I visited and researched. If what I was doing up there was trying to assemble a biography of a place and an idea, did I overlook stories that could've offered important insights because they didn't fit what I thought the Adirondacks should be?

The abolitionist John Brown is buried in the Adirondacks, next to a big rock within view of the High Peaks. In 1849, Brown moved to the area to join a community of formerly enslaved people who had established an agricultural community. He never spent much time there, but that's where he chose to be buried after he was hung for his role at Harpers Ferry. Many times I drove within a few miles of his grave. I never visited. Why not? Did I think that story wasn't Adirondack enough? Did I think it was more important to go hike another High Peak? Was that the myth speaking? By not going to see Brown's grave, I had too easily accepted a static vision of the Adirondacks—as an escape from the everyday, as a region of wilderness removed from wider social concerns—rather than trying to imagine a vision of the Adirondacks that could be malleable over time, that could accommodate people and places that conflict with the myth, that could challenge it, that could question the way we think about the region.

What else gets overlooked? The Adirondack population is, on average, poor and aging. With retirees moving in and young people moving to the flatlands to find jobs—like those twentysomethings at the bar in Tupper Lake—many towns are struggling to staff volunteer fire departments and emergency services. Despite clean air and exceptional access to world-class outdoor recreation, many towns are seeing shrinking populations; some schools have closed or merged. Although overall the Adirondacks suffers from slightly less poverty than other rural counties with comparable demographics—primarily because of the boost from tourism—many of the available jobs are seasonal and low paying, with few opportunities for advancement, and pre-pandemic many of those positions went to guest workers visiting from other countries whom business owners could pay even less. There's drug addiction, just like everywhere else, of course. There's often stark income inequality between locals and flatlanders. There's a lack of local society. Older locals I talked to expressed nostalgia for thirty to forty years ago, when towns held more off-season gatherings and had frequent funky celebrations to get through mud season and the winter. Back then there was a sense of community, the feeling of a large family getting by in a remote land. Many towns now seem to be hemorrhaging the social vibrancy that's long made them a desirable place to live. A chain of gas stations with coffee shops has spread Blue Line to Blue Line over the past few decades, at least offering a year-round if not quite homegrown place for locals in many towns to gather. One afternoon, listening to NPR while

I drove the long green blur, I caught a story about race in the Adirondacks. In the past few decades, much of rural America has begun to diversify. The Adirondacks has not. It's gradually becoming even less diverse than many other areas of rural America. The radio story recounted a racist incident in an Adirondack bar: a White bouncer confronted a Black man with a bluntly racist comment and then two weeks later a White man at Walmart repeatedly hurled racist epithets at the same man. The story went on to relate the many violent ways, subtle and direct, that minorities face racism in the Adirondacks. It was a jarring realization for me. The entire region had always felt so open to me, free and safe to roam and explore. The radio story quoted a survey that had found 90 percent of visitors to the Adirondacks are White. Some of the most popular Wilderness Areas are in Hamilton County, a massive, roughly rectangular county that occupies the most remote portion of the central Adirondacks. According to a different survey, conducted in 2021 by an Adirondack tourism organization, 96 percent of flatlanders visiting Hamilton County identified as White or Caucasian; less than 1 percent identified as Black or African American.

The popular tale of the Adirondacks is a story about environmental protection, recreation, and escape. That's not good enough. The problem with allowing such a narrow vision of a place to determine that place's story is that we crop that place's future.

The escape: If I close my eyes and think back to the first few times I drove up, I can recall the excitement of driving through Old Forge and feeling what I thought was wilderness all around me. I can feel what it was like to think of pines and boulders and silent ponds cascading into the distance and not think at all about local society or race or who cleaned the rooms at motels and whether or not their prevailing wage allowed them to feed their children fresh vegetables and buy a home with sufficient insulation for a night of −33, when, if anything, I went out of my way to avoid thinking about those issues. I could get away from the modern world, didn't have to worry about who had once lived on this land, or who lived there now, or who was excluded from enjoying time there. It was comforting to think that way because that's how most Americans have long thought about the outdoors. That's our heritage of the outdoors. The Adirondacks responds to that heritage, but it has also influenced it, even helped bolster it—might even be where it took root. If the Adirondacks is a geography that has influenced American thought about parks and wilderness and what it means to spend time there, I've realized I have to be open to the idea that influence of the Adirondacks has perpetuated or even introduced some ideas we need to change.

There are committed individuals and organizations fighting against these issues. They're making progress. But they operate within a narrative of the Adirondacks that works against them. To help, we need to find ways to think about this place that look beyond escape. If the Adirondacks has been a radical experiment in land preservation over the past century and a half, why can't it now become a radical experiment in the ways we begin to recognize that social issues are not separate from environmental issues? Why can't it become a radical experiment of social and racial justice? Why can't the Adirondacks establish a model that can challenge the entire nation to reconsider the boundaries that exist for equal access to the outdoors? Why can't the Adirondacks become a place where we demonstrate how towns and villages and their social lives and economies should be an integral part of the way we think about wilderness preservation? Truly supporting the Adirondacks for the next century demands nothing less.

I GLANCED UP FROM my notebook. Phil was still staring at me. I shuffled my feet, flipped a few pages in one direction, paused, and then flipped a few pages back. I pretended to find what I had been pretending to look for and blurted out my most pressing question, the one I'd been thinking about for the past few months: When do you remove the sun-faded letters from the black sign at the end of the season?

Phil looked at me as if I had just asked him how to tie my shoes. In a patient but irritated tone, he told me that on the morning after the last day the store is open, usually early in October, he climbs up on a ladder and takes the letters down, one by one. That's that. He goes south. Until May the sign stands blank.

His harsh tone made me question my fascination with those sun-faded letters, made me question why that easily overlooked act of removing the letters seemed so important to me, made me question why the letters had become my totem for The Roadside, how those letters had become central to how I'd been trying to rethink the past of the Adirondacks and how the ways we tell the region's history affect its future. I didn't ask Phil where he stashes those sun-faded letters all winter. I didn't ask him how long his family has used the same ones. I didn't tell him that I sat at home sometimes and thought about the letters up there, saying what they always say, that on my mental map of the Adirondacks those letters were the size of the High Peaks. I didn't tell him I thought the letters should be willed to a museum, that I thought those movable letters, those tabs on the back, those grooves on the black sign where the letters slide into place, were crucial artifacts of Adirondack history, as important as Paul Smith's or

Topridge. Actually—more so, much more so. Book after book has been written about Paul Smith's and the Great Camps. No one had yet said much about those letters, about the work they represent.

In the off-season, Phil would have enjoyed talking about all this, the importance of The Roadside in Adirondack history, how stores like his had played an important role, giving flatlanders a chance to buy the comforts of home up in the wilderness, and how cars had changed the way Americans interacted with the outdoors and how his store and his sign stood at the nexus of a complex story of money and oil and recreation and our nation's thoughts on what defines the good life.

But that day, customers swarming the aisles, all Phil wanted to do was get back to work.

144

Along the road that scribes the southern shore of Raquette Lake, there's a building that says BURKE'S. It's in big, blocky letters on the roof, light-gray shingles against green. That's how you know you're there: Burke's Marina. Boats in the woods, boats in the sun, boats tied to docks, boats stacked high on a rack in a lofty warehouse, new boats, rusty boats, rotten boats, broken boats, there are boats everywhere, pontoon boats, motor-boats, canoes, kayaks, jet skis. Burke's has been in the family since the 1940s, when Fred Burke returned from the war, bought some land, and started building. I learned this while bouncing down a sand road in the passenger seat of a golf cart, Kris Burke, Fred's grandson, driving.

I had parked at Burke's ten minutes earlier. Kris was darting around the marina's shop, trying to find something. In his late twenties, he looked slightly disheveled and fed up with the world. He was looking for a boat battery, and every time he looked somewhere for it but it wasn't there, where it should have been, he sighed. Curtly, he told me he didn't have time to chat. Next weekend was the Fourth of July, and he'd been working seven days a week since ice-out and would be doing the same thing for the next four months until the lakes froze. But he winced at the sharp tone of his own voice, and his eyes said, *Oh hell, come along.*

Kris found the battery and walked in quick steps out the door to the golf cart. We climbed in. I had to hold on, careening and clunking as we did down the dry sand road, past two rows of white rental cabins, staggered so each one had a lake view, past the ruins of Burke's hot dog stand, and then through a neighborhood of camps that resembled Bald Mountain Colony, each one on a long-term lease from Burke's. Informally, the whole area is known as Burketown. Approaching a dock, Kris hopped out with the battery before the cart came to a complete stop. A complete stop, Kris didn't have time for that.

Two guys reclined on a pontoon boat dead in the water at the dock. Waiting, the tourists sat there, all smiles, soaking in the sun. On each guy's face, that vacation look that said *This is the life*, a cooler full of beer cans in the shade.

145

If you ask a driver for a well-known parcel delivery firm what's the most remote Adirondack lake on his route—his route encompassing a good portion of what's within the Blue Line—he'll mull it over for thirty seconds, his hand on his chin, his gaze up into a nearby pine, and then tell you about it: Miles up a gravel road, a road that doesn't have a name or a gate or a sign, there's a lake, a big lake in the woods, three camps the size of mansions well-spaced around its shore. The owners of the camps paid to have the utility lines buried the length of the long road so the black, swoopy lines wouldn't spoil the scenery. Or, more pragmatically, so a tree wouldn't fall and leave the camps in the dark for three days.

146

In 1842, four members of the Piseco Lake Trout Club fished for nine days and caught 829 pounds of lake trout.

In 1845, they caught 916¾ pounds.

In 1851, the club disbanded due to a dearth of fish. In four days, the club reeled in only 109 pounds.

147

In 1893, a guide claimed that once there were so many fish in Canada Lake that a person couldn't part them to take a swim.

148

An airplane was to stock remote Bellows Lake with fish. It would fly low. The pilot would press a button or pull a lever. The fish would skydive into the lake.

The pilot missed.

149

In 1976, Silver Lake was dead. Nitrogen oxides and sulfur dioxide from Midwest power plants formed acid rain, and acid rain made the lake, and many others, too acidic for brook trout to survive.

In 1990, amendments to the Clean Air Act cut acid rain-creating emissions.

In 2002, with the lake beginning to recover, the state stocked it with the Windfall strain of native brook trout. (They didn't miss.)

In 2013, a fisherman on Silver Lake hooked a six-pound, twenty-two-inch-long brook trout, a New York state record.

150

Two stewards from the Adirondack Watershed Institute, based at Paul Smith's College, stand guard at the boat launch on Upper Saranac Lake. Most of the day, they sit, waiting. Before a boat can be launched, the stewards hop up and ask if they can inspect it, because on the hull or in the bilge that boat might harbor a stowaway: zebra mussels or spiny waterfleas or curly-leaf pondweed or European frog-bit or yellow floating heart or hydrilla or any other ruinous invasive species that Upper Saranac Lake doesn't yet have.

To intercept is the stewards' goal: keep those species out. In a garden shed nearby, there's a decontamination station, a heated pressure washer. The stewards call it DE-CON. One year the stewards inspected 1,713 boats and intercepted 26 contaminated boats. One boat had carried curly-leaf pondweed from Lake Erie. Another boat had hauled Hydrilla from the Potomac River in Maryland. A dry scrap of a weed stuck to a boat trailer, that's all it was, but the stewards caught it, and the discovery made the local news like a police raid on a meth lab.

151

A sign at a canoe launch on Little Long Lake:

HELP KEEP ZEBRA MUSSELS OUT OF OUR LAKE.
PLEASE SCRUB BOAT BEFORE LAUNCHING.

Nearby, a bottle of Shout Triple Action (36% more, Value Pack) and a cloth rag.

152–95

On a late eighteenth-century British map, the Adirondacks was labeled:

This vast
Tract of Land
Which is the Ancient
Couchsachrage, one of the Four
Beaver Hunting Countries
Of the Six Nations
Is not yet
Surveyed.

Yet today there aren't as many water bodies named Beaver as you might expect. By one count, there are nine Beaver Ponds, and I know of two Beaver Lakes, and on a map I've seen a Beaverdam Pond. One reason for the dearth of Beaver Lakes and Beaver Ponds might be that during the time when most English place-names stuck to the map, beavers were scarce.

In the 1600s, there might have been one million or so beavers in northern New York, damming streams to make even more lakes, flooding swamps, chewing down trees. Beaver felt hats became fashionable in the years to come. Continental Cocked. Clerical. The Wellington. The Paris Beau. The D'Orsay. The Regent. Native American and European trappers went into the woods and trapped as many beavers as possible. Two hundred years later, in 1800, there were about 500 beavers left in the Adirondacks, and in 1820 there were about 1,000. The nadir was 1895: 5 to 10 beavers remained. At least that's all anyone could find.

That year a state law banned further beaver trapping. A bunch of people tried to boost the population. Two owners of private estates purchased live beavers and released them. One hotel owner released a Canadian beaver into a lake. New York state sponsored the largest influx of beavers. In 1904, the state purchased seven. They were well traveled. Trapped in Canada, the beavers had been shipped to St. Louis, where they were featured in the Palace of Forestry, Fish, and Game at the Louisiana Purchase Exposition. They lived in a cement pool and ate wood, bread, green clover, and green corn. After the show, the beavers were shipped to the Adirondacks, where they spent the winter in another cement pond surrounded by a wire mesh fence. Their enclosure was in Old Forge, across the road from the Pied Piper. The Adirondack guides who took care of the beavers that winter fed them various types of wood, along with apples, carrots, turnips, beets, potatoes, and cabbages. According to one report: "Their method of eating apples was quite dainty." Before taking a bite, they peeled off all the skin, using their teeth like a paring knife.

In the spring, guides hauled the six surviving beavers into the forest in wooden crates, which I thought was a poor choice, the beavers with their long, tough teeth that could chew right through, until I learned the crates were lined with zinc. The guides released the beavers. Over the next few years, fourteen more beavers were shipped from Yellowstone to the Adirondacks.

Tourists and camp owners saw beavers as a novelty, at first, the furry brown things swimming with their broad, wedge-shaped heads just breaking the water, and then diving beneath the surface with a loud flop. The population boomed. A few seasons later, *the New York Times* ran an article titled "Want War on Beavers: Adirondack Campers Demand Season When They May Be Trapped." Camp owners wrapped metal bands around the trunks of shoreline trees to defend them from the beavers' teeth. Beaver dams barricaded popular water routes. What had been a joyride, smooth water and good views, became an obstacle course: duck and dodge and sink knee-deep in the mud. Beaver dams raised the level of lakes; shoreline trees drowned, spoiling the scenery. By 1921, New York estimated that between 15,000 and 20,000 beavers lived in the Adirondacks. Three years later, a short beaver trapping season was reopened. One owner of a camp that had been harassed by beavers was presented with a gift: a burlap sack of beaver pelts. They were made into a full-length beaver fur coat. The local history museum in Old Forge displays a stuffed beaver. It was trapped after it cut down the trees in front of a camp on a local lake.

Today, there might be between 50,000 and 75,000 Adirondack beavers.

THIRTY-TWO BEAVER PONDS: that's how many I've bush-whacked around; paddled across; stepped in, muck reeking of sulfur up to my knees; or looked at and decided I'd rather turn around and find another way. Beaver dams create the rank, thorny, ecologically critical patches of habitat we'd call soggy buggy bland. I'm grateful the beavers are back.

THE PERSON LARGELY RESPONSIBLE for bringing them back was Harry Radford. When Radford was eighteen, he founded an Adirondack magazine called, appropriately, *Woods and Waters*. The publication's rapidly increasing distribution gave Radford a platform where he could advocate for the reintroduction of iconic animals to the Adirondacks. He had convictions about what he thought should live there. Moose were first. By writing articles and cajoling friends and famous acquaintances to offer their support, Radford succeeded in getting New York to appropriate money for the project. Emboldened by his victory, Radford directed his editorial energy toward reintroducing elk, caribou, and beaver.

All of the moose died, probably of a brain disease. The state never funded the elk effort, and when private individuals released elk they were quickly shot or otherwise died. Caribou had probably been extirpated from the Adirondacks at least a hundred years earlier, so Radford had a hard time drumming up support for them.

Radford didn't live to see the extent of the beavers' success.

To Radford, the Adirondacks was a practice wilderness, the bush leagues. He desperately wanted to explore unknown lands. In 1910, he set off on a multiyear expedition in the Canadian Arctic. Two years later, Radford was dead, his remains tossed into the Arctic Ocean where islands flare atop North America like feathers in a hat. Radford had either struck or threatened one of his Inuit guides, and the guides killed Radford and a fellow explorer, George Street.

In 1917 and 1918, the Royal Northwest Mounted Police undertook an expedition to investigate the murders. Their ultimate decision was that, given Radford's explosive temper and his threats, the Inuits' actions had been justified.

196–243

In 1911, Paul Smith's Hotel Company claimed to own sixty lakes and ponds for guests to explore. Looking at contemporary maps of the 30,000 acres the company once owned, and assuming a generous definition of lake or pond, I counted only forty-eight. Maybe 1911 was a year when the rain wouldn't stop, and they tried to pawn off puddles as ponds. Or maybe it was the beavers, recently sprung, plugging any trickle of water they could find.

244

After a century-long hiatus, moose have wandered back into the Adirondacks on their own. I desperately wanted to see an Adirondack moose. Driving, I'd shout *moose!* at every stump that looked like one. On Facebook, I saw videos of moose galloping along a road I had driven the day before. That put me in a sour mood. At a restaurant one evening in Old Forge, a waitress told me she knew where I could spot one. She said locals called the moose Harold. Speaking to me like she was confiding a state secret, she told me to go to a certain lake at five-thirty in the morning.

Harold didn't show.

Chapter 14

▬

WITHOUT A DRASTIC REDUCTION in our society's greenhouse gas emissions, within the next century the climate of the Adirondacks will probably become more like the South: West Virginia, North Carolina, or even Georgia. Ecosystems (like lowland boreal forests), animals (like pine martens and moose), and recreational activities (like ice fishing and snowmobiling)—many of the things that currently make the Adirondacks the Adirondacks—might disappear.

I'm not sure how I feel about this. Part of me is curious about what'll happen. Will the look of the Adirondacks adapt? Two hundred years from now, will a PhD candidate complete a dissertation titled "Which Trees Grow Up There? The Changing Arboreal Identity of the Adirondacks, 1800–2200"? But I mourn the lives and environments that will be destroyed by this rapid change. In the pit of my stomach, I feel impending dread.

There's a wider issue at play in my uncertainty. It has lurked behind every word I've written, behind every drive I've taken up there, every mile I've walked or paddled, every thought I've ever had about the region's history and future. The Adirondacks is an idea—contested, malleable, reflecting our culture. The Adirondacks is also a cluster of environments—material, full of lives other than human, absent of ideals, intractable to us. The real, the imaginary: I've never quite figured out how to reconcile the two.

Chapter 15

TIME TRAVEL: THAT'S WHY a lot of flatlanders drive up today. It's essential to the escape. Park your car. Paddle up a darkwater stream for thirty minutes, or spend an hour walking through the woods, the pine light a soft golden green. No motorboats, no cars, no electric lights. Ignore that contrail. Silence, silence, and then the wind in the pines, a warbler singing somewhere to your left in that birch. It's 1740. The forest feels as though nothing much has happened since then.

Of course, quite a bit has happened since 1740: Logging, which removed many of the massive pines and spruce. Railroads, which made logging on private land increasingly more destructive. The automobile, which brought more tourists and resulted in the construction of more roads that sliced through. The gasoline-powered motorboat, an invention that freed hunters and fisherman from the distance restrictions imposed by their oars. Chainsaws and logging trucks and bulldozers, which meant more trees cut faster and more dirt roads dug. Off-road vehicles with knobby tires and four-wheel drive, which made it possible to drive logging roads, allowing locals and tourists to grind back into the fragments of the wilderness that had remained sequestered by distance. Dirt bikes. Floatplanes. Sleds. A strong economy, on average, that raised salaries and increased vacation time, which along with reliable cars, cheap gas, and good roads made the market for Adirondack camps boom.

By the 1950s and 1960s, the Adirondacks looked like it might become what quite a few people thought it should have always been: a recreational playground for Army surplus Jeeps and snowmobiles, and an opportunity for extensive and profitable development on private land. Other people worried that the past century had stripped the Adirondacks of its wilderness character and that the situation would only get worse.

Responding to this situation, in 1967 Laurance S. Rockefeller, chairman of New York State's Council of Parks, proposed the creation of a national park. Rockefeller hoped to core the Adirondacks like an apple. One-point-seven million acres near the middle of the Adirondacks, the part of the Adirondacks that looks most like the Adirondacks, would've become Adirondack Mountains National Park. New York would've transferred all its land within the new national park to the federal government, and the federal government would've purchased most private inholdings over the next fifteen years. Many towns within the national park would've survived as resort centers, feeding, sheltering, and supplying the massive influx of tourists expected to visit. Strict controls would've limited development and motorized use. The leftover land, the fringe, the parts of the Adirondacks that don't really look like the Adirondacks, would've formed a reduced Adirondack State Park. Like a moat, the Adirondack State Park would've surrounded Adirondack Mountains National Park.

Rockefeller's plan fell flat. No one on either side liked it. But the national park proposal sparked a conversation about the future of the Adirondacks. In 1971 the state of New York created the Adirondack Park Agency, the APA.

Each letter gets pulled out long like taffy: the A—P—A. It's a slur, it's a snarl, it's a four-letter word. It's the Adirondacks saved, just in time. It's the Adirondacks repressed, on its knees, colonized, bound in chains, just as it has always been since 1892. It's good science, ecology, and regional planning. It's a White man showing up at a public hearing dressed like an Indian and he's holding a sign that says *Now that you've taken the land, point the way to the reservation.* It's a well-trained regional planner with a polyester tie and lofty ideals and an Ivy League degree. It's threats of secession from the Adirondacks. It's a rumor of secret maps of eminent domain. It's maps, layer after layer stacked in an attempt to understand the region's complexity, and paperwork and applications and inspections and fines and lawsuits and delays and delays and delays. It's the savior of the last great wilderness east of the Mississippi. It's an attempt to buy every acre, kick everyone out, make Forever Wild into Forever Empty. It's guns drawn and protest signs and a truckload of horse shit dumped on the grass outside APA headquarters with a sign stuck in it that says *We've taken yours for three years, now here's ours.*

The state assigned the APA—a group of well-intentioned bureaucrats and planners—an extraordinarily difficult task: to design a vision for the future of every one of the almost six million acres of the Adirondacks. Here's one of those historical details that's so absurd it makes me want to laugh out loud: they were given about one year. The first step was to verify existing maps. No one really knew what was accurate or up to date.

The APA first developed a master plan for all state-owned land within the Blue Line. Most state land was designated either Wild Forest or Wilderness. Modeled after the language of the Federal Wilderness Act of 1964, wilderness designation permitted only nonmotorized travel and required the closing of roads. Wild Forest designation was more lax. Many roads remained open for travel, and snowmobiles could still be driven on some trails. Both designations remained Forever Wild.

Next, the APA zoned each acre of private land within the Blue Line, creating six different levels of permitted development. When the state had passed legislation to create the Adirondack State Park in 1892, no limits were imposed on private land. Build on it, subdivide it, cram it full of waterfront Adirondack camps—before the APA you could do pretty much whatever you wanted to do on private land. The APA's plan proposed a spectrum of development: land close to existing hamlets could accommodate dense development on small lots; more remote land could still be developed into camps, but each lot had to average about forty-three acres, keeping large parcels of forest intact. The argument went: this place was so special that it needed oversight of planning not expected for towns outside the Blue Line.

Codes, categories, and classifications; colors, lines, and labels on a map—it all sounds rather mundane. But the APA imposed a vision of the Adirondacks that attempted to balance recreation and development while preserving the expansive feel of the forest, the characteristic that most people felt defined the Adirondacks. The APA called it open space—a bland, underwhelming, bureaucratic term for the long green blur of The Roadside, for the feeling of walking all day through a forest and seeing no one else, for the feeling of paddling along a filament of dark water that sneaks through spruce where you think you might spot an Indian, a trapper, a unicorn, or a volcano.

Prior to the twentieth century, the forest that the APA hoped to preserve had been protected by distance and difficulty of travel. Motors and roads removed these barriers, opening up the Adirondacks to increasing development, with the worry that development leads to more development and then eventually the entire place would fall apart. By limiting development and access through regulation, the APA hoped to maintain the possibility of time travel. That's the kicker of Adirondack history: an area now so strongly associated with wilderness that it seems as though it has always been one and always will be one, today maintains its character through the well-reasoned actions of planners and bureaucrats. The irony of this isn't shocking. It might even be banal. Every protected area in America in the twenty-first century is like that. I still think everyone crossing the Blue Line should chant a mantra:

> *It's all held together by paper and paper pushers.*
> *It's all held together by paper and paper pushers.*
> *It's all held together by paper and paper pushers.*

That might go a long way toward breaking the myth, or at least skewing it toward something new, something that recognizes we're all still actively shaping what this place will be.

The APA was a radical move for the time, even though it was part of a larger, national dialog about regional planning in the 1960s and 1970s. Nearly everyone with a connection to the Adirondacks was angry about the APA. Locals felt they had lost the right to do what they wanted with their own land, and they also felt state land was being locked up by downstate environmentalists, who wanted again to make the Adirondacks a preserve for rich, elite wilderness lovers, much the way it had been in the late nineteenth century. Locals felt they hadn't been granted a voice in the process. Some popular camping and hunting spots that had been an easy drive into the woods were now in Wilderness Areas. Locals had been driving to those spots for generations. Now they had to park their cars at a gated road and walk the rest of the way. Local business owners felt that economic opportunities would shrink under new regulations: loggers out of business, real estate developers belly-up. Environmentalists, who had supported the APA in concept, felt that compromises made during the legislative approval process had undercut the APA's ability to control widespread development of camps and that motorized recreational access had been prioritized over wilderness. They thought the APA in its final form didn't go far enough.

Bristling, fueled by populist rage, some Adirondack property owners viewed the APA as a deliberate move by the government to crimp property rights. Adirondack newspaper editorials blasted the APA, called for its abolishment. The anti-APA League of Adirondack Citizen Rights adopted the motto, "The voice of the oppressed people of the park." The Adirondacks simmered, flared. When an APA employee told a sixty-year-old woman that she couldn't place another house trailer on her property because of the new zoning rules, she slapped him in the face, cracking his glasses. An APA employee returned to headquarters one evening to find two men splashing gasoline all over the office and about to light a match. APA employees preferred to drive unmarked cars.

It's a slur, it's a snarl, it's a four-letter word.

Today, almost fifty years since the early combative days of the APA, the militant mood has turned more reflective. Tensions have abated, mostly, though they did spike again in the 1990s after another commission tried to rectify some of the APA's original oversights, and a new round of anti-APA sentiment erupted during Trump's presidency, though so far it seems to have remained confined to bluster in social media comments. The lines drawn between APA supporters and APA protesters were never quite as clean as they had appeared. Many locals supported what the APA hoped to accomplish, and many of the loudest APA opponents were wealthy, absentee flatlanders who hoped to develop Adirondack parcels. A few protesters wanted the entire Adirondacks to feel like 1740. A few wanted unbridled development. Most were in the middle, expressing a desire to allow development and recreation to continue while not compromising the expansive, wild feel of the Adirondacks, a desire to keep it a wild land that felt different than the rest of the East Coast, a place where tourists would want to visit and where part-time Adirondackers would want to buy a camp and where families would want to live, work, and play.

One of the more prominent anti-APA protest signs, a ten-foot-square white field with APA in black letters and a red slash through it, has been removed from the house gable to which it was affixed and placed in the permanent collection of a museum. Anger is now artifact. Most locals treat the former hostilities as they might an argument they had with a good friend over some slight that seemed significant in the moment but now seems not really that big a deal. Every once in a while I talked to someone who still thought the APA was out to clear the Adirondacks of people. If that was the APA's plan, you'd think the APA would have gotten around to it by now.

If you like to snowmobile, you probably feel there are now too many Wilderness Areas where snowmobiles aren't allowed to go, too much land locked up. Or if you have a boathouse, you might be furious that you can't demolish it to build a bigger one. If you like to paddle a canoe on motor-free lakes, you probably feel there are not nearly enough of those. Even today, not many people who live in or visit the Adirondacks are absolutely happy with what the APA has done. Perhaps that's some measure of its success.

THERE'S ANOTHER IMPORTANT and often overlooked legacy of the APA.

When I spoke to locals, I noticed a generational divide. Locals who had reached adulthood before the APA more often thought of the Adirondacks in terms of individual towns or villages. In a sort of geographic tribalism, they didn't seem to think of themselves, day to day, as Adirondackers, at least not in the sense of a pan-Adirondack identity. They thought of themselves as residents of Long Lake or Old Forge or Raquette Lake. They saw the Adirondacks fractured into regions divided by political boundaries or watersheds.

Locals born in the Adirondacks in the 1980s or later—people my age or younger—or flatlanders-turned-locals who had moved to the Adirondacks after about 2000, after the worst of the anti-APA hostilities, would label themselves, proudly, as residents of the Adirondacks. It didn't matter if they were pro- or anti-APA. They were less provincial in their views, owing less loyalty to a specific locality and more to the entire park, almost as if they inhabited all of those six million acres. They expressed pride and awe toward the mosaic of private and public land, the mix of towns and working forests and wilderness areas. They talked about Old Forge and the High Peaks as elements of a larger whole and saw value in both places. It was as if those people could stand anywhere in the Adirondacks and feel the Blue Line all around them. If you look at a satellite image of the eastern United States, the Adirondacks stands out, a blob of contiguous forest and lakes and mountains. This group of locals takes that wider geographic perspective.

The APA was the catalyst. While locals hated it or loved it or just tolerated how it changed their world, the idea of the APA necessitated a shift in the scale of how people thought about the Adirondacks. If everyone within the Blue Line was to be bound by a set of land use regulations, everyone within the Blue Line had the opportunity to think of their place nested within the wider whole. Each lake, each town, each forest became one part of something larger. The APA foregrounded political, social, and ecological thinking at the regional scale. It demanded that locals step back to see the Adirondacks in the context of the rest of the East Coast.

Resistance to the APA wasn't the first episode of Adirondack revolt. In the late nineteenth century, locals had fought back against the establishment of the park, against game laws, and against No Trespassing signs. But the APA was the first contentious park-wide regulation that occurred when roads tied the different regions together, when phones and later the internet permitted coalition building. It's almost as if the Adirondacks required an act of collective resistance before more locals could view the region as a whole.

It wasn't just that resistance or that shift in thinking that instigated the rise of an identity. Because flatlanders have long propped up the Adirondacks as a cohesive unit—the Adirondacks!—locals had a multicentury history of an identity to use as a foundation. This identity has too often focused on tourism, on escape, and has too often overlooked work and the social and economic concerns of locals—but at least it was a beginning. Locals didn't have to invent an identity, didn't have to hire a marketing firm to invent one for them that would've been forced and false. Of course, the Adirondacks was an invention anyway, since the time when Emmons almost called it Aganuschioni because he thought Aganuschioni had a better sound, since Durant experimented with his rustic look, since guide rails were made out of a metal that rusts. The Adirondacks is a two-century-long humbug, one we still enjoy getting tricked by. But that invention took place so long ago that it has become something real, something that appears to have risen from the land. Adirondackers can now make it their own. This process is still in its early days. How locals continue to become Adirondackers and how they continue to develop an identity will help guide the future of the Adirondacks.

But what about those twentysomethings at the bar in Tupper Lake? In their grumblings and dreams of leaving, they lacked faith in the identity of the region. And it was their conversation and then the night of brooding at the Red Top Inn that sparked my entire effort to rethink this place. My only explanation is that the Adirondacks is still part of rural America. There are still plenty of young people who want to leave, often with good reason. The Adirondack identity isn't enough to overcome the troubling, often repressive social and economic trends of rural America. At least not yet.

Eavesdropping on that conversation meant I had started writing this book on a sour note, searching for what was sending those locals elsewhere and how that perspective conflicted with the view I had held since I stood in the limestone valley and saw that exclamation point. I could've just as easily overheard a group of twentysomethings who loved the Adirondacks and the lives they were making. I could've just as easily begun this book with hope.

I look forward to watching what this identity becomes over the next few decades. It also offers a lesson for the entire nation, an example of an identity bound to the ecological particulars of a place and expansive, intact ecosystems and its culture and politics—an identity tied to a sense of community that recognizes its boundaries as including beings beyond human, an approach we desperately need to embrace these days.

FIFTY YEARS IS ENOUGH TIME to see how the Adirondacks has changed under the APA. Since the creation of the APA, somewhere between seven thousand and twelve thousand Adirondack camps have been built, mansions and estates and condos, and there are even more in the works, some that have coopted the moniker of Great Camps as a sales gimmick. Most private shorelines have been built to capacity with camps, camp after camp all around, and now that the lakeshores are full, flatlanders are building camps higher on mountain slopes, marring previously pristine views and washing sediment into lakes after each storm—a situation the APA wasn't designed to address and can't seem to control. And yet, through conservation easements and outright purchase, more than a million acres of land has been protected from development and opened for public access, and the shorelines of wild rivers remain forested, and Wilderness Areas and Wild Forests still permit time travel. As many scholars of the Adirondacks have pointed out over the past few decades, the Adirondacks is both more developed and better protected than it was fifty years ago.

The Forest Preserve, Forever Wild, the Adirondack Park, the A—P—A: since the late nineteenth century the Adirondacks has been the site of a string of ambitious, controversial experiments in environmental regulation. In 1891, a reporter said these experiments had started a war in the Adirondacks, locals mad and fighting back against flatlanders telling them what to do. The APA is just another battle in that war. Given the challenges the Adirondacks might face during the next century—aquatic and terrestrial invasive species, water pollution, rising temperatures, shrinking local populations, owners of coastal vacation homes fleeing to new getaways as oceans rise, the siting of solar panels within the Blue Line—the APA will probably not be the last.

It's still a scapegoat for all economic problems, even though the region's economic problems are similar to those of other rural areas. It's chronically underfunded and understaffed, to the point that it has a difficult time enforcing its own regulations. It's struggling to address vital water-quality concerns, like leaky septic systems from all those aging waterfront camps. It's unable to curb the cumulative effect of smaller developments and subdivisions, what some analysts call "death by a thousand cuts." It's responsible for zoning plans that permit concentrated development along The Roadside, which is then what most tourists see and makes them think the whole forest is turning into condos. It's struggling to reach a balance between ecology and economy that offers tourists a wilderness to roam and offers locals good-paying, year-round jobs. But the APA has allowed the Adirondacks to remain a contentious tangle, a complicated land of contrasts and conflicts, which is what the Adirondacks has always been and probably, hopefully, will always be.

· **245**

In 1979, New York expanded Pharaoh Lake Wilderness Area to include Crane Pond but excluded the dirt road that led to the pond. Seven years later, the road was lumped in and deemed a nonconforming use. In December 1989, 2.1 miles of the road were closed. Locals were livid. They had been driving up to Crane Pond for generations to hunt and fish and camp. To them, this was about tradition and family and memory. A local town sued the state to keep the road open. The local town lost. In 1990, the state placed a row of boulder bollards to block the road where it entered the Wilderness Area. Locals removed the boulders and hauled them to an anti-APA protest. The boulders were dubbed the "stones of shame." When the state tried to place new boulders, protesters blocked the way. This was June 19.

To celebrate the Fourth of July, locals planned a demonstration. Organizers encouraged attendees to bring their rifles, "in case rabid animals should be in the area." Armed but peaceful, the protest inadvertently turned into a Fourth of July parade: red, white, and blue, and a glint of gun metal, knobby tires, and diesel exhaust; protesters drove their trucks up the closed road to see the wilderness pond. Over Labor Day weekend, Earth First!, a radical environmental group, blocked Crane Pond Road. A group of pro–open road protesters got mad. Maynard Baker, an elected official from a nearby town, punched one of the Earth First! protesters in the face. A local newspaper wrote that Baker's electorate "must be very proud of their leader, who is a problem-solver of the Neanderthal order."

Crane Pond Road is still closed but open.

Out of curiosity, after visiting the road I called a local towing company and asked how much extraction would cost. The man who answered said, "Aw, no. Are you in that mud hole way back there? We're not going up there. Good luck."

246

Orrando P. Dexter, a Yale graduate, a lawyer, a recluse, and the son of a millionaire, began amassing an Adirondack estate in the 1880s. By 1891 he owned 7,000 acres. Dexter Lake sat in the middle. Dexter fenced his land, tacked up No Trespassing signs, and posted guards. Before Dexter's tenure, locals had hunted, fished, cut firewood, and traveled roads on that land, and locals kept doing all that after Dexter had bought the land. Dexter had violators arrested, or at least he tried to when he could get local officials to respond, which was rarely. One day Dexter was driving his wagon to the post office and someone shot him to death. Locals wouldn't say who had done it.

On the lake, Dexter had built a camp modeled after the home of Albrecht Dürer, a Renaissance artist who died in 1582. While Dürer's house probably fit in perfectly fine in Nuremburg, Germany, the facsimile placed in the Adirondack wilderness looked whimsical. Country star Shania Twain and Robert "Mutt" Lange purchased the camp and property in 1994. Carpenters had recently restored the camp, giving fastidious attention to recreating historic details and matching original materials. Twain and Lange knocked it down. They built a mansion and a recording studio but failed to secure the proper APA permits. The APA fined Twain and Lange $45,000, and the couple had to restore a damaged wetland. Twain and Lange later said that their confrontation with the APA encouraged them to sell their Adirondack camp. They listed the camp for $9 million and bought a vacation home in Switzerland.

247

Hacked an illegal trail. Cut 14 Forever Wild trees to build a camp. Used a chainsaw in a Wilderness Area. Landed a floatplane on a remote pond in the same Wilderness Area. That's the rap sheet of two hunters busted by forest rangers in 2020.

248–50

New York recently purchased the land around Boreas Ponds, a shallow impoundment with long views north to the High Peaks. A paper company had owned the land and cut trees to make paper. On the shoreline of Boreas Ponds, the company had built a lodge as a corporate retreat, which the state has since knocked down: Forever Wild. The lake and its immediate shoreline will be classified wilderness. A gravel road crosses the property to access the ponds.

The most contentious debate was: How close to the ponds should the parking lot be? Or, in other words, and to phrase the question in a way that smugly sums up the recent history of wilderness in the Adirondacks: For a Wilderness Area to feel like wilderness, how far should someone have to walk from a car to get there: three miles, one mile, or one-tenth of a mile?

Chapter 16

▮▮▮

IT WAS A BEAUTIFUL DAY, the sun a crisp flare in a pale sky. The forest smelled like a long, slow thaw. Things were starting to wake up from the deep dark of winter: salamanders, birds, woodland flowers, pines and spruce and maples, a few bears. But I felt that the drive had been pointless, that I would have been better off staying at home, that I didn't even get a look at anything but The Roadside and the long green blur. I drove and drove and drove, and then I saw a loon.

On my way up a day earlier I had been stuck in a tractor jam behind a manure spreader. I crossed the Blue Line and saw a forest still without leaves. I had driven from spring up into late winter. Red and yellow plastic debris littered the yard of a mobile home. At a glance, the yard looked like a tulip garden. I stopped at a scenic overlook and read a sign: *Welcome to the largest park in the United States outside of Alaska.* Nearby on the road, a man in a green flannel shirt rode his ATV. The day felt fresh. I took a deep breath of the pine and balsam air that poured in, thumping, through my windows.

At a trailhead I parked and hiked up a trail to the cliffs of Panther Mountain. A kid, five or six, and his dad showed up on the top a bit later, and the kid said, "Wow! You can see a lot!" You could, you really could, a long view of lakes and trees lit by the spring sun. I recognized the tone of the kid's voice, that excitement, that joy to be up here. He saw the exclamation point, or would someday.

I walked back down the trail to my car, got back on the road. My windshield smashed so many small, black bugs that I thought the blue sky was dropping rain. Flakes of yellow paint peppered the roadside sand and gravel: paint chipped by snowplow blades; and in the grass nearby, there were dots of yellow coltsfoot flowers. Mile after mile I drove, the whole way lined with white pines, it seemed, pines tight against brainstorm camps and rental cabins, rust-colored pine needles heaped on picnic tables, roofs, gutters, junk cars stashed in front of homes, motel parking lots. In the shade of some pines, someone had planted daffodils. I caught them at peak bloom. I thought I saw a magnolia blooming in a camp's front yard, pale moons of tropical flowers in the shade, which felt a bit incongruous, up there, but I wasn't quite sure if I saw it or not and I couldn't find anyplace to turn around to get a second look. I made a note to look again the next time I drove by.

At motel after motel, workers were getting ready for the season, planting petunias in plastic pots and in the wedges of mulch pinched by curbs, steam-cleaning carpets, replacing rotten window frames, sweeping away pine needles from porches and welcome mats. I thought about this happening at every motel within the Blue Line, locals busy getting the whole place ready for summer. A few hours later, every motel I drove by featured workers now sitting on tailgates drinking beer, feet propped up, laughing, enjoying the end of their day.

I was glad that Adirondack Mountains National Park doesn't exist. It would have ruined what I like best about the Adirondacks.

I've spent many wonderful days in our national parks, from Alaska to Utah to Maine, hiking, sleeping in rustic lodges that reminded me of the Adirondacks, driving around to look at the scenery. I like the Adirondacks better. National parks can feel like trinkets sequestered on a shelf, set aside to help us reminisce about a past we only wish had once existed. They're often too perfect, too curated, almost artificial in the way they forge an identity around the ecosystems and geological oddities they're meant to preserve. They can be awe-inspiring and fun, and they've changed many lives and led to a greater appreciation of the natural world. But national parks take themselves too seriously. Visitors only hear the curated story.

The Adirondacks suffers from some of these same problems, in places, and often the APA and other associated committees are the worst offenders, trying to shoehorn the Adirondacks into the image of its myth. Yet the Adirondacks maintains a complexity that's missing from national parks. The Adirondacks isn't a relic of a time that never existed. In the Adirondacks—if you try to peer beyond the myth—you see wealth and poverty, gas stations and grocery store parking lots, farms and woodlots and white tractor trailers hauling woodchips. You see vast, intact ecosystems where lives other than human thrive. You see neighborhoods and schools and town highway maintenance garages. You see neon signs and a pine tree that pops the top of a building. You see success stories of forests recovering from rampant logging, and you see forests sustainably harvested to boost the local economy. You see mistakes, plenty of them, ill-considered developments of camps that make you cringe. You have the opportunity to walk in a trackless wilderness or to sit on the maroon-and-teal, sun-faded vinyl bench seat of a pontoon boat. You can stroll through a town. You can commute from your home to a job in a nearby city. The Adirondacks sets all these objects and environments and activities in relationship with each other, foregrounding the value of seeing and appreciating the whole. That's what the Adirondacks has to offer the ongoing and increasingly important conversation about how we should protect the North American landscape.

Perhaps that line of thought—comparing the Adirondacks to national parks where very few people today live—is misguided. A better comparison might be between the Adirondacks and other rural areas. The mid-Hudson Valley. The West Virginia highlands. The limestone valley where I grew up in Pennsylvania. The Flint Hills of Kansas. Doing that makes it easier to see what the Adirondacks gets right: the coexistence of human communities and intact environments, some used responsibly for profit and some set aside, wild. And a sense that the land can recover from even the most egregious damage if we set policies that dwell in spans of time longer than our own.

What if throughout the country there were six-million-acre tracts of land that mixed public and private land and adopted the same ethos? Doing so would require rewriting American history and our own stories of what we think we are on this land. It would also require cash, since what props up the communities of the Adirondacks is cash from the state and from flatlanders flocking north. Also, this idea I'm proposing overlooks Indigenous rights and claims, and also overlooks that the only reason the Adirondacks wasn't swamped by settlers on our nation's first rush west was because the region was too rocky and too cold and too remote to successfully farm cash crops.

Ignore all of that, for now. Take the Adirondacks—this six-million-acre fractured mosaic of public and private land, bound by (or protected by) rigid regional planning, and an identity bolstered by two centuries of tourists—and place a similar model in each major ecosystem type across the country. Put one on the Atlantic Coast. Put one in the Colorado

Rockies. One in the Pacific Northwest. One in Iowa. One on the Appalachian Plateau. How would that change the way we view the land?

The story of the Adirondacks, even with its flaws and conflicts, stands out as one of the more successful experiments in land protection in the United States. What if it didn't stand out as exceptional? What if in the second half of the nineteenth century, when our country was figuring out how it might protect parts of the nation for future generations, when we developed monuments and then national parks, this was the model that had been adopted?

I kept driving, my windshield playing an Adirondack time lapse, a blurry glimpse of rocks and pines and spruce and camps and signs that still said SEE YOU NEXT YEAR. I drove past where Paul Smith's used to be, past Fish Creek and Knapp's Trading Post, the sign a black void against a blue sky and pine shadows. I drove and drove and drove, trying not to fall into the trap of the myth and also trying desperately to find the myth, an impossible effort that put me in a bad mood.

The loon—when I saw it I pulled a hard U-turn, parked, grabbed my binoculars. Twenty feet off the sandy shore, the loon floated, bright and buoyant in the sun, a part-time Adirondacker back north for the summer. The loon flapped its wings, chirped, tipped its head back. It dove. A smooth radiating circle on the wind-rippled lake formed where the loon had been. I tried to guess where it might pop up, that loon in about the middle of the big dark woods.

A floatplane was docked near a red shack to my right. A sign advertised scenic flights, and beyond was the motel neon sign that might as well say MURRAY. Up the lake a worker was pressure washing the moss and mildew from the walls of a boathouse, and the view beyond was of the distant, jagged High Peaks. The sun was warm, but it was getting on in the day and the shadows had grown long and held a chill that felt like winter still hadn't quite let go.

I stood there on the shore and watched the loon dive again and thought about how summer would soon arrive. Green growing back. Loons nesting. Pontoon boats tied to docks, beer cans in the cooler. Motel neon signs humming, flickering, and snapping on in the pines. The piper back on the roof, the moose head on the pine. Summit Stewards and Bicknell's thrush flitting about the highest peaks. The corner of the brainstorm booth at Fish Creek hammered back toward square, maybe a new speed bump where a thirty-below night had heaved the asphalt. Phil Knapp up on a ladder, placing each letter on the sign, one by one, to say what they always say. A carpenter repairing a boathouse would fall off a ladder and say *Oh buddy! That's cold!* as he crawled out of the water. Herds of tourists would soon drive up along every road, featherweight canoes strapped to some of the cars, maybe a guideboat or two. I tried to think of the months to come: mud season, bug season, hectic summer weekends, every campfire lit, every camp wood stand stacked full, the warm days and cool nights of fall, every maple leaf turning red at once, the ice and the cold slamming back down.

The loon popped up with a splash, shook its head, reared back as if it was about to wail.

I thought back through stories told about this place, about all the visions of what it might become and what it once was and what we thought it should be. I thought back through Bald Mountain Colony and Great Camps and railroads built to get to the scenery faster, back through Colvin, back through cougars and lynx and wolves, that howling wilderness so many flatlanders still hope to see, the howling wilderness I thought I would find. The idea, the environment: they blurred. Maybe they were, after all, inseparable, and maybe that's what I liked best, maybe that's why I kept going back—why I keep going back—and why the exclamation point still pops into my head. I didn't have to choose between the myth and what's actually up there. I could travel in the tension between what the land is and what we've pretended it to be.

Guides and sports. Trappers and farmers. The Algonquian, the Haudenosaunee. I was falling through time. Pines thinned, grew scraggly. Maples fled south. Spruce scattered, grew in snarled clumps. Tundra. Lichen. Heaps of rock. Ribbons of sand. Glaciers barreled through. A deep, dull rattle. A low, low grind.

But in that moment, the whole of the Adirondacks was a lull, like the slack in some great turning, a moment of peace between the thaw and the high season—a lull and a loon and a line of long pine shadows on the far edge of the lake.

ACKNOWLEDGMENTS

MY PARENTS GET THE first thanks. For good reason. Somewhat unsure why I was spending so very much time wandering the Great North Woods, they were nonetheless supportive in every possible way, as they've always been. My mom long ago taught me how to write, despite my vocal preteen protests; my dad taught me to get out and go see places for myself.

Along a trail, on top of a High Peak, in a campground, in a grocery store, in front of an ice cream stand, in the loon knickknack aisle of a souvenir shop: I had conversations with a few hundred people during my Adirondack travels. Their experiences and stories, their awe and, occasionally, their indifference for the Adirondacks—the place where they lived or worked or were just visiting—helped inform what I've written here. For taking the time to gab with a stranger, thank you.

For leading me through a topic or slice of geography, much appreciation to (in no particular order) Joyce and Carrol Turner at Turner Camps; Andi Smith, formerly of Kenmore Housekeeping Cottages; the staff of Hoss's Country Corner; Kris Burke at Burke's Marina; the late Jim Kammer, historian of Raquette Lake; Karyn Norwood, formerly of Adirondack Architectural Heritage; Scott Thompson at Beaver River; Phil Knapp and Jackson Rockefeller at Knapp's Trading Post; Wendy Newtown and Savana Li at Fish Creek Ponds Campground; and Dona Stryszowski at Long Lake Motel and Cottages.

I did most of my archival research at Adirondack Experience: The Museum on Blue Mountain Lake. Thanks to Jerry Pepper and then Ivy

Gocker for their help in the library, and also thanks to Hanna Person for assisting with many of the photographs that appear in the book's gallery. I was fortunate to spend a few afternoons at the Goodsell Museum in Old Forge; thanks to Kristy Rubyor and Kate Lewis. Michelle Tucker at the William Chapman White Memorial Adirondack Research Room at the Saranac Lake Free Library kindly assisted me in person and then later tried to track down a copy of a letter that describes Verplanck Colvin's office. I also spent time at Piseco Historical Society, Cornell University's Division of Rare and Manuscript Collections, Cornell University's Mann Library and Olin Library, Long Lake Library, Raquette Lake Library, Keene Valley Library Archives, Penfield Homestead Museum, and Caroga Historical Society.

Two reviewers, Phil Terrie and Doug Klein, read a late draft of this book. I very much appreciate their suggestions and advice that helped refine the final draft. Any remaining errors are my own, of course.

In pre-pandemic times, I benefitted from a community of writers that met under the banner of HAW! (Historians Are Writers!) at Cornell University. Many people in the group commented on specific portions of this book, and through discussion on the practice of writing, the entire group shaped the way I write. In particular, thank you to Molly Reed, Ryan Purcell, and Joe Giacomelli. Endless (yet completely insufficient) thanks to Aaron Sachs, who read an early draft and guided the next one in a much better direction.

Eric Myers of Myers Literary Management took a chance on me and on this book. Thanks for sharing your experience and knowledge along the way. At Fordham University Press, Fredric Nachbaur, Nancy Basmajian, Mark Lerner, and Eric Newman were all essential in getting this book to publication.

Erin, Henry, Willa: all three showed me patience with this project and helped me through it. Willa (our super mutt) showed up while I was writing a first draft to take me on long lunchtime walks. Henry (my now three-year-old son) arrived somewhere in the middle and brought me, along with immense joy, the lesson that the world does not revolve around prepositional phrases. Erin (longtime travel partner, now spouse) read every word of multiple drafts, offered critical comments kindly, and was the go-to daycare commuter so I had a few more minutes each day to write. Most importantly, all three kept me from forgetting what matters most: that not far beyond the back edge of my dinged wooden desk there's a boisterous and beautiful world of gardens and grackles and gorges. Thank you, thank you, thank you.

NOTES

1

p. 2   "Tupper Lake, population 3,500": This is the approximate population of the village of Tupper Lake. The town of Tupper Lake, formerly known as Altamont, is closer to 5,700. In New York, the term "town" is used instead of the more widely used "township." A village represents a small, denser area within a geographically larger town.

p. 2   "built a railroad and then a giant sawmill": Louis J. Simmons and Carol Payment Poole, *"Mostly Spruce and Hemlock,"* 2nd ed. (Saranac Lake, NY: Hungry Bear, 2009), 27.

p. 3   "Where 1920s silent film directors": Mary MacKenzie and Lee Manchester, *The Plains of Abraham: A History of North Elba and Lake Placid* (Utica, NY: Nicholas K. Burns, 2007), 355.

p. 3   "zero traffic lights": Philip G. Terrie, *Contested Terrain: A New History of Nature and People in the Adirondacks*, 2nd ed. (Syracuse, NY: Syracuse University Press, 2008), 165.

p. 3   "adventurous escape from such things": See "The Adirondacks," *New York Times*, September 11, 1871. In the same issue, also see "The Adirondacks: Advantages of a Rough Life."

p. 3   "hop onto a train at seven in the evening": For more on departure from New York City, see William Gove, *Logging Railroads of the Adirondacks* (Syracuse, NY: Syracuse University Press, 2006), 68.

p. 4   Adirondack geology: See *Adirondack Journal of Environmental Studies: A Journal of the Adirondack Research Consortium* 21 (2016). In my review of glaciers in this paragraph, I'm compressing multiple glaciations into a single sentence. Each successive period of glaciers is thought to wipe away evidence of the previous episode.

p. 5   "Fifteen thousand years ago": Depending on the source and the location within what is now the Adirondacks, this melting might have begun between 19,000 and 12,000 years ago.

p. 5   "stagnant ice": See Mike Storey, *Why the Adirondacks Look the Way They Do: A Natural History* (self-published, 2006), 41.

p. 5 "Before trees migrated back north": On how the forest changed through time after the glaciers, see Edwin H. Ketchledge, "The Great North Woods," in *Adirondack Archangels: Guardians of the High Peaks*, ed. Christine Bourjade and Alex Radmanovich (Lake George, NY: Adirondack Mountain Club, 2016), 213–24.

p. 5 "wanted to make some noise": For rolling rocks from mountaintops in the Adirondacks, see *Adirondack Life*, December 1991, 31, confirmed with a letter to the publication in February 1992, 3. Also see MacKenzie and Manchester, *Plains of Abraham*, 7. Another source for rolling rocks is "A Note on Adirondack Boulders: Dr. Charles E. Betts Explores a Mystery," *The Adirondac*, January–February 1962, 51.

p. 5 "the budget for dynamite was a thousand bucks": Simmons and Poole, "*Mostly Spruce and Hemlock*," 301.

p. 5 Tree types by habitat and elevation: See Barbara McMartin, *The Great Forest of the Adirondacks* (Utica, NY: North Country Books, 1994), 7–14.

p. 5 "might be the largest intact temperate forest left in the world": This claim gets lobbed around as a tag line for various articles and news stories. Many Adirondack environmental groups also insert it into their publications. I've never seen this quantified, but given the lack of large, intact temperate ecosystems in the world, the Adirondacks must, at the very least, be among the largest.

p. 6 "captioned each of the postcards": My example is drawn from the work of well-known Adirondack photographer Henry M. Beach. There are other examples of this marketing approach, both early and later, and including even today. Nineteenth-century printmakers also used the "In the Adirondacks" title. For more on Beach, see Robert Bogdan, *Adirondack Vernacular: The Photography of Henry M. Beach* (Syracuse, NY: Syracuse University Press, 2003).

p. 6 For size comparisons of national parks: Glacier is about 1,000,000 acres; Yellowstone is about 2,200,000; Grand Canyon is about 1,200,000; and Everglades is about 1,500,000. Death Valley is about 3,400,000 (the largest national park outside Alaska); Olympic is about 922,000; Yosemite is about 760,000; Great Smoky Mountains is about 520,000.

p. 7 "approached the boundaries of their local knowledge": George Washington Sears, *Canoeing the Adirondacks with Nessmuk: The Adirondack Letters of George Washington Sears* (Syracuse, NY: Syracuse University Press, 1993), 160.

p. 7 "white tractor trailers": During my time in the Adirondacks, I saw many more white tractor trailers hauling woodchips from shredded trees than more-traditional log trucks. I connected it to the logging of a younger forest, or possibly to a market more interested in woodchips than in logs, but perhaps it was just some quirk of what I happened to see.

p. 8 "a protection embedded within the state's constitution since 1894": Forever Wild language appeared earlier, in 1885, but wasn't in the state constitution until 1894. Forever Wild also exists outside the Adirondacks, in the Catskills, for example. Much of that other Forever Wild land receives almost no attention from anyone except locals. I think this is because it falls outside of a larger, widely known place like the Adirondacks. For more discussion on this, from the perspective of a study on the Catskills, see David Stradling, *Making Mountains: New York City and the Catskills* (Seattle: University of Washington Press, 2010), 117–20.

p. 8 "landowners who loved the wild woods": Louise A. Halper, "'A Rich Man's Paradise': Constitutional Preservation of New York State's Adirondack Forest, a Centenary Consideration," *Ecology Law Quarterly* 19, no. 2 (1992): 246–48.

p. 8   TIMOs: See Tim Rowland, "Molpus Woodlands Is the Park's Largest Landowner," *Adirondack Explorer*, January 3, 2018, https://www.adirondackexplorer.org/stories/molpus -woodlands.

p. 9   "hard to tell what's public and what's private": Protesters against new private land regulations have called for private landowners to post private land with blue flags or No Trespassing signs, to show how much of the Adirondacks is actually private. The goal: for tourists to see this. For more on these protests, see Barbara McMartin, *Perspectives on the Adirondacks: A Thirty-Year Struggle by People Protecting Their Treasure* (Syracuse, NY: Syracuse University Press, 2007).

p. 9   "most complicated and contested park in the country": For more on the idea of the Adirondacks as a contested place, see Terrie, *Contested Terrain.*

p. 9   "No one really wanted it": See Barbara McMartin, *The Privately Owned Adirondacks: Sporting and Family Clubs, Private Parks and Preserves, Timberlands and Easements* (Utica, NY: North Country 2004), 6; and Norman J. Van Valkenburgh, *The Forest Preserve of New York State in the Adirondack and Catskill Mountains: A Short History*, rev. ed. (Fleischmanns, NY: Purple Mountain, 1996), 13, 14.

p. 9   "At least 130,000 people": Population numbers in the Adirondacks are often inaccurate. Political boundaries do not align with the boundary of the Adirondacks, so the boundary of the Adirondacks splits census tracts. In Jerry Jenkins, *The Adirondack Atlas: A Geographic Portrait of the Adirondack Park* (Syracuse, NY: Adirondack Museum/Syracuse University Press, 2004), there's an estimate of 150,000. Other sources indicate a lower population. I've tried to use a number roughly in the middle of reliable estimates.

p. 9   Montana acres per person: I'm calculating the Montana figures from a population of about 1,000,000 (slightly rounded down) and the size of Montana as 94,105,000 acres, a slight rounding.

p. 9   Alaska acres per person: I'm calculating the Alaska figures from a population of 740,000 (an approximate population) and the size of Alaska as 424,500,000 acres.

p. 9   "commute to jobs": *Adirondack Atlas*, 114.

p. 9   "'could turn his hand to in the woods'": Quote is from William Helms, a resident of Long Lake, during a cross-examination in a trial: "Q: What was your occupation during the years from 1870 to 1880? A. I was guiding, hunting and fishing, and anything that a man could turn his hand to in the woods." *The People of the State of New York vs. Jennie H. Ladew and Joseph H. Ladew*, 413 (1239).

p. 9   "around 200,000": See Abigail M. Larkin and Colin M. Beier, "Wilderness Perceptions versus Management Reality in the Adirondack Park, USA," *Landscape and Urban Planning* 130, no. 1 (2013): 2. This article places the permanent population at 132,000, roughly the number I used earlier.

p. 10   "84 million people live within a day's drive": A map in the Adirondack Park Agency's online map collection shows this figure. See "Population within a Days [*sic*] Drive," Maps & Geographic Information Systems (GIS), Adirondack Park Agency, accessed February 22, 2022, https://apa.ny.gov/gis/#MapCollection.

2

p. 15   Native American history in the Adirondacks: See Melissa Otis, *Rural Indigenousness: A History of Iroquoian and Algonquian Peoples of the Adirondacks* (Syracuse, NY: Syracuse University Press, 2018); Curt Stager, "Hidden Heritage," *Adirondack Life*, June 2017; Lynn

Woods, "A History in Fragments," *Adirondack Life*, December 1994; David R. Starbuck, *Archeology in the Adirondacks: The Last Frontier* (Hanover, NH: University Press of New England, 2018), 15–30.

p. 15   "virgin land of jewels and precious metals": Mary MacKenzie and Lee Manchester, *The Plains of Abraham: A History of North Elba and Lake Placid* (Utica, NY: Nicholas K. Burns, 2007), 59.

p. 15   "feared it might harbor unicorns": Philip G. Terrie, *Wildlife and Wilderness: A History of Adirondack Mammals* (Fleischmanns, NY: Purple Mountain, 1993), 34–36; Philip G. Terrie, *Forever Wild: A Cultural History of Wilderness in the Adirondacks* (Syracuse, NY: Syracuse University Press, 1994), 19.

p. 15   "first European to cross the Adirondacks": Paul Jamieson, "Poncet: The First White Man in the Western Adirondacks," in *Adirondack Pilgrimage* (Glens Falls, NY: Adirondack Mountain Club, 1986), 53.

p. 15   "maps on birch bark": Jeptha R. Simms, *Trappers of New York* (Albany, NY: Joel Munsell, 1851), 149.

p. 16   "'This Country by reason of Mountains'": Quote is from Lewis Evans, "A General Map of the Middle British Colonies, in America," 1755.

p. 16   "One bought four million acres": Barbara McMartin, *The Great Forest of the Adirondacks* (Utica, NY: North Country Books, 1994), 16.

p. 16   "decided to eyeball the rest": Louis J. Simmons and Carol Payment Poole, *"Mostly Spruce and Hemlock,"* 2nd ed. (Saranac Lake, NY: Hungry Bear, 2009), 5.

p. 16   "clear three or four acres of forest per year": Ted Aber and Stella King, *The History of Hamilton County* (Lake Pleasant, NY: Great Wilderness Books, 1965), 26.

p. 16   "floated them to flatland cities": Aber and King, *Hamilton County*, 928–29.

p. 16   Report of volcanoes: See Ebenezer Emmons, *Geology of New York. Part II, Comprising the Survey of the Second Geological District* (Albany, NY: W&A White and J. Visscher, 1842), 222.

p. 17   "he thought Aganuschioni had a better sound": Ebenezer Emmons, "Report of E. Emmons, Geologist of the 2d Geological District of the State of New-York," in "February 20, 1838 Communication from the Governor, relative to the Geological Survey of the State," 242.

p. 17   History of Adirondack as a name: There's a lot of conflict over the history of "Adirondack" and "Adirondacks," and how exactly the name ended up being applied to this region. What's told here is an abbreviated (and, depending on your source, disputed) version. For more, see Stephen Sulavik, *Adirondack: Of Indians and Mountains, 1535–1838* (Fleischmanns, NY: Purple Mountain, 2005), 51, 52, 164–67; Philip Terrie, "Introduction," in Russell M. L. Carson, *Peaks and People of the Adirondacks* (Glens Falls, NY: Adirondack Mountain Club, 1973), xxxv–xxxvii; Murray Heller, *Call Me Adirondack* (Saranac Lake, NY: Chauncy, 1989), 24; Nathaniel Sylvester, *Historical Sketches of Northern New York and the Adirondack Wilderness* (Troy, NY: W. H. Young, 1887), 39, 40.

p. 17   "'as little known and as inadequately appreciated'": O. L. Holley, "Report of the Surveyor-General to the Canal Board, in relation to the public lands, &c." Presented to NY Senate, March 10, 1840, 12.

p. 17   *"Ho! For the woods!"*: "Life in the Adirondack: Number 6," *New York Times*, August 23, 1858.

p. 17   "Wearing coarse woolen shirts and cowhide boots": Wardrobe from this era comes from "The Lakes of the Wilderness," *Great Republic Monthly*, April 1859, 335–50.

p. 17   "trout stuffed with salt pork": Charles Brumley, *Guides of the Adirondacks: A History* (Utica, NY: North Country Books, 1994), 16, 17.

p. 17   "'It was wonderful how those solemn mountains'": "The Wilderness and Its Waters, Chapter 1: The Threshold," *The Crayon*, March 14, 1855, 163.

p. 17   *"Cut out and get out"*: Rather than pay land taxes, loggers abandoned their land, which by default reverted to the state. For more, see Louise A. Halper, "'A Rich Man's Paradise': Constitutional Preservation of New York State's Adirondack Forest, a Centenary Consideration," *Ecology Law Quarterly* 19, no. 2 (1992): 207.

p. 17   "porch became prized real estate": Karen Ann Dietz, "A Home in the Woods: Summer Life in the Adirondacks" (PhD diss., University of Pennsylvania, 1992), 132.

p. 18   "Some said the Adirondacks was now ruined": Even in 1860 (and earlier, too), a few visitors to the Adirondacks were complaining about how worn and overused and crowded the place felt. For one example, see Maitland De Sormo, *Summers on the Saranacs* (Saranac Lake, NY: Adirondack Yesteryears, 1980), 27. Reading Adirondack travel articles published from 1860 on will also reveal similar sentiments. Also see "The Sportsman Tourist: The Adirondacks in 1853," *Forest & Stream*, October 22, 1891.

p. 18   "guides sank a few in protest": Elizabeth Folwell, "Scorched Earth: Arson in the Adirondacks: A Hot Topic for Two Centuries," in *Short Carries: Essays from Adirondack Life* (Jay, NY: Adirondack Life, 2009), 92.

p. 18   "sometimes a steamboat got stuck": See Harold K. Hochschild, *Adirondack Steamboats on Raquette and Blue Mountain Lakes* (Blue Mountain Lake, NY: Adirondack Museum, 1962), 6.

p. 18   "imposed regulations and game laws": Halper, "'A Rich Man's Paradise,'" 246–64; Norman J. Van Valkenburgh, *The Forest Preserve of New York State in the Adirondack and Catskill Mountains: A Short History*, rev. ed. (Fleischmanns, NY: Purple Mountain, 1996), 31.

p. 18   "Some still did. Most got away with it.": For more on this era, see Karl Jacoby, *Crimes against Nature: Squatters, Poachers, Thieves, and the Hidden History of American Conservation* (Berkeley, CA: University of California Press, 2001/2014), 11–78.

p. 18   "cut more Forever Wild trees to pay the fine": Ted Aber and Stella King, *Tales from an Adirondack County* (Prospect, NY: Prospect Books, 1981), 171.

p. 18   "On menus it was Mountain Mutton": Frank Graham Jr., *The Adirondack Park: A Political History* (New York: Alfred A. Knopf, 1978), 82; "Law Breakers in the Adirondacks" (and response), *Recreation* 9 (November 1898): 385.

p. 19   "dinner on July 24, 1909": Menu items are from Childwold Hotel. Menu can be found in the clippings folder for the hotel at Adirondack Experience, Blue Mountain Lake, New York.

p. 19   "Importing mounted moose heads": Mention of moose heads in hotels when Adirondack moose had all been killed appears in a footnote of Robert Bogdan, *Adirondack Vernacular: The Photography of Henry M. Beach* (Syracuse, NY: Syracuse University Press, 2003), 88.

250 Adirondack Lakes, 1–16

p. 20   "Six real estate agents": This was a billboard for Herron Realty. Their logo includes a heron, which makes the agents standing in the water even better. The billboard has since been taken down, for what I find obvious reasons, and the one that replaced it has the agents sitting on a bench, dry.

3

p. 25   "panther might have been the last killed": Shot, stuffed, the cougar crouched in a hotel and was then stored in an attic until it was purchased and moved to the mansion. See Rainer H. Brocke, "Reintroduction of the Cougar (*Felis concolor*) in Adirondack Park: A Problem Analysis and Recommendations" (Endangered Species, New York State Department of Environmental Conservation, 1981), appendix 4. For a photo of the stuffed panther on the fireplace, see Harold K. Hochschild, *Adirondack Railroads Real and Phantom* (Blue Mountain Lake, NY: Adirondack Museum, 1962), 18. For a photo of the chimney, after Forest Lodge was burnt but before the chimney was knocked down, see Robert Engel, Howard Kirschenbaum, and Paul Malo, *Santanoni: From Japanese Temple to Life at an Adirondack Great Camp* (Utica, NY: North Country Books), 191.

p. 25   "as a footstone for his grave": This is mentioned in Charles Howard Burnett, *Conquering the Wilderness: The Building of the Adirondack and St. Lawrence Railroad by William Seward Webb, 1891–1892* ([Norwood, MA]: Plimpton, 1932), 57.

p. 25   "a township named after him": New York has slightly confusing town and township usage. Technically, there's a town named after Webb: The Town of Webb. But, in New York, "town" is used similarly to the way most places use "township."

p. 26   "The state torched the mansion": There were two reasons why the camp was burnt. First, the family selling the property requested that it be destroyed. Second, Forever Wild regulations wouldn't permit enclosed structures to remain. Only later did the state legislature pass a bill that declared under certain circumstances historic structures could remain on Forever Wild land.

p. 26   Guideboats: Most of the material on guideboats comes from Kenneth Durant and Helen Durant, *The Adirondack Guide-Boat* (Blue Mountain Lake, NY: Adirondack Museum, 2015); and Stephen Sulavik, *The Adirondack Guideboat: Its Origins, Its Builders, and Their Boats* (Peterborough, NH: Bauhan, 2018). My choice of spelling (guideboat over guide boat or guide-boat) is based on usage in Sulavik.

p. 27   "Twelve to fifteen feet long": These guideboat measurements are from browsing appendix A of Durant and Durant, *Adirondack Guide-Boat*. The appendix is a long list of guideboats from one builder. But this is the best information I've been able to find. Larger guideboats hauled cargo or bussed children to school or took people to church.

p. 27   "A crook is shaped like half of a smile": The cut of a crook follows the bent grain of the crook to avoid the need for cross-bracing.

p. 28   "Guideboats were the pickup trucks": This is a common claim. See, for example, "Guide Boats Return to the Adirondacks," *New York Times*, September 17, 1985.

p. 28   "didn't pay much attention to guideboats until they leaked": Durant and Durant, *Adirondack Guide-Boat*, x.

p. 28   "Gradually guideboats became pleasure craft": See Charles Brumley, *Guides of the Adirondacks: A History* (Utica, NY: North Country Books, 1994), 22, for how guideboats were used as pleasure craft, and see 213 for guideboats being replaced by boats with outboard motors.

p. 29   "Adirondack Boats Cranky": "Adirondack Boats Cranky, Easiest Thing in the World to Get a Ducking, If You Are Not Careful," *New York Times*, July 12, 1908, "Resort," 4.

p. 29   "Nessmuk pushed him to build them lighter": Alice Wolf Gilborn, foreword to George Washington Sears, *Canoeing the Adirondacks with Nessmuk: The Adirondack Letters of George Washington Sears*, ed. Dan Brenan (Syracuse, NY: Syracuse University Press,

1993). For more on the story of Nessmuk and Rushton, see Atwood Manley, "The Go-Light Brotherhood," in *Rushton and His Times in American Canoeing* (Syracuse, NY/Blue Mountain Lake, NY: Syracuse University Press/Adirondack Museum, 1968).

p. 29   "'use it for a soap dish'": This quote appears as "soup dish" in some sources and "soap dish" in others. For "soup dish," see Hallie Bond, *Boats and Boating in the Adirondacks* (Syracuse, NY: Syracuse University Press, 1998), 98. For "soap dish," see Sears, *Canoeing the Adirondacks*, 25.

p. 30   "'like a scared loon'": Sears, *Canoeing the Adirondacks*, 34.

p. 31   "been sued for trespass just to make a point": The former editor of *Adirondack Explorer*, Phil Brown, has advocated for the reopening of historic navigation rights. For a while, it seemed he might win his legal disputes (with good reason). But he lost the case. See Phil Brown, "A Twenty Year Standstill," *Adirondack Explorer*, June 18, 2010. In December 2018, a judge ruled that the water route in that case should not be considered public. More recently, see Michael Virtanen, "Judge Rules for Landowners in Paddling Case," *Adirondack Explorer*, December 21, 2018, https://www.adirondackexplorer.org/stories/judge-rules-for-landowners-in-paddling-case.

p. 31   Beaver River: See Pat Thompson, *Beaver River: Oasis in the Wilderness* (Eagle Bay, NY: Beaver River, 2000); and Anne L. Bowes, "The Beaver River Flow Country," *The Conservationist* (June–July 1965): 18–20.

p. 32   *"In the Heart of the Frontier"*: "A Last Frontier of Wild Life" is the subtitle of this publication. (Beaver River, NY: Norridgewock Lake Club, 1941[?]). A copy is available in the vertical files of the Adirondack Experience archives in Blue Mountain Lake, New York.

p. 32   Population of Beaver River: At the time of my visit the population was six. A more recent piece by NPR has Scott Thompson saying it's only four. See Doyle Dean, "Scene Up North: Welcome to Beaver River Station, Pop. 4," North County Public Radio, September 17, 2018, https://www.northcountrypublicradio.org/news/story/37022/20180914/scene-up-north-welcome-to-beaver-river-station-pop-4.

p. 32   "For a few decades": Phil Brown, "Crisis in Beaver River," *Adirondack Explorer*, September 2001, 12–13.

250 Adirondack Lakes, 17–105

p. 37   Floating decks (or docks, depending on your source): Mary Thill, "Pier Group: Star Lake's Dock Culture Comes Undone," *Adirondack Life*, July/August 2003, 76–81.

p. 37   "'Star Lake, *star*-like'": E. R. Wallace, *Descriptive Guide to the Adirondacks (Land of the Thousand Lakes) and to Saratoga Springs; Schroon Lake; Lakes Luzerne, George, and Champlain; the Ausable Chasm; Massena Springs; and Trenton Falls*, rev. ed. (Syracuse, NY: W. Gill, 1894), 140.

p. 38   Stoner/Stink Lakes: See Carol Parenzan Smalley, *Around Caroga Lake, Canada Lake, and Pine Lake* (Mount Pleasant, SC: Arcadia, 2011), 53. Also see Verplanck Colvin, *Report on the Adirondack and State Land Surveys to the Year 1884* . . . (Albany, NY: Weed, Parsons, 1884), 57. Also worthwhile to look at for an early account of this story is Jeptha R. Simms, *Trappers of New York* (Albany, NY: Joel Munsell, 1851), 169.

p. 38   "probably a hardscrabble farmer": See Barbara McMartin, *Caroga: An Adirondack Town Recalls Its Past*, 2nd ed. (Caroga, NY: Lake View, 1998), 213. On that page, there's a listing of Stoner's estate in 1820: "1 mare, 1 cow, 3 hogs, 1 calf, some fowl, 13 traps for hunting, some old knives, some pots and kettles, tea cups and crockery, 1 plough and 1 iron chain."

p. 38   "Forty-three Mud Ponds, and sixteen Clear": Murray Heller, *Call Me Adirondack* (Saranac Lake, NY: Chauncy, 1989), 124.

p. 38   Jock and Jocks Lake: See Simms, *Trappers of New York*, 253; Joseph F. Grady, *The Adirondacks, Fulton Chain–Big Moose Region: The Story of a Wilderness*, 3rd ed. (Utica, NY: North Country Books, 1972), 22; Dwight A. Webster, "An Unusual Lake of the Adirondack Mountains, New York," *Liminology and Oceanography* 6, no. 1 (1961): 88–90.

p. 39   Adirondack League Club: See Edward Comstock and Mark C. Webster, *The Adirondack League Club, 1890–1990* (Old Forge, NY: Adirondack League Club, 1990).

p. 39   "changed the lake's name to Honnedaga": By this change, one historian wrote, Jock was thus "deprived of immortality on the map of the forest." See Grady, *Adirondacks*, 65.

p. 39   "I hoped the club was magnanimous": Before the last decades of the nineteenth century, the Adirondacks was a vast commons, the few locals, European or Native American, venturing where they pleased. Wealthy clubs and families then purchased massive estates and blocked local access to the land. Large areas have been barricaded behind Posted and No Trespassing signs ever since. The Adirondack League Club is just one example. Locals and tourists could no longer hunt or fish or paddle through, a change that triggered resentment and even violence from locals. During the first few dry summers following this change, fires scorched swaths of the forest, some sparked by locals seeking revenge. For more, see Karl Jacoby, *Crimes against Nature: Squatters, Poachers, Thieves, and the Hidden History of American Conservation* (Berkeley, CA: University of California Press, 2001/2014), 11–77.

p. 40   Okara Lakes and the name change: Most information is from the vertical file on Okara at Goodsell Museum in Old Forge. Goodsell Museum has a beautiful color rendering of one of the camp models.

p. 40   "He wore a long feather headdress": Thanks to Jerry Pepper for pointing this out to me one day while we talked at the Adirondack Museum (before it became Adirondack Experience) library one afternoon. The brochure's cover can be seen in Philip G. Terrie, *Contested Terrain: A New History of Nature and People in the Adirondacks*, 2nd ed. (Syracuse, NY: Syracuse University Press, 2008), 144.

p. 40   "mimicked elements from traditional Japanese architecture": Details such as the graceful, curving hips of an irimoya-zukuri roof; vertical wooden beams that poked through the porch roof; open, airy floor plans that visually pulled the forest indoors.

p. 41   Lake Ozonia: See William Gerald McLoughlin, *Lake Ozonia: An Informal History* (n.p.: V. D. McLoughlin, 1997). Another source on Heath and the lake is a collection of clippings and photocopies titled "The Heath Family and Fernwood Hall," n.d., MS 09–121, Adirondack Experience, Blue Mountain Lake, New York. The story about locals hollering is on page 50 of McLoughlin's book.

p. 41   Eskers: See Paul F. Jamieson, "Adirondack Eskers," in *Adirondack Pilgrimage* (Glens Falls, NY: Adirondack Mountain Club, 1986), 130–43, and George Halcott Chadwick, "Adirondack Eskers," *Bulletin of the Geological Society of America* 39, no. 4 (1928): 923–30.

p. 42   Big Moose Lake: See Jane A. Barlow et al., *Big Moose Lake in the Adirondacks: The Story of the Lake, the Land, and the People* (Syracuse, NY: Syracuse University Press, 2004).

p. 42   Anne LaBastille: See her series of *Woodswoman* books (*Woodswoman: Living Along in the Adirondack Wilderness*, *Woodswoman II: Beyond Black Bear Lake*, *Woodswoman III: Book Three of the Woodswoman's Adventures*, and *Woodswoman IIII: Book Four of the*

Woodswoman's Adventures). There also are some secondary sources to check out: "Woman's Work," *Adirondack Explorer*, August 1999, 20–21; Peggy Lynn and Sandra Weber, *Breaking Trail: Remarkable Women of the Adirondacks* (Fleischmanns, NY: Purple Mountain, 2004), 156–61; and one of LaBastille's obituaries: Paul Grondahl, "Anne LaBastille, 1933–2011," *Adirondack Explorer*, August 22, 2011, https://www.adirondackexplorer.org/stories/anne -labastille-1933-2011.

p. 42   Vision quest: I changed the name listed in this note.

4

p. 44   "thirty-five or so other Adirondack campgrounds": The flexibility in this number is that the state has, at various times, considered closing or reducing the season of certain campgrounds in the Adirondacks. For background on Adirondack campgrounds, see Jonathan D. Anzalone, *Battles of the North Country: Wilderness Politics and Recreational Development in the Adirondack State Park, 1920–1980* (Amherst: University of Massachusetts Press, 2018), 36–60 and 112–18. Much of the information about campgrounds presented here is informed by Anzalone's book, and that's where I'd recommend beginning any further research for anyone so inclined.

p. 44   The rise of Adirondack campgrounds: The best source for tracing the rise of campgrounds in the Adirondacks is the various annual reports of New York government departments responsible for managing the Adirondacks. However, Norman J. Van Valkenburgh, *The Forest Preserve of New York State in the Adirondack and Catskill Mountains: A Short History*, rev. ed. (Fleischmanns, NY: Purple Mountain, 1996) presents a more accessible and brief narrative.

p. 44   "some tourists slept along the road": To place these Adirondack-specific concerns within a national context of cars and the outdoors (and to learn more about campground design and the automobile, and wilderness as it relates to driving), see Paul S. Sutter, *Driven Wild: How the Fight against Automobiles Launched the Modern Wilderness Movement* (Seattle: University of Washington Press, 2005). For more on camping in the United States, see Terence Young, *Heading Out: A History of American Camping* (Ithaca, NY: Cornell University Press, 2017), and Dan White, *Under the Stars: How America Fell in Love with Camping* (New York: St. Martin's, 2017).

p. 45   "clustered campsites were easier to monitor and maintain": Anzalone, *Battles of the North Country*, further explores this idea.

p. 45   "respected the intent of Forever Wild": See Anzalone, *Battles of the North Country*, especially the "City of Tents" chapter. Van Valkenburgh, *Forest Preserve*, 152, 153.

p. 45   "almost 83,000 people were turned away": For the figures in this sentence, see Van Valkenburgh, *Forest Preserve*, 211. The actual number in 1954 was 82,861.

p. 48   Loons in the Adirondacks: A good place to begin is Nina Schoch, "The Common Loon in the Adirondack Park: An Overview of Loon Natural History and Current Research" (Wildlife Conservation Society working paper no. 20, 2002). A more recent book that covers loons across a wider geographic area is James D. Paruk, *Loon Lessons: Uncommon Encounters with the Great Northern Diver* (Minneapolis: University of Minnesota Press, 2021). Also see Judith W. McIntyre, *The Common Loon: Spirit of Northern Lakes* (Minneapolis: University of Minnesota Press, 1988). For more on the specific environmental problems that threaten loons, see C. A. Spilman et al., "The Effects of Lakeshore

Development on Common Loon (*Gavia immer*) Productivity in the Adirondack Park, New York, USA," and N. Schoch et al., "The Impact of Mercury Exposure on the Common Loon (*Gavia immer*) Population in the Adirondack Park, New York, USA," *Waterbirds* 37 (Special Publication 1): 94–101; 133–46.

p. 48   "'that damned fish eater'": Elizabeth Folwell, "New Loon: How Adirondacks' Favorite Fowl Went from Vilified to Glorified," in *Short Carries: Essays from Adirondack Life* (Jay, NY: Adirondack Life, 2009), 193–98. The 1970s shooting of loons comes from Kip Taylor, "The Loon," *Adirondack Life*, Spring 1974, 30–37, 44.

p. 49   "At least one has flown to Florida": N. Schoch, D. C. Evers, and A. K. Sauer, "Restore the Call: New York Status Report for the Common Loon" (Portland, ME: Biodiversity Research Institute, 2015), 3. Available at https://www.adkloon.org/reports.

p. 50   "lead sinkers": New York has outlawed the sale of small lead sinkers, but some people still have stocks of them, and not all surrounding states have banned their sale.

p. 50   "has tracked a stable population": Schoch, "Restore the Call."

250 Adirondack Lakes, 106–33

p. 53   Good Luck Lake: See Jeptha R. Simms, *Trappers of New York* (Albany, NY: Joel Munsell, 1851), 169.

p. 53   Bisby lakes: See E. R. Wallace, *Descriptive Guide to the Adirondacks (Land of the Thousand Lakes) and to Saratoga Springs; Schroon Lake; Lakes Luzerne, George, and Champlain; the Ausable Chasm; Massena Springs; and Trenton Falls*, rev. ed. (Syracuse, NY: W. Gill, 1894), 54.

5

p. 56   Colvin: Start with Nina Webb, *Footsteps through the Adirondacks: The Verplanck Colvin Story* (Utica, NY: North Country Books, 1996). Also be sure to check out an unpublished biography, written by Joseph M. Jillisky, *What the Rocks and Mountains Tell Me: Verplanck Colvin and the Exploration of the Adirondack Mountains*. Jillisky researched Colvin extensively, including reading widely in scientific books of Colvin's era to be able to contextualize Colvin's work. The manuscript ran many hundreds of pages in length. Jillisky unfortunately died before the work was ever published. A copy is available in the archives of Adirondack Experience. (For more on Jillisky, see James M. Odato, "Mountainous Obsessions: Verplanck Colvin and his Amateur Biographer," *Adirondack Explorer*, August 13, 2021, https://www.adirondackexplorer.org/stories/the-little-known -story-of-a-driven-colvin-biographer.) I relied on Jillisky's account of Colvin as I thought my way through Colvin's contributions to Adirondack history. Beyond these two books, it's worthwhile to read Colvin's own words, both in his reports and articles and in his journals.

p. 57   "Colvin and his crew had to flee": For more on the fire, see Verplanck Colvin, *Annual Report on the Progress of the Topographical Survey of the Adirondack Region, 1874–1878* (Albany, NY: Weed, Parsons, 1880), 124.

p. 57   "named one of the computers Colvin": I had always thought this was a myth. But, according to the APA's own website, it's true. See "The 'Cart Room,'" Adirondack Park Agency, accessed February 22, 2022, https://apa.ny.gov/gis/. The source doesn't precisely say the decade in which these computers were named, but from the details provided, it was probably the 1980s or 1990s. I went with 1990s since the computers would have hung around for that long.

p. 58   "'for should the streams become frozen'": This quote appears in the entry for October 30 in Verplanck Colvin, *Report on the Topographical Survey of the Adirondack Wilderness of New York, for the Year 1873* (Albany, NY: Weed, Parsons, 1874).

p. 58   "'Gazing out upon a wealth of mountains'": Colvin, *Report on the Topographical Survey . . . for the Year 1873*, 26.

p. 59   "'splintered branch provoked some fresh displeasure'": This account of Lake Tear-of-the-Clouds can be found in Russell M. L. Carson, *Peaks and People of the Adirondacks* (Glens Falls, NY: Adirondack Mountain Club, 1973), 138.

p. 60   Colvin's map: See Jillisky, part 3; Colvin, *Annual Report . . . 1874–1878*, 105; 1872 report, 39.

p. 60   "erase and erase and erase": I'm basing this primarily on Colvin's use of reconnaissance maps and small-scale sketches and maps that were intended to inform the larger map. This seems to be the iterative drawing process on which he relied. See, for example, Colvin, *Report on the Topographical Survey . . . for the Year 1873*, 37.

p. 60   John Wesley Powell in the Adirondacks: Powell would later lead a USGS survey in the Adirondacks, which in many ways took over Colvin's work after the state cut his survey's funding. See Carson, *Peaks and People*, 220.

p. 61   "Blake had camped for thirty-seven days": See Carson, *Peaks and People*, 65.

p. 61   Colvin's office: See Jillisky's manuscript, at the start of the epilogue. Jillisky cites a letter that's found in Donaldson's notes. Despite multiple visits to the archive that houses the letters, I've never been able to find the source he cites.

p. 62   "'The desert has blossomed'": "The Wilderness," *New York Times*, August 3, 1872. "Reveling" is spelled "revelling" in the actual quote. The article also states: "Now, there was a time when the 'Adirondacks,' as the northern part of New-York State is comprehensively called, constituted a particularly howling wilderness. At all events, it sheltered a large number of wild animals, abundantly capable of howling to any desired extent."

p. 64   "Some scholars credit Colvin": Phil Terrie primary among them.

p. 64   "was dipped into 250 Adirondack lakes": The paddle and 250 lakes appear in a number of sources: Tom Lewis, *The Hudson: A History* (New Haven, CT: Yale University Press, 2005), 33, mentions Colvin exploring 250 lakes in one year, but no paddle. A 1980 *Sports Illustrated* article titled "No Landscape More Brightly Gemmed" mentions that Colvin signed the paddle on his deathbed. Most reliably, it appears in the unpublished manuscript written by Jillisky, in part 4, which unfortunately doesn't have page numbers. I also believe that the paddle is currently housed in the collections of Adirondack Experience in Blue Mountain Lake, New York.

p. 65   "the Algonquian and Haudenosaunee peoples": As mentioned earlier, see Melissa Otis, *Rural Indigenousness: A History of Iroquoian and Algonquian Peoples of the Adirondacks* (Syracuse, NY: Syracuse University Press, 2018); Curt Stager, "Hidden Heritage," *Adirondack Life*, June 2017; Lynn Woods, "A History in Fragments," *Adirondack Life*, December 1994.

p. 66   "Donaldson's book argued": Otis further explores this idea in *Rural Indigenousness*, 2.

p. 66   Mitchel Sabattis: See the very thoroughly researched material in Otis, *Rural Indigenousness*, 121–28. (My use of Mitchel rather than Mitchell is based on the usage in Otis's book.) Also see L. E. Chi Chittenden, *Personal Reminiscences Including Lincoln and*

Others (New York: Richmond, Croscup, 1894), 139–58, and Charles Brumley, *Guides of the Adirondacks: A History* (Utica, NY: North Country Books, 1994), 152–57.

250 Adirondack Lakes, 134–42

p. 70   "Only later did someone realize": Verplanck Colvin, *Annual Report on the Progress of the Topographical Survey of the Adirondack Region, 1874–1878* (Albany, NY: Weed, Parsons, 1880), 184.

p. 70   "Kwĕnōgā'mäk by the Abenaki": See J. Dyneley Price, "Forgotten Indian Place-Names in the Adirondacks," *Journal of American Folk-Lore* 13 (January–March, 1900): 126.

p. 71   "On May 9, 2015, the Crew found bolt number 180": Information on the Upper Preston Pond bolt comes from the Recovery report from the Colvin Crew, which I found on their website under the "Past Recoveries" section: http://www.colvincrew.org/.

p. 71   "Pāskāngā'mäk, which meant": See Price, "Forgotten Indian Place-Names," 125, 126.

p. 71   "Colvin and his guides lucked out": Colvin, *Annual Report . . . 1874–1878*, 146–48.

p. 71   Moss Lake: There's a sequence of articles in the *New York Times* that covers the episode at Moss Lake between August 19, 1974, and October 25, 1981. This quote is from Richard Severo, "Mohawks Fight to Regain Land," *New York Times*, July 6, 1975. The image of the sign appears in Sam Howe Verhovek, "Standoff Ends, but Not Mohawk Defiance," *New York Times*, April 14, 1990.

p. 72   "shivering in the breezes of the mountains": See Verplanck Colvin, *Report on a Topographical Survey of the Adirondack Wilderness of New York*, March 10, 1873, 40. On Lake Tear of the Clouds: See Russel Carson, *Peaks and People of the Adirondacks* (Glens Falls, NY: Adirondack Mountain Club, 1973), 138–44; *Heaven Up-h'isted-ness! The History of the Adirondack Forty-Sixers and the High Peaks of the Adirondacks* (Cadyville, NY: Adirondack Forty-Sixers, 2011), 178; Colvin, *Annual Report . . . 1874–1878;* and Colvin, *Report on a Topographical Survey* (1872).

6

p. 73   Blue Line: Some sources say the line was first drawn in 1891 but then the map was published in 1892. See Norman J. Van Valkenburgh, *The Forest Preserve of New York State in the Adirondack and Catskill Mountains: A Short History*, rev. ed. (Fleischmanns, NY: Purple Mountain, 1996), 49. For more on the Blue Line, see Barbara McMartin, "The Thin Blue Line: Tracing the History of a Problematic Perimeter," *Adirondack Life*, February 1994, 16. The Blue Line almost was red. The Red Line would have bounded more of the wild forest that remained in northern New York. Logging interests made sure the Blue Line was chosen, leaving more trees for them to cut and float downstream to the mills. Which is what they did, according to McMartin's essay.

p. 74   "a tale of the past fifty years": *The Future of the Adirondacks: The Reports of the Temporary Study Commission on the Future of the Adirondacks* (Blue Mountain Lake, NY: Adirondack Museum, 1971), 37. The report states there were no signs along many roads, and that people might start to recognize they were in the Adirondacks if signs existed.

p. 75   "to brown with yellow words": See *Adirondack Life*, May/June 1978, 7. As the blurb in *Adirondack Life* says, this change in sign design required a variance from the Federal Highway Administration.

p. 75   "Highway departments are replacing them": See "Guidelines for the Adirondack Park," published by the New York State Department of Transportation Engineering Division. In appendix L, there's a section titled "Aesthetic Guide Rail Treatment" that includes details on replacing rustic guide rails. Also, various local news sources first carried the story of the guide rails failing and creating a safety hazard.

p. 76 *"use color schemes harmonious with natural environments"*: The Adirondack Park in the *Twenty-First Century* (State of New York, Commission on the Adirondacks in the Twenty-First Century, 1990). For more context, it's worthwhile to take a look at "Strengthening the APA: Ideas for a Better Adirondack Park" (2014), a special publication from *Adirondack Explorer*, available at https://www.adirondackexplorer.org/apa_book.

p. 77 Lake Luzerne: See Lester St. John Thomas, *Timber, Tannery, and Tourists: Lake Luzerne, Warren County, New York* (Lake Luzerne, NY: Committee on Publication of Local History, 1979).

p. 78 "first became a popular thing for Americans to do": On the origins of American tourism, see John F. Sears, *Sacred Places: American Tourist Attractions in the Nineteenth Century* (New York: Oxford University Press, 1989). On the development of early tourism more specifically in Lake George, see Theodore Corbett, "The Reluctant Resort: Caldwell on Lake George," in *The Making of American Resorts: Saratoga Springs, Ballston Spa, and Lake George* (New Brunswick, NJ: Rutgers University Press, 2001).

p. 78 "example of what the entire region might soon become": Supporters of regional planning held an exhibit with photographs of Lake George. See Frank Graham Jr., *The Adirondack Park: A Political History* (New York: Alfred A. Knopf, 1978), 239.

p. 79 "Some call it the first motel built in the Adirondacks": I first saw this claim in Lynn Woods, "An Adirondack Auto Biography," *Adirondack Life*, May/June 1996.

7

p. 83 White Pine Camp: A good place to start is Howard Kirschenbaum, *White Pine Camp: The Saga of an Adirondack Great Camp and Summer White House* (Keeseville, NY: Adirondack Architectural Heritage, 2018). Further sources include the wonderful guided tours that are offered at White Pine Camp during the summer months; "By Mountainside and Lake . . . ," *New York Times*, July 4, 1909; "Large House Party Given at the House of Archibald White in the Adirondacks," *New York Times*, July 11, 1911; and at White Pine Camp, in the guest rooms, a self-published collection of stories from the camp. (As far as I can tell, that volume isn't available anywhere else.) During the summer of 2020, a fire destroyed some of the buildings at White Pine Camp. They're currently being rebuilt.

p. 83 Brainstorm: Much of this history comes from Tom Henry and Howard Kirschenbaum, "Siding with Tradition: The Real Story behind a Staple of Adirondack Style," *Adirondack Life*, 2005 Collectors Issue, 6–11.

p. 84 "the term 'brainstorm' was hot in the news": On the murder, see "Thaw Reaches Danger Point," *New York Times*, February 19, 1907, 1; "Thaw Murders Stanford White," *New York Times*, June 26, 1906, 1; "The Girl, the Swing and a Row House in Ruins," *New York Times*, November 4, 2007, 6. That "brainstorm" was hot in the news appears in Henry and Kirschenbaum, "Siding with Tradition." Here's more on the murder and the rise of "brainstorm" at the trial: Harry Thaw, the son of a rich Pittsburgh family, killed Stanford White on the rooftop garden theater of the second Madison Square Garden, a building Stanford had designed. Thaw killed White near the end of *Mamzelle Champagne*, a musical comedy. In response to the murder, the manager of the show apparently yelled, "Go on playing! Bring on that chorus!" One witness described Thaw before the shooting as "on the verge of delirium tremens." Thaw had tried to have White brought to justice for seducing and maybe assaulting young women, including Thaw's wife, Evelyn Nesbit, but Thaw claimed to have had no desire to kill White until the moment he shot him. Thaw pleaded that a temporary episode of insanity, a brainstorm, had caused him to commit the murder. At the first trial, the jury couldn't reach a verdict. In the second trial, Thaw was declared not guilty by reason of insanity. Sent to a mental institution, he later escaped, fled to Canada, and was then extradited back to the United States. In 1915, he was declared sane and set free. For the first jury, see "In the Jury Room by Juror No. 6," *New York Times*, April 13, 1907. On the second, see "Thaw Lays Killing to a 'Brainstorm,'" *New York Times*, July 30, 1909, 1. For remainder of story, see "Thaw Wins Fight for Jury Test," *New York Times*, June 19, 1915, 18; and "Thaw, Free, Flirts with the Old Life as Mother Waits," *New York Times*, July 17, 1915, 1.

p. 84 "'amid an elaborate pyrotechnic display'": This quote is from "Paul Smith's: Sylvan Play Produced amid Sylvan Surroundings," *New York Times*, July 11, 1909.

p. 84 On the holdup: See "Desperate Coach Hold-Up," *New York Times,* July 21, 1912.

p. 84 On the wider context of White Americans pretending to be Indians: See Philip J. Deloria, *Playing Indian* (New Haven, CT: Yale University Press, 1999).

p. 86 "No one paid them much attention": For a good review of when Great Camps became a popular category (and the various ways in which the state and private organizations have sought to purchase or preserve them) see chapter 10, "State Stewardship," in Robert Engel, Howard Kirschenbaum, and Paul Malo, *Santanoni: From Japanese Temple to Life at an Adirondack Great Camp*, 2nd ed. (Utica, NY: North Country Books, 2009).

p. 86 Great Camps: The literature is extensive. If you want to learn about a specific Great Camp, turning to the organization that owns that camp—if the camp still survives—is sometimes the best bet, because often there are site-specific interpretive brochures (or even on-site tours) that offer a level of detail not present in wider studies. Depending on the site, there could be a National Historic Landmark application/report available, which will typically offer extensive building-by-building histories of a site. Many of these are available online. For more of an overview of Great Camps, the best place to begin is Harvey H. Kaiser, *Great Camps of the Adirondacks* (Boston: David R. Godine, 2020)—as well as the earlier, 1982/1990 version of that book—and Gladys Montgomery, *An Elegant Wilderness: Great Camps and Grand Lodges of the Adirondacks* (New York: Acanthus, 2011). Although I've been told that, in places, Montgomery's book is unreliable, the images alone are worth the time to read the entire thing.

p. 86 "'it looked more like an Adirondack Great Camp'": See *Adirondack Explorer*, Holiday Issue 1998, 3. The article continues: "Preliminary plans for the store sported a New England-style clapboard exterior. 'Not for us,' said the [village planning] board. 'This is the Adirondacks.'"

p. 87 Pine Knot: There's some debate over whether his father started Pine Knot and William West Durant took over in 1877, or if it was all along the younger Durant's idea. Sources for Pine Knot and Durant include Craig Gilborn, *Durant: The Fortunes and Woodland Camps of a Family in the Adirondacks* (Sylvan Beach, NY: North Country Books; Blue Mountain Lake, NY: Adirondack Museum, 1981); and "Camp Pine Knot National Historic Landmark Nomination," United States Department of the Interior, National Park Service. I've also relied on the photographic collections of Pine Knot in the Adirondack Experience photograph archives.

p. 87 "shows him descending a wooden staircase": The photograph on which this description is based was taken by well-known Adirondack photographer Seneca Ray Stoddard, probably in 1890. It appears as figure 47 in Gilborn, *Durant*, and is reproduced in the photo gallery in this volume.

p. 88 "the resort of the future": This is quoted in Gilborn, *Durant*, 5.

p. 88 "even the half he had stolen from his sister": When Durant's father died in 1885 and when Durant sold his father's railroad and land, he robbed his sister, Heloise "Ella" Durant Rose, of her share. When she later sued Durant, she rightly won. Durant owed her $754,000, one-third of a fortune he had already spent making the wilderness into a resort. For the $754,000 figure see Harold K. Hochschild, *Life and Leisure in the Adirondack Backwoods* (Blue Mountain Lake, NY: Adirondack Museum, 1962), 62.

p. 91 "'. . . I have it yet to hear about'": Quote is from Fannie B. Merrill, "Life at Paul Smith's," in *Forest and Stream*, June 18, 1891, 433. There's an 1890 date in the author's signature at the end, which is why I'm dating Smith's quote to that year.

p. 91 "Paul Smith's wasn't above boasting": This quote comes from an ad on page iv of the *New-York Daily Tribune*, June 4, 1911. The headline of the page is "THE ADIRONDACKS, A SUMMER PARADISE."

p. 92 "advertising a brand of whiskey": The whiskey story is from an article, "Paul Smith's Whiskey," that appeared in the *Malone Palladium*, July 19, 1906, 1. It seems that the story was printed widely across New York, and that it first appeared in the *Tupper Lake Herald*. That he sought damages is from page 1 of the *Adirondack News*, St. Regis Falls, July 21, 1906. Resolution of this lawsuit appears in *Norwood News*, December 25, 1906, 1; and then in other papers at later dates. All these newspaper sources I found through the website NYS Historic Newspapers.

p. 92 "'when he died they were full of millionaires'": This is from the *Evening Post*, December 16, 1912, 6, though it's also a commonly seen quote in many other sources on Paul Smith and the Great Camps.

p. 93 Paul Smith's Electric Railway: Distances and timeline of train connections and Paul Smith's Electric Railway come from William Gove, *Logging Railroads of the Adirondacks* (Syracuse, NY: Syracuse University Press, 2006), 138. For greater detail, see the section on Paul Smith's Electric Railway in Michael Kudish, *Where Did the Tracks Go in the Central Adirondacks?* (Fleischmanns, NY: Purple Mountain, 2007), 493–99.

p. 93 Paul Smith: Most of the details in what I've written come from articles from Paul Smith's era, of which there are too many to list. For some, see below notes on Hunter's Home. Also see Geraldine Collins, *The Biography and Funny Sayings of Paul Smith* (Paul Smiths, NY: Paul Smith's College, 1965).

p. 93 Hunter's Home: Most of these details come from Zab. Boylston Adams, "The Sportsman Tourist: The Adirondacks in 1853, a Story Told by Paul Smith," *Forest and Stream*, October 22, 1891, 266; "Life on the St. Regis Lake," *New York Evangelist*, August 17, 1876; "Shooting in the Adirondack," *All the Year Round*, September 29, 1860; "Paul Smith's Hotel," *New-York Tribune*, June 15, 1902; "Paul Smith's: The Great Pleasure Park of the Adirondacks on the St. Regis Lakes," *New-York Tribune*, June 12, 1898; Harold D. Leslie Sr., "Apollos (Paul) Smith: A Yankee Guide for High Society," *New York State Conservationist*, December–January 1965–66, 6–9. I've seen the establishment's name written as both "The Hunter's Home" and "Hunter's Home."

p. 94 "Paul Smith kicked out an encampment": Curt Stager, "Hidden Heritage," *Adirondack Life*, June 2017.

p. 94   Lydia Smith: See Peggy Lynn and Sandra Weber, *Breaking Trail: Remarkable Women of the Adirondacks* (Fleischmanns, NY: Purple Mountain, 2004), 28.

p. 95   "It's still known for both": Yet—it almost got a different name. In 2015, a donor, Joan Weill, offered to give the financially struggling college a $20 million gift. Weill and her husband, Sanford, owned a camp nearby and had already given the school gifts for a library and a student center. The new gift required the school to change its name to Joan Weill–Paul Smith's College. The school was in favor of the change but the original donation by the Smith family said the school had to forever keep Paul Smith's as its name. A judge ruled against the school, and it's still called Paul Smith's. See "College Will Get $20 Million, If It Changes Its Name," *New York Times*, August 18, 2015.

8

p. 97   "'Am I going to sue the bastards?'": See Phil Brown, "If It Floats Is It a Boat?" *Adirondack Explorer*, July/August 2007, 4.

p. 97   "A steamboat, from Durant's era": See Harold K. Hochschild, *Adirondack Steamboats on Raquette and Blue Mountain Lakes* (Blue Mountain Lake, NY: Adirondack Museum, 1962).

p. 97   "*$120,000—Great hunting camp*": The camp descriptions presented here in italics are slightly modified (for length) entries found in Adirondack real estate catalogs.

p. 99   "The apogee of Adirondack rustic": See Gladys Montgomery, *An Elegant Wilderness: Great Camps and Grand Lodges of the Adirondacks* (New York: Acanthus, 2011), 217.

p. 99   "A ten-and-a-half-foot-tall plate glass window": Fifteen workers installed the window. A sonic boom from an Air Force jet later shattered the window, and the federal government sent Post a $3,600 check. See Harvey H. Kaiser, *Great Camps of the Adirondacks* (Boston: David R. Godine, 1990), 213.

p. 99   "usually once every few years": See Evelyn Farley, "Working in a Camp on Upper St. Regis Lake," *Franklin Historical Review* 20 (1983).

p. 99   "Two maids spent four hours": See Montgomery, *Elegant Wilderness*.

p. 99   "three moving vans hauled": See Craig Gilborn, *Adirondack Camps: Homes Away from Home, 1850–1950* (Syracuse, NY: Syracuse University Press, 2000), 181.

p. 99   Topridge and Jakubowski: See Harold Faber, "State Sells Its Lavish Camp in Adirondacks for $911,000," *New York Times*, August 1, 1985; and Harold Faber, "'Great Camp' in Adirondacks Is Passing into Private Hands," *New York Times*, November 14, 1985. In the second article, Jakubowski is quoted as saying, "Look at me, a Polish kid from Camden. It's unbelievable." Also see Gilborn, *Adirondack Camps*, 305.

p. 99   Idems and the St. Regis Yacht Club: See Hallie Bond, *Boats and Boating in the Adirondacks* (Syracuse, NY: Syracuse University Press, 1998), 134–35. There's more information available in the archives of Adirondack Experience.

p. 100   "to the stern attached a wooden hot dog": See "Our Towns: Upper St. Regis," *Adirondack Life*, July/August 2005, 12.

p. 100   "'I should own the entire Adirondack Park, that's what I think'": Quote is from James Howard Kunstler, "The Man Who Would Be King: Roger Jakubowski's Dream of an Adirondack Empire," *Adirondack Life*, October 1987, 40.

250 Adirondack Lakes, 143

p. 101   "'Then, almost as by magic'": This quote appears in "A Night-Hunt in the Adirondacs [*sic*]," *Putnam's Monthly*, August 1868. It also appears in Burroughs's *Wake-Robin* (New York: Houghton, Mifflin, 1887), which says that the journey took place in 1863.

9

p. 102   Adirondack Loj: See Sandra Weber, *The Finest Square Mile: Mount Jo and Heart Lake* (Fleischmanns, NY: Purple Mountain, 2003).

p. 103   "They call themselves the Adirondack 46ers": How they spell it, though, varies. Most people seem to prefer Adirondack 46ers, but sometimes it's Adirondack 46rs or even ADK 46ers. According to the club's articles of organization (printed in *Adirondack Peeks* Fall/Winter 1963/1964), the group should officially be called the Adirondack 46ers, but sometimes they refer to themselves as the Adirondack Forty-Sixers, and they also refer to the whole of the club and its members as the forty-sixers or 46ers informally. On top of that, the club was originally referred to as the Forty-Sixers or the Forty-Sixers of Troy, New York, and only later became the Adirondack 46ers.

p. 104   "serves forty-six types of sandwiches": It's called Big Mountain Deli and Creperie and is in Lake Placid.

p. 104   Bob Marshall's Adirondack explorations: See Phil Brown, "Bob Marshall: Wilderness Advocate," in *Adirondack Archangels: Guardians of the High Peaks*, ed. Christine Bourjade and Alex Radmanovich (Lake George, NY: Adirondack Mountain Club, 2016), 41–48; and Phil Brown, ed., *Bob Marshall in the Adirondacks: Writings of a Pioneering Peak-Bagger, Pond-Hopper, and Wilderness Preservationist* (Saranac Lake, NY: Lost Pond, 2006).

p. 104   "might have been inspired to hike the peaks": Marshall's father owned a copy of an early Colvin report, shelved in the library of the Marshall family's Adirondack camp, Knollwood. See *Heaven Up-h'isted-ness! The History of the Adirondack Forty-Sixers and the High Peaks of the Adirondacks* (Cadyville, NY: Adirondack Forty-Sixers, 2011), 16.

p. 104   "Marshall wrote a short book": *The High Peaks of the Adirondacks* ([Albany, NY]: Adirondack Mountain Club, 1922). It's reprinted in Brown, *Bob Marshall in the Adirondacks*.

p. 104   For another account of the High Peaks in the 1920s: See Robert S. Wickham, *Friendly Adirondack Peaks* ([Binghamton, NY]: Adirondack Mountain Club, 1924).

p. 104   "to find medicinal plants": Melissa Otis, *Rural Indigenousness: A History of Iroquoian and Algonquian Peoples of the Adirondacks* (Syracuse, NY: Syracuse University Press, 2018), 47.

p. 104   "his book is the founding document": *Heaven Up'histed-ness*, 27.

p. 104   "The trio founded the club": *Heaven Up'histed-ness*, 33, notes that the first mention of the Forty-Sixers was in a newspaper in 1937.

p. 104   For more on the High Peaks: A good place to begin to dig deeper into the High Peaks and the region's history is *Heaven Up'histed-ness*. Russell M. L. Carson, *Peaks and People of the Adirondacks* (1927; repr. Glens Falls, NY: Adirondack Mountain Club, 1973), also offers much historical information, even though it was written almost a century ago. The Forty-Sixers and/or the Adirondack Mountain Club have created a series of self-published, comprehensive histories of the area. I found the 1970 one, *The Adirondack High Peaks*, to be quite helpful. Details on these publications can be found in the early pages of *Heaven Up'histed-ness*. It's also worthwhile to take a look at the Forty-Sixers' official publication, *Adirondack Peeks*. The magazine offers good insights into the 1960s and 1970s damage on the peaks and trails. In particular, see the spring issue of 1966, page 4, for more on the existential crisis I mention, though issues from the '60s and '70s also offer an important record of it.

p. 105   "New York didn't make much of an effort": Some of this timeline I'm drawing from *Heaven Up'histed-ness* and some is from "Technical Report 5, Recreation," in *The Future of the Adirondacks: The Reports of the Temporary Study Commission on the Future of the Adirondacks* (Blue Mountain Lake, NY: Adirondack Museum, 1971). Also see Philip G. Terrie, *Contested Terrain: A New History of Nature and People in the Adirondacks*, 2nd ed. (Syracuse, NY: Syracuse University Press, 2008), 126.

p. 105   "private organizations blazed routes": See Karen Doman, "The Adirondack Trail Improvement Society: 118 Years and Counting," in Bourjade and Radmanovich, *Adirondack Archangels*, 233–38.

p. 105   "just above 13,000": Number of 46ers comes from 46ers official website, which keeps an updated list: https://adk46er.org.

p. 106   "The rack included brochures": This bit on the brochure is in *Adirondack Peeks*, Fall 1964.

p. 108   "And yet it caught on": *Heaven Up-h'isted-ness*, 159.

p. 108   Grace Hudowalski: A good introduction is the documentary *The Mountains Will Wait for You*, 2013. It must have been filmed and created earlier, based on the aspect ratio, the people interviewed, and the quality of the footage, as well as the surprising fact that Johnny Cash narrates a portion. Also see Peggy Lynn and Sandra Weber, *Breaking Trail: Remarkable Women of the Adirondacks* (Fleischmanns, NY: Purple Mountain, 2004), 123–29.

p. 108   "pale-blue-and-white-checked shorts": Hudowalski's shorts are in the collection of the Adirondack Experience, Blue Mountain Lake, New York.

p. 109   Esther McComb: Sandra Webb, *The Lure of Esther Mountain, Matriarch of the Adirondack High Peaks* (Purple Mountain, 1995). Also see *Heaven Up-h'isted-ness*, 557–63.

p. 109   Noah John Rondeau: See *Heaven Up'histed-ness*, 45–47; Maitland C. De Sormo, *Noah John Rondeau: Adirondack Hermit* (Saranac Lake, NY: North Country Books, 1969); and William J. O'Hern, *Noah John Rondeau's Adirondack Wilderness Days* (Cleveland, NY: Forager, 2009). There's a letter that says Hudowalski climbed "Couchee [Couchsachraga]" from Cold River in *Heaven Up'histed-ness*, 41.

p. 110   "'occupied a hole in a woodpile'": Quote is from an article by Clayt Seagear, "The Hermit of Cold River," which is reprinted in De Sormo, *Noah John Rondeau*, xii–xvi.

p. 110   "was only decoded in the 1990s": See O'Hern, *Noah John Rondeau's Adirondack Wilderness Days*, especially chapter 3, "The Scratchings of an Inebriated Hen," and chapter 5, "Decoded."

p. 110   Whiteface toll road: See Jonathan D. Anzalone, "A Mountain to Climb," in *Battles of the North Country: Wilderness Politics and Recreational Development in the Adirondack State Park, 1920–1980* (Amherst: University of Massachusetts Press, 2018).

p. 111   William Nye: Most of this information on Nye comes from *Heaven Up-h'isted-ness*, 337. That source is confirmed by Charles Brumley, *Guides of the Adirondacks: A History* (Utica, NY: North Country Books, 1994), 140–41, and Mary MacKenzie and Lee Manchester, *The Plains of Abraham: A History of North Elba and Lake Placid* (Utica, NY: Nicholas K. Burns, 2007), 194–95. Frémont's expedition: See David Roberts, *A Newer World: Kit Carson,*

John C. Fremont, and the Claiming of the American West (New York: Simon and Schuster, 2001).

p. 111   "'from all parts of the civilized world'": Phelps's obituary is reprinted in *The High Peaks of Essex: The Adirondack Mountains of Orson Schofield Phelps*, ed. Orson Schofield Phelps and Bill Healy (Purple Mountain, 1992), 101. The book mostly consists of a found manuscript of a book Phelps wrote about (mostly) the High Peaks. For more on Phelps see Annie Stoltie, "An Adirondack Icon Revealed," *Adirondack Life* (December 2011).

p. 111   "there was a kegger": Mike Lynch, "Hiker Ticketed after Keg Party atop Adirondack High Peak," *Adirondack Explorer*, October 14, 2015, https://www.adirondackalmanack.com /2015/10/hiker-ticketed-by-dec-after-keg-party-on-phelps.html. The 46er received a ticket but not for the keg. He was issued a ticket by the state because he was part of a group that exceeded the size of a group allowed in the wilderness area.

p. 111   Adirondack Mountain Reserve: See Edith Pilcher, *Up the Lake Road: The First Hundred Years of the Adirondack Mountain Reserve* (Centennial Committee for the Trustees of the Adirondack Mountain Reserve, 1987).

p. 113   "summit patches of tundra-like plants": The exact acreage is hard to pin down, likely based on different methods of measurements and also because, faced with a warming climate, the area is changing. In the 1980s and 1990s it was thought to be 85 acres. There was even a guidebook published in 1993 titled *85 Acres: A Field Guide to the Adirondack Alpine Summits*. The more recent edition of the guidebook drops the number and is called *Adirondack Alpine Summits: An Ecological Field Guide*. In *Adirondack Archangels*, 30, it says there are 173 acres. The most reliable estimate, in my opinion, is in Bradley Z. Carlson, Jeffrey S. Munroe, and Bill Hegman, "Distribution of Alpine Tundra in the Adirondack Mountains of New York, U.S.A.," *Arctic, Antarctic, and Alpine Research* 43 (2011): 331–42. Their estimate was 65 acres. This study relied on GIS delineated polygons that were recorded during field visits to twenty peaks, but the study didn't include Whiteface because it considered the alpine environment there to be too disturbed by human activities and structures. Which is a fair point. So, between all these sources, and with some vegetation still recovering from pre-Ketchledge days of hiker trampling, and maybe some areas of the alpine zone being conquered by trees because of rising temperatures, my best guess is that it's somewhere between 65 acres and 75 acres. On the role of climate change on alpine plants, see the discussion on page 340 of the above-mentioned "Distribution of Alpine Tundra."

p. 113   "or traveled back in time ten thousand years": There are many sources on regional vegetation history. I really like Donald R. Whitehead and Stephen T. Jackson, *The Regional Vegetational History of the High Peaks* (Adirondack Mountains) New York (Albany: New York State Museum, 1990).

p. 113   "Similar plant communities can be found elsewhere": For a wonderful collection of writing and information about alpine areas in the East, see Mike Jones and Liz Willey, eds., *Eastern Alpine Guide: Natural History and Conservation of Mountain Tundra East of the Rockies* (Hanover, NH: University Press of New England, 2018).

p. 114   Edwin Ketchledge: Ketchledge actively worked on the project for so long that there's a very broad and informed literature to draw from for both his work and his life. Here's a selection of what I found the most helpful: Bourjade and Radmanovich, *Adirondack Archangels*, has a number of chapters either written by Ketchledge or written about Ketchledge and his work, including a few chapters written by his children and another chapter written by a scientist who has continued some of Ketchledge's work; Sandra Weber, "Savior of the Summits," *Adirondack Explorer*, July 1999, 20–21, 31; Tony Goodwin, "Savior of the High Peaks, *Adirondack Explorer*, September–October 2010, 31; E. H. Ketchledge et al., "Rehabilitation of Alpine Vegetation in the Adirondack Mountains of New York State," United States Department of Agriculture (Forest Service) publication, Research Paper NE-553, 1985; "Adirondack Insights: The Sensitive Summits," *Adirondac*, August 1982, 20; "Adirondack Insights: Summit Stability," *Adirondac*, December 1982, 22; and "Adirondack Insights: The Alpine Flora," *Adirondac*, June 1984, 17. A more recent review of the areas that Ketch worked to restore can be found in Sean C. Robinson, "A 23-Year Assessment of Vegetation Composition and Change in the Adirondack Alpine Zone, New York State," *Rhodora: Journal of the New England Botanical Club* 112 (2010): 355–77. (As an interesting side note for people who read broadly in environmental literature, Robin Wall Kimmerer, author of the excellent *Braiding Sweetgrass*, is a coauthor for that paper.) Also, the Adirondack Park Agency has a 2011 presentation online, titled "Adirondack Alpine Ecology," which shows many Before restoration and After restoration photos of High Peaks. Also worth looking at, for information on the stability of alpine plant communities when there is little or no disturbance from hiker traffic: E. H. Ketchledge and R. E. Leonard, "A 24-Year Comparison of the Vegetation of an Adirondack Mountain Summit," *Rhodora: Journal of the New England Botanical Club* 86 (October 1984): 439–44.

p. 114 "Over the next three decades": On Ketch working on the summits for three decades, see Bourjade and Radmanovich, *Adirondack Archangels*, 12. On half of the alpine zone being seeded like a garden, see James Grant, "Tundra on the Top," *Adirondack Life*, July/August 1987, 52–57.

p. 114 "Ketch didn't like that": For Ketch's thoughts on visiting these summits, see "The Four Rewards of Visiting Alpine Summits," in Bourjade and Radmanovich, *Adirondack Archangels*.

p. 115 History of Summit Steward program: See Bourjade and Radmanovich, *Adirondack Archangels*, 46–66.

p. 115 "600,000 conversations": This statistic is from a post on the official Facebook page of the Adirondack Mountain Club, July 16, 2021.

10

p. 118 "the Fools thought it was a thing they should do": I'm basing this idea, that Murray's Fools shot at loons, on a comment from Nessmuk, who would later ask his readers, beg them, actually, to not follow Murray's example of shooting at loons. Maybe it was precautionary, but I'm guessing he had heard stories or seen people do it. See George Washington Sears, *Canoeing the Adirondacks with Nessmuk: The Adirondack Letters of George Washington Sears* (Syracuse, NY: Syracuse University Press, 1993), 155.

p. 120 "Long Lake was the largest settlement": For more on this time in Long Lake, visit the Long Lake Public Library. They have a number of unpublished documents. Settlers had cleared 744 acres by 1855, most of it cut for hay to feed animals. In 1844, there were eighteen families; between 1844 and the Civil War, some of the families left. For other early views of Long Lake, see Joel Headley, *The Adirondack: Or, Life in the Woods* (1861) and John Todd, *Long Lake* (1845).

p. 121 "When Hoss's Country Corner needed more space": At Hoss's, there's a binder of photographs that show the entire progress of how the tree has changed through time. If you ask *really* nicely at the counter, and the day isn't too busy, sometimes they'll share it with you.

p. 121   "'the best rendezvous of the wilderness'": This is in Murray, *Adventures in the Wilderness* (1869), 47.

p. 123   On the most remote spot in the Adirondacks: I'm relying on the work done by Remote Footprints. See https://remotefootprints.org/. The Adirondack Park Agency has also published a map that shows areas of the Adirondacks that are more than three miles from a road.

11

p. 126   Roadside firewood stands: The history of roadside firewood sales in the Adirondacks was difficult to trace. Although I was never able to speak to anyone who sold firewood, I talked to a bunch of locals and campground forest rangers; each offered fragments of the story. Everyone agreed that there has always been a market for firewood—for at least as long as they had been alive—and most people agreed that in the past decade or so, since invasive species have become a more prominent issue and the regulations more regularly enforced, more and more campwood stands have popped up along the roads.

12

p. 130   "unofficially modified a yellow diamond road": New York has since repaved Route 28 and, unfortunately, replaced all the rustic guide rails.

p. 130   Fulton Chain steamboats and Route 28: See Charles Herr, *The Fulton Chain: Early Settlements, Roads, Steamboats, Railroads, and Hotels* (Utica, NY: North Country Books, 2017).

p. 132   "white cloth napkins curled into cones": This description comes from a photograph taken by Henry Beach around 1910 that's currently in Adirondack Experience's collection, photograph # P002397, which can be found on their online database at http://adirondack .pastperfectonline.com.

p. 133   Bald Mountain House and why it transitioned to Bald Mountain Colony: See the vertical files of the Goodsell Museum, Old Forge, New York.

p. 136   The Woods Inn/The Wood: For more on this building, see Herr, *Fulton Chain*, and Bruce P. Bonfield, *Fourth Lake Early Camps and Hotels* (Utica, NY: North Country Books), 2016. For more on the recent rehab of the hotel, see Lee Manchester, "Historic Adirondack Inns," in *Adirondack Heritage: Travels through Time in New York's North Country* (available online). For more on the recent history of the hotel, see Jane Mackintosh, "Wood Turners," *Adirondack Life*, 2005 Collectors Issue, 64–69.

p. 140   Brown's Tract mud: see Kenneth Durant and Helen Durant, *The Adirondack Guide-Boat* (Blue Mountain Lake, NY: Adirondack Museum, 2015), 145.

13

p. 146   "the Adirondacks as a healthful and adventurous but safe": For a more contextualized look at this idea, see Daegan Miller, *This Radical Land: A Natural History of American Dissent* (Chicago: University of Chicago Press, 2018).

p. 147   "fire departments and emergency services": The point about emergency services is a problem I encountered while talking to people in the region. On February 22, 2022, North Country Public Radio ran a story that digs a bit deeper into an instance of this issue as well as a glance at causes. "This rural EMT says that 'no career path' is holding back the North Country EMS workforce." Further, in early 2022, Big Moose, a village not far from Old Forge, shuttered its all-volunteer ambulance company due to a lack of volunteers.

p. 148 "becoming even less diverse": I was first made aware by these two stories: Peter Nelson, "Racial and Socioeconomic Diversity and the Adirondacks," *Adirondack Almanack*, January 11, 2014, https://www.adirondackalmanack.com/2014/01/hidden -adirondack-issue-racial-socioeconomic-diversity.html; and Pete Nelson, "Diversity and the Adirondacks: A Demographic Stasis, *Adirondack Almanack*, February 1, 2014, https://www .adirondackalmanack.com/2014/02/diversity-adirondacks-demographic-stasis.html.

p. 148 "The radio story recounted a racist incident": This story can be found at Brian Mann, "Are Black Visitors Really Welcome in the Adirondack Park?," North Country Public Radio, August 26, 2016, https://www.northcountrypublicradio.org/news/story/32452/20160826 /are-black-visitors-really-welcome-in-the-adirondack-park. Also see Brian Mann, "Nearly Half of Adirondack Tourists Could Be People of Color," North Country Public Radio, August 29, 2016, https://www.northcountrypublicradio.org/news/story/32460/20160829 /nearly-half-of-adirondack-tourists-could-be-people-of-color.

p. 148 "less than 1 percent identified as Black or African American": The survey is titled "Leisure Travel Study—Lake Placid, Essex and Hamilton Counties, Saranac Lake, and Tupper Lake; 2021 County Visitor Profiles & Regional Return on Marketing Investment Analysis". and was released in July 2022 by the Regional Office of Sustainable Tourism, Lake Placid, New York.

250 Adirondack Lakes, 144–244

p. 151 Burke's: Some of this stuff on Burke's is from talking to Kris Burke; some is from Ruth Timm, *Raquette Lake: A Time to Remember* (Utica, NY: North Country Books, 1989), 103; some is from postcards Kris's grandfather printed that people local to the area have shown me.

p. 152 "the club reeled in only 109 pounds": Ted Aber and Stella King, *The History of Hamilton County* (Lake Pleasant, NY: Great Wilderness Books, 1965), 194.

p. 152 "couldn't part them to take a swim": Barbara McMartin, *Caroga: An Adirondack Town Recalls Its Past*, 2nd ed. (Caroga, NY: Lake View, 1998), 239.

p. 153 "The pilot missed": McMartin, *Caroga*, 239.

p. 153 Acid rain in the Adirondacks: See Jerry Jenkins et al., *Acid Rain in the Adirondacks: An Environmental History* (Ithaca, NY: Comstock, 2007).

p. 153 The record numbers and story both come from "Record Brook Trout Caught in Adirondack Wilderness Area," *Adirondack Almanack*, May 30, 2013, https://www .adirondackalmanack.com/2013/05/record-brook-trout-caught-in-adirondack-wilderness -area.html.

p. 153 "invasive species that Upper Saranac Lake doesn't yet have": At the time I'm writing this, inspections are still voluntary across most of the Adirondacks, though there have been efforts to make them compulsory within the Blue Line.

p. 153 "One boat had carried curly-leaf pondweed": See Adirondack Watershed Institute's website (http://www.adkwatershed.org/invasive-species/ais-prevention-program/aispp -inspections) as well as the reports listed on that site, one of which was a 2018 report for the year 2017 of this boat launch.

p. 153 On hydrilla: Brendon Quirion, executive director of the Adirondack Park Invasive Plant Program, said, "Hydrilla is considered by many to be the Godzilla of aquatic invasive plants.

It is probably one of the most . . . pernicious aquatic invasive plants on the planet." This quote comes from Pat Bradley, "Boat Stewards Prevent Aggressive Aquatic Invasive from Entering Upper Saranac Lake," WAMC, Northeast Public Radio, August 3, 2017.

p. 154 *"This vast Tract of Land"*: Karen Ann Dietz, "A Home in the Woods: Summer Life in the Adirondacks" (PhD diss., University of Pennsylvania, 1992), 254; Philip Terrie, *Wildlife and Wilderness: A History of Adirondack Mammals* (Fleischmanns, NY: Purple Mountain, 1993), 41.

p. 154 Waterways named after Beaver: Many of these are from my own observations, but also see Murray Heller, *Call Me Adirondack* (Saranac Lake, NY: Chauncy, 1989), 126.

p. 154 "One reason for the dearth of Beaver Lakes": On the history of Adirondack beavers, see Cheryl Lyn Dybas, "Appetite for Construction," *Adirondack Life*, March/April 2001, 61–67.

p. 154 "might have been one million or so beavers": This guestimate is from Harry V. Radford, *Artificial Preservation of Timber and History of the Adirondack Beaver* (Albany, NY: J. B. Lyon, 1908). Despite some relief from the discovery of an alternate source of felt, the nutria or coypu, in South America, and changing hat fashion, the population of Adirondack beavers continued to fall even as numbers started to bottom out.

p. 154 "One hotel owner released a Canadian beaver": He had to try three times: Local camp owners deemed the first beaver a pest and shot it. The hotel owner got another beaver. This one swam down the AuSable River to AuSable Forks, outside the Blue Line at the time, where the beaver attracted swarms of curious locals and tourists. The hotel owner tried again. The third beaver settled down to start a family.

p. 155 "and ate wood, bread, green clover, and green corn": What they ate comes from David Rowland Francis, *The Universal Exposition of 1904*, Volume 1 (Louisiana Purchase Exposition Company, 1913).

p. 155 Sources for the increasing numbers of beavers include "Want War on Beavers: Adirondack Campers Demand Season When They May Be Trapped," *New York Times*, July 13, 1913; "Beavers Multiplying in the Adirondacks," *New York Times*, July 4, 1915; "Editor, Guides Credited with Saving Adirondack Beaver from Extinction," *Utica Daily Press*, June 1916 (an article I found in the Harry Radford file at Goodsell Museum); "The Renaissance of the Beaver: From an Interesting Experiment in 1905 the Restocking of These Industrious Animals Has Become a Vexatious Problem in the Adirondacks Today," *Forest and Stream*, April 1921, 152; as well as the Terrie source mentioned above.

p. 155 "a full-length beaver fur coat": This story is from Lucia Meigs Andrews, *Big Wolf Lake, 1916–1966*. A copy is available in the collection of the Adirondack Experience, Blue Mountain Lake, New York.

p. 155 "between 50,000 and 75,000 Adirondack beavers": This number comes from "Beaver," Adirondack Ecological Center, ESF Newcome Campus, accessed February 12, 2022, http://www.esf.edu/aec/adks/mammals/beaver.htm.

p. 156 Beaver reintroduction: See Radford, *History of the Adirondack Beaver*, and Terrie, *Wildlife and Wilderness*.

p. 156 On caribou in the Adirondacks: "History, Food Habits and Range Requirements of the Woodland Caribou," in *Transactions of the North American Wildlife Conference* 22 (1957): 485–501; "Implications of a Bayesian Radiocarbon Calibration of Colonization Ages for Mammalian Megafauna in Glaciated New York State after the Last Glacial Maximum," *Quaternary Research* 85 (2016): 262–70; James De Kay, *Natural History of New York*, Part 1 (1842), 122, mentions that there's a chance they existed in the region at one time.

p. 156 Some more background on Radford: When Radford was young, his father abandoned him and his mother. Radford and his mother grew quite close. Energetic, ambitious, skilled in the outdoors, and a bit of an impatient, brash fool, Radford desperately wanted to be an explorer. He wanted to see the unseen. He wanted to be widely known and honored. But to explore would mean abandoning his mother for years. Radford sated his desire to explore by wandering the Adirondacks. When his mother died, Radford inherited enough money to live comfortably. He quickly made plans to explore the Canadian arctic.

Solo, he headed north in 1910. He wandered around west and northwest of Hudson Bay, gathering specimens of birds and insects and plants, and taking photographs. He discovered a herd of wood bison, a species previously thought to be extinct, and he shot one of them. ("New Herd of Bison Interests Scientists: Radford's Discovery of Supposed-Extinct Animals Causes Much Comment," *New York Times*, September 9, 1912.) The skeleton eventually ended up at the Smithsonian. ("The Wood Bison," *New York Times*, September 15, 1913.) Toward the end of his multiyear exploration, Radford hoped to map what he called "the last strip remaining unexplored of the continental coast of North America," a sliver of the continent up against the Arctic Ocean. (Quote is from "Further News of the Explorer Radford's Death," *Geographical Review* 2 [October 1916]: 302.)

Radford convinced another explorer, George Street, to go along. Radford and Street left Fort Resolution, on Great Slave Lake, and headed northeast across the tundra. Two natives guided the explorers about two hundred miles to Artillery Lake but then abandoned them. Which was the start of the explorers' bad luck. They hired two different native guides, who only had a small birch bark boat and couldn't help haul much of the explorer's gear and food. Radford poisoned one of his fingers with the arsenic he used to preserve zoological specimens. The arsenic spread to Radford's hand and then arm. Lame, Radford couldn't do much work, and then the two new guides abandoned Radford and Street. Street did all of the work for a while, hauling 1,300 pounds of gear and food around rapids. Street also performed minor field surgery on Radford, which improved his condition greatly. By luck, Street and Radford stumbled into another group of Inuit, who agreed to guide them to Chesterfield Inlet on Hudson Bay, where Radford had arranged for a steamboat to drop off additional supplies. Not far south of the Arctic Circle, Radford and Street overwintered in the igloo of Chief Akulak.

In March 1912, the explorers and their guides left camp and headed northwest across a land of ice and snow and rock and sand toward the Arctic Ocean. They had a difficult time finding food to feed their sled dogs because there weren't many caribou around. At Bathurst Inlet, sheltered from the Arctic Ocean by the complex of islands that tops North America, Radford and Street met another group of Inuit. Three Inuit agreed to guide the explorers west along the Arctic coast to the Mackenzie River delta, where the explorers planned to head south and eventually reach the outpost of Dawson City, former Klondike boomtown, and then make their way through Alaska and back home.

At the last minute, one of the guides wouldn't go. His wife might have been sick or injured. The guide didn't want to leave her. Confusion. Frustration. Tension. An impatient Radford who needed to get quickly back to civilization to make a name for himself in the press and who thought this guide was just being indolent. Anger. Shouting. Maybe a crack of a dog whip as the guide trudged away. Maybe a crack of that dog whip across the guide's face. Maybe wild, frantic gestures attempting to bridge their languages: I'll throw you into that deathtrap in the ice if you try to leave. One of the Inuit stabbed Radford in the back. Street tried to help. An Inuit stabbed him, too, and Radford and Street died from their wounds. Their remains were eventually thrown into the Arctic Ocean to scuttle any investigation.

On Radford and Radford and Street's expedition, see James J. Walsh, "A Young Catholic Explorer," *Records of the American Catholic Historical Society of Philadelphia* 26, no. 2 (June 1915): 111–30; *Report of the Royal Northwest Mounted Police, 1913*, 1914, 40–41; Madge Macbeth, "The Radford-Street Expedition," *Canada Monthly*, November 1913, 12–13, 65–67; "Forsaken Explorer in Arctic Wilds," *New York Times*, March 9, 1912; Captain William Campbell, *Arctic Patrol Stories of the Royal Canadian Mounted Police* (1936), 116–22; and Francis J. Dickie, "The World's Longest Man Hunt," *Popular Mechanics*, April 1917, 549–51. The official report is *Report of the Bathurst Inlet Patrol, Royal Northwest Mounted Police, 1917–1918*. See pages 3–32 for various reports and interviews.

p. 156   "Company claimed to own sixty lakes and ponds": The figure of sixty ponds comes from a full-page advertisement in the *New-York Daily Tribune*, June 4, 1911, which was printed on page iv of a supplement titled "The Adirondacks: A Summer Paradise."

14

p. 158   Climate change and the Adirondacks: See Jerry Jenkins et al., *Acid Rain in the Adirondacks: An Environmental History* (Ithaca, NY: Comstock, 2007), especially 28–70.

15

p. 159   "By the 1950s and 1960s": On views of the Adirondack Park in the mid-twentieth century, see a series of three articles in *The Conservationist*, October–November 1963, December–January 1963/64, April–May 1964; as well as "The Selfish People, *The Adirondac*, January–February 1962, 4, 5, 19; in the same issue, "Motorized Transport in the Forest Preserve," 58–60, 68; "The Forest Preserve and the Gasoline Engine," *The Conservationist*, August–September 1963; Eleanor Brown, *The Forest Preserve of New York State: The Great Adirondack and Catskill Public Forests, and Their Protection through a Century of Conflict: A Handbook for Conservationists* (Lake Placid, NY: Adirondack Mountain Club, 1985), 169–76.

p. 160   "proposed the creation of a national park": See Conrad Wirth, "A Report on a Proposed Adirondack Mountains National Park," 1967. A copy is available at the Adirondack Experience archives. On the Adirondack Mountains National Park plan, see Frank Graham Jr., *The Adirondack Park: A Political History* (New York: Alfred A. Knopf, 1978), 219–29; Murray Schumach, "Huge U.S. Park Urged in Adirondacks," *New York Times*, July 30, 1967; William F. Porter and Ross S. Whaley, "Public and Private Land-Use Regulation of the Adirondack Park," in *The Great Experiment in Conservation: Voices from the Adirondack Park*, ed. William F. Porter, Jon D. Erickson, and Ross S. Whaley (Syracuse, NY: Syracuse University Press, 2009). For the New York Conservation Department's response to the proposal, see "Conservation Department Replied to the National Park Proposal," *The Conservationist* (January–February 1968), 26–28. On the life and reception of the national park proposal, see Norman J. Van Valkenburgh, *The Forest Preserve of New York State in the Adirondack and Catskill Mountains: A Short History*, rev. ed. (Fleischmanns, NY: Purple Mountain, 1996), 255–62. On the connection between the National Park proposal and APA, see Van Valkenburgh, *Forest Preserve*, xii.

p. 160   Adirondack Park Agency: There are so many sources on the APA that it's difficult to decide even where to begin. A recent study that's incredibly detailed and insightful is Brad Edmondson, *A Wild Idea: How the Environmental Movement Tamed the*

Adirondacks (Ithaca, NY: Cornell University Press/Three Hills, 2021). I'd also recommend looking at Jonathan D. Anzalone, *Battles of the North Country: Wilderness Politics and Recreational Development in the Adirondack State Park, 1920–1980* (Amherst: University of Massachusetts Press, 2018), 105–70; Barbara McMartin, *Perspectives on the Adirondacks: A Thirty-Year Struggle by People Protecting Their Treasure* (Syracuse, NY: Syracuse University Press, 2007); Philip G. Terrie, *Contested Terrain: A New History of Nature and People in the Adirondacks*, 2nd ed. (Syracuse, NY: Syracuse University Press, 2008); and Graham, *Adirondack Park*. For a sense of pre-APA efforts at land use planning, look into the Pomeroy Committee, also called the Joint Legislative Committee, which in the 1950s called for a system of Adirondack Wilderness Areas, and also thought motorized vehicles were a threat to the Forest Preserve; see Edmondson, *Wild Idea*; McMartin, *Perspectives*, 25; Van Valkenburgh, *Forest Preserve*, 206. That group's ideas were later adopted by the APA. But, about the same time, there was in 1952 a "zoning" plan that would have permitted logging on state land, essentially undercutting Forever Wild. See Van Valkenburgh, *Forest Preserve*, 205. In 1963, the committee released a report that prompted the state to ban motors or Forest Preserve land (Van Valkenburgh, *Forest Preserve*, 229, 230), but the committee continued with different leadership and in 1966 made a new proposal that only 30 percent of state land should be wilderness, with the rest used intensively for wildlife management, recreational development, and timber harvesting (Van Valkenburgh, *Forest Preserve*, 240, 241). I'd also highly recommend a visit to the Adirondack Experience to see their collections of documents related to these times. For another recent take on the APA and its legacy, see "Strengthening the APA: Ideas for a Better Adirondack Park" (2014), a special publication from *Adirondack Explorer*.

p. 161, 36.

p. 163 "two men splashing gasoline": "2 Accused of Adirondack Arson," *New York Times*, October 21, 1976.

p. 163 "preferred to drive unmarked cars": McMartin, *Perspectives*, 40.

p. 163 "One of the more prominent anti-APA protest signs": Peter Crowley, "Adirondack Experience Museum Acquires Anti-APA Sign," *Adirondack Daily Enterprise*, July 20, 2017, http://www.adirondackdailyenterprise.com/news/local-news/2017/07/adirondack -experience-museum-acquires-anti-apa-sign/.

p. 164 Adirondack identity: See Elizabeth S. Vidon, "The Call of the Wild: Power and Ideology in the Adirondack Park," in *Political Ecology and Tourism*, ed. Sanjay Nepal and Jarkko Saarinen (London: Routledge, 2016). It's also worthwhile to read all of McMartin's *Perspectives*, as it also hints at this developing sense of identity. For more on identity related to the APA, see John S. Banta, "The Adirondack Land Use and Development Plan and Vermont's Act 250 after Forty Years," *John Marshall Law Review* 45 J. Marshall L. Rev. 417 (2012): 433; McMartin, *Perspectives*, 13; and "What Makes This a Park?," printed in the 2014 *Adirondack Explorer* APA special issue mentioned above.

p. 166 "another battle in that war": See Karl Jacoby, "Class and Environmental History: Lessons from 'The War in the Adirondacks,'" *Environmental History* 2 (July 1997): 324–42, and Karl Jacoby, *Crimes against Nature: Squatters, Poachers, Thieves, and the Hidden History of American Conservation* (Berkeley: University of California Press, 2001/2014), 11–78.

250 Adirondack Lakes, 245–50

p. 168   Crane Pond: There's some debate as to the timeline of these events at Crane Pond. The "1992 Pharaoh Lakes Wilderness Unit Management Plan" (published by DEC), 2–3, presents a slightly different timeline than is found in "Crane Pond Access Closed to Motor Vehicles," *Altamont Enterprise*, June 28, 1990. The quote about "rabid animals" is from this article. Also see Barbara McMartin, *Perspectives on the Adirondacks: A Thirty-Year Struggle by People Protecting Their Treasure* (Syracuse, NY: Syracuse University Press, 2007), 146–47. The quote "problem-solver of the Neanderthal order" is from McMartin, *Perspectives*, 147.

p. 169   Orrando P. Dexter: Sources include Barbara McMartin, *The Privately Owned Adirondacks: Sporting and Family Clubs, Private Parks and Preserves, Timberlands and Easements* (Utica, NY: North Country Books, 2004), 108–9; Karl Jacoby, *Crimes against Nature: Squatters, Poachers, Thieves, and the Hidden History of American Conservation* (Berkeley: University of California Press, 2001/2014), 41; William Gerald McLoughlin, *Lake Ozonia: An Informal History* (n.p.: V. D. McLoughlin, 1997), 57–62; and Neal S. Burdick, "Who Killed Orrando P. Dexter?" *Adirondack Life*, June 1982, 23–26, 48, 49.

p. 169   Twain and Lange: See Historic Saranac Lake's Localwiki page titled "Dexter Lake Camp," which includes the text of their 1994 sales brochure and an article from December 4, 1998, in the *Adirondack Daily Enterprise*. For further details see "Fed Up and Moving On," *Adirondack Explorer*, August 1998, 12; "Most Famous Resident," *Adirondack Explorer*, September 1998, 12; "Shania Settles," *Adirondack Explorer*, January 1999, 3; and "Staff Report," *Adirondack Explorer*, July 1999, 6.

SOURCE ESSAY

In major research libraries you'll find shelves stacked full of books about the Adirondacks, and at nearly every bookseller within or near the Blue Line, you'll find the same: biographies, memoirs, local histories, tomes of tall tales, academic studies, field guides, even meticulously researched accounts of, say, logging camps in one river valley. This book is built on that literature. I read as much of it as I could.

While the notes to this book offer further reading related to the subjects I wrote about, below you'll find a more general account of what I consider to be the most helpful books and periodicals. Go to the notes if you're looking for something specific. Start here if you want to continue learning more generally about the region.

Start with Phil Terrie's *Contested Terrain: A New History of Nature and People in the Adirondacks*. While Terrie is an academic historian, his writing is very readable. A newer and more journalistic take, also from Terrie, is *Seeing the Forest: Reviews, Musings, and Opinions from an Adirondack Historian.*

Elizabeth Folwell's *Short Carries: Essays from Adirondack Life* and Paul Jamieson's *Adirondack Pilgrimage* both offer entertaining, well-written, and informative collections of Adirondack essays. Also see Bill McKibben's *Wandering Home: A Long Walk across America's Most Hopeful Landscape.*

Adirondack Life and *Adirondack Explorer*: both magazines offer extensive coverage of the region, reflecting on its current condition and its past, and both have been around for a while—*Adirondack Life* since 1970 and *Adirondack Explorer* since 1998; it's now possible to study these past issues as historical documents that speak to how the region has changed.

The best introduction I've found to Adirondack natural history is Mike Storey's *Why the Adirondacks Look the Way They Do: A Natural History*. There are a number of Adirondack-specific field guides out there, for birds, trees, wildflowers, and the like, but Storey's book excels at communicating a narrative of the region. Also check out Edward Kanze's *Over the Mountain and Home Again: Journeys of an Adirondack Naturalist* and *Adirondack: Life and Wildlife in the Wild, Wild East*.

Two recent publications examine race in Adirondack history. I recommend both: Sally Svenson's *Blacks in the Adirondacks: A History* and Melissa Otis's *Rural Indigenousness: A History of Iroquoian and Algonquian Peoples of the Adirondacks*.

Jerry Jenkin's *The Adirondack Atlas: A Geographic Portrait of the Adirondack Park* offers an abundance of fascinating information about the region. Even though parts of it are dated, it still offers plenty of insights.

The most recent take on the APA is Brad Edmondson's *A Wild Idea: How the Environmental Movement Tamed the Adirondacks*. Although the book has a narrower focus than the title suggests, it offers a stunningly detailed account of the rise of the APA. For more on the political background of the Adirondacks, see Frank Graham Jr.'s *The Adirondack Park: A Political History*. For a more focused account of the political battles over recreation during the twentieth century, see Jon Anzalone's *Battles of the North Country: Wilderness Politics and Recreational Development in the Adirondack State Park, 1920–1980*.

On Great Camps, the best place to start is Harvey Kaiser's *Great Camps of the Adirondacks*. A first edition was published in 1982, launching the movement to preserve Great Camps. A new edition was published in 2020. The two editions differ significantly. If you're interested in learning more about Great Camps, it's worthwhile to read both editions to gain more historical perspective on the preservation of camps. Also see *Santanoni: From Japanese Temple to Life at an Adirondack Great Camp* by Robert Engel, Howard Kirschenbaum, and Paul Malo.

I mentioned Barbara McMartin's *The Great Forest of the Adirondacks* earlier. I'd also recommend her *Perspectives on the Adirondacks: A Thirty-Year Struggle by People Protecting Their Treasure*; *Hides, Hemlocks and Adirondack History: How the Tanning Industry Influenced the Growth of the Region*; and *The Privately Owned Adirondacks*.

But as important as all of that: go visit. Park your car and take a stroll, stand on the sandy shore of a lake and think about glaciers, climb an esker, find the moose pine in Old Forge and see if the owners have raised the price, listen to the wind whoosh in a spruce, spot your favorite neon motel sign and learn what it looks like at dusk on a stormy day, paddle a feather-weight canoe or a guideboat. Better yet, a clunker of a kayak.

INDEX

Matt Dallos is a PhD candidate at Cornell University, where he teaches environmental writing seminars. He lives in the Finger Lakes of New York.

EMPIRE STATE EDITIONS SELECT TITLES FROM EMPIRE STATE EDITIONS

Colin Davey with Thomas A. Lesser, *The American Museum of Natural History and How It Got That Way*. Forewords by Neil deGrasse Tyson and Kermit Roosevelt III

Wendy Jean Katz, *Humbug: The Politics of Art Criticism in New York City's Penny Press*

Lolita Buckner Inniss, *The Princeton Fugitive Slave: The Trials of James Collins Johnson*

Mike Jaccarino, *America's Last Great Newspaper War: The Death of Print in a Two-Tabloid Town*

Angel Garcia, *The Kingdom Began in Puerto Rico: Neil Connolly's Priesthood in the South Bronx*

Jim Mackin, *Notable New Yorkers of Manhattan's Upper West Side: Bloomingdale–Morningside Heights*

Matthew Spady, *The Neighborhood Manhattan Forgot: Audubon Park and the Families Who Shaped It*

Robert O. Binnewies, *Palisades: 100,000 Acres in 100 Years*

Marilyn S. Greenwald and Yun Li, *Eunice Hunton Carter: A Lifelong Fight for Social Justice*

Jeffrey A. Kroessler, *Sunnyside Gardens: Planning and Preservation in a Historic Garden Suburb*

Elizabeth Macaulay-Lewis, *Antiquity in Gotham: The Ancient Architecture of New York City*

Ron Howell, *King Al: How Sharpton Took the Throne*

Phil Rosenzweig, *Reginald Rose and the Journey of "12 Angry Men"*

Jean Arrington with Cynthia S. LaValle, *From Factories to Palaces: Architect Charles B. J. Snyder and the New York City Public Schools*. Foreword by Peg Breen

Boukary Sawadogo, *Africans in Harlem: An Untold New York Story*

Alvin Eng, *Our Laundry, Our Town: My Chinese American Life from Flushing to the Downtown Stage and Beyond*

Stephanie Azzarone, *Heaven on the Hudson: Mansions, Monuments, and Marvels of Riverside Park*

Ron Goldberg, *Boy with the Bullhorn: A Memoir and History of ACT UP New York*. Foreword by Dan Barry

Peter Quinn, *Cross Bronx: A Writing Life*. Foreword by Dan Barry

Jill Jonnes, *South Bronx Rising: The Rise, Fall, and Resurrection of an American City, Third Edition*. Foreword by Nilka Martell

Mark Bulik, *Ambush at Central Park: When the IRA Came to New York*

Brandon Dean Lamson, *Caged: A Teacher's Journey Through Rikers, or How I Beheaded the Minotaur*

For a complete list, visit www.fordhampress.com/empire-state-editions.